Henry James Morgan

The Tour of H.R.H.; the Prince of Wales

Through British America and the United States

Henry James Morgan

The Tour of H.R.H.; the Prince of Wales
Through British America and the United States

ISBN/EAN: 9783744744270

Printed in Europe, USA, Canada, Australia, Japan

Cover: Foto ©Andreas Hilbeck / pixelio.de

More available books at **www.hansebooks.com**

THE TOUR

OF

H. R. H. THE PRINCE OF WALES

THROUGH

BRITISH AMERICA

AND

THE UNITED STATES.

BY A BRITISH CANADIAN,

Montreal:
PRINTED FOR THE COMPILER BY JOHN LOVELL,
ST. NICHOLAS STREET.
1860.

TO

The Honourable Philip M. Vankoughnet,

COMMISSIONER OF CROWN LANDS FOR CANADA;

In acknowledgment of his sterling and brilliant abilities as a Statesman, and as

THE MOVER IN THE LEGISLATIVE COUNCIL

. OF

THE ADDRESS TO THE QUEEN INVITING

Her Majesty

TO VISIT CANADA,

This Work is humbly and respectfully INSCRIBED by his obliged, obedient, and humble servant,

THE COMPILER.

BIOGRAPHICAL SKETCH

OF

THE PRINCE OF WALES.

Albert Edward, Heir Apparent to the British throne, was born at Buckingham Palace on the 9th of November, 1841. He is consequently nineteen years of age.

The titles of the Prince of Wales are Duke of Saxony, Prince of Saxe Coburg Gotha, Duke of Cornwall and Rothsay, Earl of Chester, Carrick, and Dublin, Baron Renfrew, and Lord of the Isles. These titles he derives partly by inheritance and partly from creation, from the circumstance of King Edward I. having, in politic concession to the Welsh chieftains, created his heir "Prince of Wales," a few days after his birth, which took place in Caernarvon Castle. This was the unhappy Edward II., who was so barbarously murdered by Mortimer in Berkeley Castle. A few days afterwards he was created Earl of Chester, which title has been retained up to the present time. The Scottish titles of the Prince are derived from Robert III., in whose reign they were vested in the Heir Apparent of the Crown of Scotland. His Irish titles were conferred on the present Prince of Wales by Queen Victoria, on the 10th of September, 1849, in commemoration of her visit to Ireland. In the House of Lords he is known as the Duke of Cornwall.

Dod, the great authority on all these questions, thus defines the rank and position of the Prince of Wales :—" The Prince of Wales has ever been regarded as the first subject in the realm, the nearest to the throne, the most dignified of the Peers of Parliament, and, though not exercising any political power beyond his vote as a legislator, yet regarded by all men as the most eminent person in the State next after the Sovereign."

The Princes of Wales, previous to the present subject of our memoir, have for more than a century been all placed in false positions. Since the accession of the Georges, they have invariably been in opposition to their father. The evil conduct of George IV. had sadly tarnished the high distinction: let us hope the present bearer of that high title will redeem it.

The education of Albert Edward has been conducted under the immediate supervision of the Queen. In the languages, classics, natural philosophy, mathematics, jurisprudence, and other branches, His Royal Highness has had the most eminent professors of the day; and it is stated that after his tour in America he will return to his studies at Oxford.

On the 9th of November, 1858, the Prince of Wales, having, on that day, completed his seventeenth year, was appointed colonel in the army. The *Gazette* of the following Friday contained the subjoined announcement:—

"The Queen taking into her royal consideration that His Royal Highness Albert Edward, Prince of Wales, Knight of the Most Noble Order of the Garter, and, by virtue of the statutes of the said order, constituent member thereof, has not as yet assumed the stall assigned to the Prince of Wales in the Royal Chapel of St. George, at Windsor, and having, as sovereign of the said order, the inherent right of dispensing with all statutes, ordinances, and regulations in regard to installation, Her Majesty has been pleased, by letters patent under her Royal Sign Manual and the Great Seal of the Order, bearing date this day, to give and grant to His Royal Highness Albert Edward, Prince of Wales, full power and authority to wear and use the Star, and also to wear and use the Collar and all other Ornaments belonging to the said Most Noble Order, and to sit in the stall assigned to the Prince of Wales in our Royal Chapel of St. George, at Windsor, and to exercise all rights and privileges belonging to a Knight Companion of the said Most Noble Order, in as full and ample manner as if His Royal Highness had been formally installed; any decree, rule, or usage, to the contrary notwithstanding."

Having thus fairly entered upon the duties of manhood, His Royal Highness determined upon pursuing his studies, for a time at least, at Rome. Accordingly, after a brief visit to his illustrious sister at Berlin, the Princess Frederick William of Prussia, he proceeded on his journey to Italy. On his way thither, he performed the first public act of his life, by presenting colors to the 100th or Prince of Wales' Royal Canadian Regiment of Foot, then stationed at Shorncliffe, near Folkestone. His Royal Highness took occasion to make the following appropriate speech to the assembled officers and men :—

"Lord Melville, Colonel de Rottenberg, and Officers and Soldiers of the 100th Regiment,—It is most gratifying to me, that, by the Queen's gracious permission, my first public act since I have had the honour of holding a commission in the British army, should be the presentation of colors to a regiment which is the spontaneous offering of the loyal and spirited Canadian people, and with which, at their desire, my name has been specially associated. The ceremonial on which we are now engaged, possesses a peculiar significance and solemnity; because, in confiding to you for the first time this emblem of military fidelity and valor, I not only recognize emphatically your enrollment into our national force, but celebrate an act which proclaims and strengthens the unity of the various parts of this vast empire under the sway of our common Sovereign. Although, owing to my youth and inexperience, I can but very imperfectly give expression to the sentiments which this occasion is calculated to awaken with reference to yourselves and to the great and flourishing province of Canada, you may rest assured that I shall ever watch the progress and achievements of your gallant corps with deep interest, and that I heartily wish you all honour and success in the prosecution of the noble career on which you have entered."

The Prince arrived in the Eternal City in the latter part of January, 1859, and, having spent some time in exploring ancient and modern Rome, proceeded quietly and unostentatiously to his studies. Before doing so, however, he paid a visit to the Pope. His appearance at the Vatican is worthy of note, inasmuch as a Prince of the blood-royal of England had not made a similar visit for some centuries. Agreeably to the expressed wish of Her Majesty, the reception was conducted with little ceremony. His Holiness rose on the entry of the Prince, and, coming forward to the door of the apartment to meet him, conducted him, in the most affable manner possible, to a seat, and entered into conversation with him in French. Col. Bruce was the only other person present at the interview; which was brief, and limited to complimentary expressions and subjects of local interest, but perfectly satisfactory to all parties. On the Prince rising to take his leave, the Pope conducted him again to the door with the same warmth of manner which he had testified on receiving him. The stay of His Royal Highness in Rome being interrupted by the outbreak of the war in Italy, he travelled to Gibraltar, and thence to Spain and Portugal. He returned to England on June 25, 1859.

On his return, he took up his residence at Oxford to pursue his studies. On the 9th of July last, he embarked, with his suite, at Devonport, on board the *Hero*, ship of war, and sailed for America on the following morning.

PREFACE.

THE fact of the late visit of His Royal Highness the Prince of Wales being attended, in British America, with all the loyal devotion which a happy and contented people could pay to the representative of the best of Sovereigns, irrespective of the interest which necessarily attached to H. R. H. as being Heir Presumptive to the British Throne,—and in the United States, with acts of unbounded courtesy and kindness,—has induced the Compiler to collect together the most interesting details of the Royal tour, and to present them in the following simple form, trusting that it will be full of interest, not only to the Canadian people, but to others "at home," and to "our cousins across the line"; and that it will form an acceptable *memento* of the Royal visit.

If the work, as an accurate panoramic view of the events which have taken place, give satisfaction to the great mass of the people, who were so deeply interested in the Prince's very successful sojourn in Canada, then will the Compiler be amply rewarded for his trouble; but if some too discriminating critic detect a flaw, it must be remembered that

"We all are prone to err."

INTRODUCTION.

The Canadians in general, have, apart from their industrial and commercial pursuits, always been celebrated for their steady adherence to the British Crown, as is witnessed in the transfer of the French to the English rule over the native Canadians, who now live in peaceful and on the best of terms with the great mass of the English residents; bearing towards the Queen the most unfeigned feelings of reverence, and towards the Constitution that deference to which it is entitled.

No republican spirits lurk in the midst of the Canadians,— except it be a few fanatics, too weak for action, and who are unable to augment their numbers by their silly, boisterous, and attempted agitation-talk. The great majority of the inhabitants laugh at these silly people, who, to attain a brazen notoriety, attempt to mar our happiness. No! every true inhabitant of this our home, bears towards Britain true allegiance, which neither time can work upon, nor future events affect.

Persons unacquainted with the history of the Province, may aver, that the disturbance of 1837 in Canada, and many things tending to its advance, are evidence to the direct contrary. To this we give an unequivocal denial; for, in the first place, every person *in* Canada is aware that that rebellion was concocted by a few persons totally unacquainted with the Province, except by business or debased political ties. Certainly there were persons connected with it who were natives of the Province; but such disaffected persons are to be found in every community, no matter how respectable, ready, at any moment of weakness, to endeavour to take advantage of the existing form of government.

It was such persons, by their idle, interested misrepresentations concerning England and Canada, that led many others to err; and a few were led, from a mistaken sense of danger, to co-operate with them, who to their death will, no doubt, always regret having taken arms against their country, and her fair young Queen.

The fact of many of these latter persons now being our leading and best of citizens, and moreover ever ready to support the Queen and the Constitution, proves, we think, that our statement is correct.

Again, look at the terrible numbers that bore arms against them, in defence of their homes and country, and the valiant band, in the war of 1812, that defended both sea and land from the aggressors,—every capable man bearing a musket, ready to spill his last drop of blood in defence of Canada and the King. And look at the great bulk of the population of Upper Canada, the noble and patriotic United Empire Loyalists, who forsook their homes, their all, in the disaffected colonies (now the United States); enduring as they did every privation, rather than serve under the flag that supplanted ours.

These, and many other acts of valour, prove beyond all doubt, that the inhabitants of Canada are worthy of the confidence and esteem of their Queen. Indeed, no sovereign on earth ought to be so satisfied with her subjects as Victoria with her Canadian ones, and no people so proud (as we really are) of our Queen; and we doubt not, that no ruler is so venerated and esteemed as Victoria is, by not only the Canadians, but the great mass of the American colonists.

It was, then, this feeling of loyalty and veneration which dictated the address from our Houses of Parliament, praying Her Gracious Majesty to visit us; to see us as we are, to see the improvements effected by British bone and sinew, without capital, without help; in a land given to our forefathers in a comparative state of wildness; to witness her administration of our industry, and to give us occasion to prove our attachment to her Throne and Person, by entertaining her in a land which we have battled for and preserved to her, and which, we doubt not, may ere long justify the remark, that it is indeed "the brightest gem in the British Crown."

What, then, were our feelings when we became aware of the noble response to our humble address? Her Majesty, unable to come herself, would depute her eldest son and heir to witness those noble advancements in a land, from barbarism to civilization.

If our loyalty and allegiance to her could at all increase, then did they upon the receipt of the joyful intelligence.

From cities to towns, from towns to remote villages, and even far away into the recesses of the forest, where the solitary settler was effecting "a clearing," did the good news travel fast, and throughout the length and breadth of the land did it receive a joyous welcome; and need we add, that the Queen was blessed and blessed again. One regret, and only one, pervaded the whole colony,—that Her Majesty herself could not come; yet we would receive the Prince her son, and our future King, in a fitting manner,—in a manner to fully demonstrate to him, that he was indeed her son and heir.

We imagined that His Royal Highness (being brought up under his royal mother's watchful eye) was a young gentleman of sound mind and "excellent understanding," capable of appreciating the hearty welcome we intended for him. In this we have not been disappointed, for he has proved to be all that we could wish; all that a son of Her Majesty, and the future ruler of Great Britain, ought to be.

His noble qualities have endeared him to us tenfold; he has received an ovation, which has been declared by members of his suite, and by others from the other side of the Atlantic, to be the grandest and most cordial they ever heard of or witnessed, and let us hope worthy of him; and we rejoice exceedingly, knowing as we do that to Canada, and the members of our present Administration, is the whole of civilized America indebted for the honour of the visit of Prince Albert Edward of England.

We cannot conclude without mentioning the great debt Canada owes to the Hon. Messrs. Vankoughnet and Cartier, the chief promoters of this memorable event. Let us always remember, that, but for them, it is as likely as not that we would never have seen the Prince of Wales in America.

To Mr. Commissioner Rose the country is under deep obligations, for the elaborate arrangements perfected to receive the royal prince; worthy of His Royal Highness, and worthy the great spirit that projected them and carried them out.

THE TOUR

OF

H. R. H. THE PRINCE OF WALES.

In 1858, a person named Norris, whether to show his loyal attachment to England, or to obtain a certain amount of notoriety through the undertaking, got up a memorial to Her Majesty, praying her to allow the Prince of Wales to visit our shores, and open the Crystal Palace at Toronto. In doing this he made a very serious blunder, consequent on his extreme haste to *honour himself.*

The following is the memorial :—

TO THE QUEEN'S MOST EXCELLENT MAJESTY.

The humble Petition of the undersigned Inhabitants of Toronto, and Inhabitants of Canada generally,

Most respectfully showeth,—

That your Petitioners desire to approach your Royal Majesty with an expression of devoted loyalty and attachment to your royal person and family. That your Petitioners beg leave to inform your Majesty that a Crystal Palace, similar in design, but of smaller dimensions, to those of London and Paris, for the exhibition of the products of Canadian industry and skill, is in course of erection in Toronto, and will be completed about the 1st October next. That your Majesty has been graciously pleased to honour the inauguration of similar undertakings in England, and elsewhere, with your royal presence. Therefore your Petitioners most humbly pray that your Most Gracious Majesty will confer a mark of favour and distinction on your loyal subjects in Canada—of which they will always entertain the most grateful remembrance—by conferring your authority on His Royal Highness the Prince of Wales, or some other member of your Majesty's Royal Family, to proceed to Canada, and to represent your Majesty in opening the Crystal Palace in this the most important dependency of your Majesty's Empire.

And your Petitioners, &c.

To this Mr. Norris succeeded in obtaining some very influential names, some of the leading persons of the Province; but in signing it, they little *understood* his intentions.

Instead of having the document forwarded to Her Majesty through the Governor General, Mr. Norris, to the astonishment of the gentlemen who had signed it, deputed himself.

Sir E. B. Lytton, no doubt, was somewhat surprised on receiving a document of such magnitude from a private individual, who had constituted himself our "ambassador"; and with such a lack of what ambassadors invariably possess, education and good breeding, he must have been sorely puzzled at the good people he partly presided over.

However, on an insight into the matter, the truth eked out, and Mr. Norris received such a rebuke, as we fancy he will not easily forget, and which was conveyed in the following official letter from Downing Street:—

DOWNING STREET, 11th September, 1858.

SIR,—I cannot but regret that the Petition from the citizens of Toronto, and inhabitants of Canada generally, which I had the honour to receive from you, was not transmitted, according to usage, through the Governor of the Province. But, as the time within which it was necessary that this Petition should receive an answer, would not allow of my consulting the local Government on the subject of it, I have deemed it my duty to lay the Petition before the Queen, who has been pleased to receive it very graciously; and I am commanded by Her Majesty to state, that, while under the necessity of declining the request that His Royal Highness the Prince of Wales, or some other member of Her Majesty's Family, should proceed to Canada, with the view of opening the Crystal Palace at Toronto, which is to be completed about the 1st of October, Her Majesty appreciates the loyalty to the Crown, and the attachment to her Person and Family, which prompted the wish of the Petitioners.

I have also to add the expression of Her Majesty's sincere good wishes for the Exhibition itself, which Her Majesty trusts will produce important and useful results to Canada.

I have the honour to be, Sir,

Your obedient servant,

EDWARD BULWER LYTTON.

The object of the Prince of Wales' visit, to use the words of his illustrious father the Prince Consort, was "to inaugurate that stupendous work of engineering skill, the Victoria Bridge," we may say the eighth wonder of the world.

It is hardly necessary to observe, that Mr. Norris' memorial was got up for the purpose of inviting His Royal Highness to open the Palace of Industry at Toronto, and in which an Exhibition was held in 1858.

We are infinitely happy that Mr. Norris did not succeed in his undertaking in inviting the Prince of Wales; for had His Royal Highness visited us at that time, he would have found us in a comparatively depressed commercial state, consequent on the great money-panic of 1857; not but that our loyal countrymen would have given their last shilling towards entertaining him, but we would not have been enabled to give him the reception which he has since received,—an ovation which the Canadians have done their utmost to make worthy of so illustrious a guest, but which in 1858 we could not have given if we would. Besides, in that year the Victoria Bridge was not completed; and he would have left our shores without giving the concluding touch to that immortal monument of Stephenson's skill, of British capital, and Canadian industry.

Then again, he would not have had the pleasure of witnessing in a suitable manner the productions of both sections of our flourishing and go-a-head Province, which he has lately done in the Crystal Palaces at Montreal, C. E., and Hamilton, C. W.; moreover, the people would not have had sufficient time for the preparation attending a royal visit, had he come to inaugurate the Toronto Exhibition.

Thus was the time of the late visit not only propitious, but we were entirely prepared for the honour conferred upon us by our Gracious Sovereign, to welcome the Prince of Wales in a manner, which we doubt not, has not only been acceptable to him, but has reflected the highest credit on ourselves; and been a source of pride and satisfaction to us.

On the last day of the session of the Provincial Parliament, May 14, 1859, held at Toronto, the following address was unanimously carried in both Houses of Parliament, on motion (in the Legislative

Council) of the Hon. P. M. Vankoughnet, Commissioner of Crown Lands; who, in introducing the subject, said that in the previous year he had signed a memorial to Her Majesty, praying her to allow His Royal Highness the Prince of Wales to visit this portion of her dominions, which memorial was got up by a man named Norris; but when he (Mr. Vankoughnet) signed that document, he understood it was to be forwarded through His Excellency the Governor General. He now regretted having signed the memorial alluded to, because it was carried over by this Norris himself.

The opening of the great Victoria Bridge was now a fitting opportunity to invite Her Majesty hither.

The Address was moved in the Assembly by the Hon. Mr. Cartier the Premier, and seconded by the Hon. Mr. Foley, and carried in both Houses with the greatest unanimity and exultation; and the Speaker of the Assembly (the Hon., now Sir Henry Smith) was deputed to present, in his official capacity, the same to Her Majesty.

The Address is as follows:—

To the Queen's Most Excellent Majesty:—

MOST GRACIOUS SOVEREIGN,—We, Your Majesty's most dutiful and loyal subjects, the Legislative Council and Assembly of Canada, in Provincial Parliament assembled, hereby approach Your Majesty with renewed assurances of devotion and attachment to Your Royal Person and Government.

We have long hoped that Your Majesty would be graciously pleased to honour with your presence Your Majesty's subjects in British North America, and to receive the personal tribute of our unwavering attachment to your rule; and we trust that, while Your Majesty's presence would still more closely unite the bonds which attach the Province to the Empire, it would gratify Your Majesty to witness the progress and prosperity of this distant part of your dominions.

The completion, in the year 1860, of the Victoria Bridge, the most gigantic work of modern days, would afford to Your Majesty a fitting occasion to judge of the importance of your Province of Canada; while it would afford the inhabitants the opportunity of uniting in their expressions of loyalty and attachment to the Throne and Empire.

We therefore most humbly pray that Your Majesty will vouchsafe to be present upon the occasion of the opening of the Victoria Bridge, with Your Majesty's Royal Consort, and such members of Your Majesty's August Family as it may graciously please Your Majesty to select to accompany you.

Legislative Council,
 Wednesday, 4th May, 1859.

We are confident in saying, that no better man could have been selected to perform the pleasing duty of presenting this Address, than Sir Henry Smith, a gentleman in the true sense of the word, and possessing everything that is requisite to make a gentleman and an ambassador. What a difference between the would-be self-important Mr. Norris, and the Speaker of the House of Assembly! Sir Henry Smith left for England shortly after the prorogation of Parliament, and, as every one is well aware, was perfectly successful in his mission; and to him, to the truly-inspiring Address of our Canadian Senators, and to its originator (Mr. Vankoughnet), we owe the visit of the Prince of Wales.

The following despatch in reply was received by the Governor General:—

CANADA, No. 6.

DOWNING STREET, 30th January, 1860.

SIR,—As the two Houses of the Canadian Legislature will soon re-assemble for the Despatch of Business, it becomes my duty to inform you that the Joint Address, to which they agreed at the close of their last Session, was duly presented to the Queen, and was most graciously received by Her Majesty.

In that Address, the Legislative Council and Commons of Canada earnestly pray the Queen to receive in person the tribute of their un-wavering attachment to Her rule, and to honor with Her presence Her subjects in British North America upon the occasion of the opening of the great Victoria Bridge, accompanied by the Prince Consort, and such members of the Royal Family as it may please Her Majesty to attend Her on the occasion.

Her Majesty values deeply the attachment to Her Person, and the loyalty to Her Crown, which have induced this Address; and I am commanded to assure the Legislature, through you, how lively an interest is felt by the Queen in the growing prosperity of Canada, in the welfare and contentment of Her subjects in that important Province of Her Empire, and in the completion of the gigantic work which is a fitting type of the successful industry of the people.

It is therefore with sincere regret that Her Majesty is compelled to decline compliance with this loyal invitation. Her Majesty feels that Her duties at the Seat of the Empire prevent so long an absence, and at so great a distance, as a visit to Canada would necessarily require.

Impressed, however, with an earnest desire to testify to the utmost of Her power, Her warm appreciation of the affectionate loyalty of Her Canadian subjects, the Queen commands me to express Her hope, that, when the time for the opening of the Bridge is fixed, it may be possible for His Royal Highness the Prince of Wales to attend the ceremony in Her Majesty's name, and to witness those gratifying scenes in which the Queen is Herself unable to participate.

The Queen trusts that nothing may interfere with this arrangement; for it is Her Majesty's sincere desire that the young Prince, on whom the Crown of this Empire will devolve, may have the opportunity of visiting that portion of Her Dominions from which this Address has proceeded, and may become acquainted with a people, in whose rapid progress towards greatness, Her Majesty, in common with Her subjects in Great Britain, feels a lively and enduring sympathy.

I have the honor to be,
Sir,
Your most obedient humble servant,
NEWCASTLE.

Governor,
The Right Honorable
SIR EDMUND WALKER HEAD, Bart.,
&c., &c., &c.

What joy was diffused throughout British America, on the announcement that Our Gracious and Beloved Queen had so nobly responded to our call! Unable to leave England herself, she would send Her beloved Son, our future King, as Her substitute. Oh, what feelings actuated the breasts of the truly loyal! Now and for ever we support thee, Beloved Queen. We would spill our last drop of blood to do thee service. Wonder not, strangers, at seeing such marvellous displays in Canada, in honor of the Heir Apparent: the love and attachment which are entertained for Victoria, and the Royal Family, are not equalled on earth towards any ruler, except it be to the Omnipotent One above.

As soon as the news was received in the Lower Provinces, their respective Parliaments adopted Addresses to Her Majesty, praying, that, if His Royal Highness the Prince of Wales should visit Canada, they also should be honoured in like manner.

Newfoundland, Prince Edward's Island, New Brunswick, Nova Scotia, and we believe the West Indies, all petitioned.

To these Her Majesty, ever generous, replied that their requests would be complied with. The city of New York, U. S., invited the Prince thither, as did also the President of the United States, as appears in the subjoined correspondence.

The President of the United States invited him to Washington, and the authorities of the city of New York "did likewise," as appear in the subjoined correspondence:—

President Buchanan to Queen Victoria.

To HER MAJESTY QUEEN VICTORIA,—

I have learned from the public journals that the Prince of Wales is about to visit your Majesty's North American dominions. Should it be the intention of His Royal Highness to extend his visit to the United States, I need not say how happy I should be to give him a cordial welcome to Washington. You may be well assured that everywhere in this country he will be greeted by the American people in such a manner as cannot fail to prove gratifying to your Majesty. In this they will manifest their deep sense of your domestic virtues, as well as their convictions of your merits as a wise, patriotic, and constitutional sovereign.

Your Majesty's most obedient servant,

JAMES BUCHANAN.

Washington, June 4, 1860.

Queen Victoria to President Buchanan.

BUCKINGHAM PALACE, June 22, 1860.

MY GOOD FRIEND,—

I have been much gratified at the feelings which prompted you to write to me, inviting the Prince of Wales to come to Washington. He intends to return from Canada through the United States, and it will give him great pleasure to have an opportunity of testifying to you in person that these feelings are fully reciprocated by him. He will thus be able, at the same time, to mark the respect which he entertains for the Chief Magistrate of a great and friendly State and kindred nation.

The Prince of Wales will drop all royal state on leaving my dominions and travel under the name of Lord Renfrew, as he has done when travelling on the continent of Europe.

The Prince Consort wishes to be kindly remembered to you.

I remain ever your good friend,

VICTORIA R.

LEGATION OF THE UNITED STATES,
London, June 22, 1860.

SIR,—My letter of the 8th instant will have informed you of the step taken by me to apprise the Prince of Wales of the desire expressed by the Common Council of New York that he should visit your great city at the close of his public duties in Canada. I have now the honour to transmit a note addressed to me in answer to my communication by Her Majesty's principal Secretary of State for Foreign Affairs, conveying the gratifying assurance that His Royal Highness, with the high sanction of his illustrious mother and her Government, will meet the wishes of your community. With the highest respect.

Sir, your most obedient servant,

G. M. DALLAS.

To His Excellency Fernando Wood, Mayor of New York.

The undersigned, Her Majesty's principal Secretary of State for Foreign Affairs, has the honour to acknowledge a communication addressed to him by Mr. Dallas, Envoy Extraordinary and Minister Plenipotentiary of the United States, containing a resolution expressive of the wish of the Municipality of New York and of its important and wealthy community to receive a visit from His Royal Highness the Prince of Wales, on the occasion of His Royal Highness' presence in the colonial possessions of Her Majesty. The undersigned, having laid these documents before Her Majesty and the Prince of Wales, is commanded by them to express to Mr. Dallas the high sense which they entertain of the importance of strengthening, by every means, the relations of friendship and regard which bind this country to the United States of America. When, therefore, the public duties, for the performance of which the Prince undertakes the voyage across the Atlantic to Her Majesty's North American Colonies, shall be concluded, both the consideration above referred to and the natural desire on the part of the Prince to visit some of the institutions and some of the most prominent objects of interest in the United States, will prompt His Royal Highness, on his return from the Upper Province of Canada, to direct his route through a portion of that great country; and that route will include a visit to the important city of New York. The time allowed for this journey will, however, under all circumstances, be necessarily very limited, and it will be out of the power of His Royal Highness to make a prolonged stay.

His Royal Highness will, on leaving the British soil, lay aside all Royal state and exchange his title, as he has done on former journeys to foreign countries, for that of Lord Renfrew. While thus dispensing with any ceremony which might be inconvenient to the communities which he hopes to visit, he trusts to be enabled as a private gentleman to employ the small amount of time at his disposal in the study of the interesting objects in the United States, and of the ordinary life of the American people.

The undersigned is directed to request that Mr. Dallas will communicate to His Excellency Fernando Wood, the expression of the satisfaction felt by the Prince of Wales upon receiving the resolution of the

Municipality of New York, and of his hope that towards the latter end of September he may be enabled to pay a visit to the city they represent, and to the mercantile community who have given to him so welcome a testimony of their friendly regard.

The undersigned requests Mr. Dallas to accept the assurance of his highest consideration.

J. RUSSELL.

What can be more kind than the letter from our "American Cousins," and what more truly reciprocal than that from Queen Victoria! Truly we are more than infinitely blest with such a Queen.

THE PRINCE LEAVES ENGLAND.

His Royal Highness the Prince of Wales embarked on board the royal yacht *Victoria and Albert* at Osborne, for Plymouth, on 9th July, 1860. He was accompanied to Plymouth by his royal father, the Prince Consort; and as far as the *Victoria and Albert*, in Cowes Roads, by the Queen, Princess Alice, and Prince Arthur, who remained in the *Fairy* and sailed after the royal yacht for some distance, and then returned. The *Victoria and Albert* arrived at Plymouth Sound on the same day. The Channel Squadron was drawn up in two lines outside the Breakwater, to receive the yacht. Yards were manned, and a royal salute fired by Her Majesty's ships *Hero, Ariadne, St. George,* and *Emerald*.

An Address was shortly afterwards presented to the Prince of Wales, by the Mayor and Corporation of Davenport, to which His Royal Highness replied :—

" Mr. MAYOR AND GENTLEMEN,—I thank you warmly for this Address, for the expressions of your loyalty and devotion to the Queen, and for the kind sentiments to myself, which characterize this farewell from your important town on the eve of my departure for a short time from my native land.

" You may well look back with pride to the fact, that so many eminent colonists have embarked on their great mission from your shores. It shall not be my fault if I fail to convey to our brethren across the Atlantic the feelings entertained by the Queen and the people of England for the descendants of those men, and for the countries which they founded. I go to the great possessions of the Queen in North America with a lively anticipation of the pleasure which the sight of a noble land, great works of nature and of human skill, and a generous and active people, must produce; and I shall endeavour to bring home with me such information as may in future be of use to me in all my associations with my countrymen. Again I thank you for your good wishes for my safe voyage and happy return."

The Prince of Wales having embarked on board H. M. S. *Hero*, 91, Captain Geo. H. Seymour, C. B., and the Prince Consort having returned to Osborne in the royal yacht, the *Hero*, accompanied by the *Ariadne*, 26, Captain E. W. Vansittart, weighed anchor, and sailed for Newfoundland. Salutes were fired by H. M. S. *St. George* and *Emerald*, by the Artillery in Plymouth Citadel, and by the Cornish Royal Volunteers, from a field-battery near Mount Edgecumbe Park.

About a league and a half south-east of the Eddystone, the *Hero* was joined by Vice Admiral Sir Charles Fremantle's Channel Squadron, which escorted it a short way and then returned.

RECEPTION AT NEWFOUNDLAND.

The *Flying Fish*, 6, Commander Hope, which left England on the 1st July, in advance of the squadron, arrived at St. Johns, on the 17th of the same month.

The *Hero* and *Ariadne* made it about 4·30 on the evening of July 23, and anchored opposite the city at 7 P.M. They were received by a royal salute from the Citadel, by the ringing of bells, and by the lusty and loyal cheers of the populace of St. Johns and the surrounding country, who crowded the wharves and every available spot where they could obtain a good view of the war-vessels. Flags were displayed in profusion, every house appeared decorated and illuminated, and the greatest enthusiasm prevailed among the whole of the inhabitants. In the evening an illumination took place, and which for magnificence was all that could be desired.

For the information of our readers, we append here a few extracts from the Log of the Ariadne :—

Tuesday, July 10th, 1860.—Left Plymouth; joined at 7 a.m.; met the Fleet outside the Breakwater; formed in two lines, and saluted as the Hero and Ariadne passed down between them.

At 4.20 p.m., the Fleet fired a salute and hoisted colors. Wind light from S.E. Weather thick.

11th.—Under steam part of the day; wind from N.W., and moderate smooth sea. Exchanged colors with the American ship "Parliament" of Boston.

12th.—Under steam part of the day; wind from S.W. to N.W. Fresh, with thick fog; sea getting up.

13th.—Under steam until 2 p.m., drew up screw-propeller and proceeded under sail only. Wind strong from W.N.W., with foggy weather. A good deal of sea running.

14th.—Wind strong from W.N.W. A good deal of sea running; weather thick; under sail only.

15th.—Wind strong from W.N.W. A good deal of sea running; fine weather; under steam the latter part of the day.

16th.—Wind moderate from N.W.; sea going down; steamed until 8 p.m., then up propeller and proceeded under sail. Weather thick.

17th.—Wind strong from N.W.; under sail until 7 p.m., then down propeller and steamed. Weather overcast and thick; sea moderate.

18th.—Wind fresh from N.W.; thick fog; steamed all day; sea moderate.

19th.—Wind moderate from W.N.W., with fog. At 7 a.m., took Hero in tow and proceeded at an average rate of 7¼ knots; sea moderate.

20th.—Wind variable; thick fog. 1.30 p.m., cast off Hero; wind fresh from W.S.W.

21st.—Strong north winds, with thick fog; sea moderate.

22nd.—Strong west winds, with thick fog; sea moderate.

23rd.—Fresh west winds, with bright clear weather. At noon took Hero in tow, she being short of fuel. At 7 p.m., anchored at St. Johns harbour.

Tuesday morning (24th) was ushered in with naught but rain and dark foreboding clouds. By noon, however, everything had become bright and beautiful again, the sun appeared, and shone with increased lustre, adding to the scene of magnificence about to follow. Shortly after the Prince and suite, which was composed of His Grace the Duke of Newcastle, Secretary of State for the Colonies; Earl of St. Germains, Lord Chamberlain; Major General Hon. Robert Bruce, Governor to H.R.H.; Dr. Auckland, Physician to H.R.H.; G. Engleheart, Esq., Secretary to the Duke of Newcastle; Major Teesdale, and Capt. Grey, Equerries in Waiting, landed from the *Hero*. The booming of cannon from the citadel, the *Ariadne*, and the *Flying-Fish*, and the cheers from the sailors and populace, proclaimed Albert Edward representative of our

Queen. The yards of H.M. ships were manned, and the city and harbour presented a fine appearance, as every house and ship was decorated. Every body turned out in his best to do the Prince honour.

The landing took place on the Queen's Wharf, which was densely crowded with fashionably-dressed ladies, who hailed the Prince " with their spotless handkerchiefs, and indulged in the warmest expressions of joy and gladness." The Prince and suite were received by the Governor, Sir Alexander Bannerman, who led them to carriages. The Masonic body, the St. George's, St. Andrew's, British Mechanics', Coopers', Temperance, Native, and Irish Societies, Phœnix Volunteer Fire Company, a Guard of Honour of the Royal Newfoundland Corps, and of the 1st, 2nd, and 3rd Volunteer Rifle Companies, composed the procession, which passed through many beautiful arches and gorgeous decorations, to the Government House, a fine substantial building.

At three o'clock His Royal Highness held a grand levee, when two hundred persons were presented; also many Addresses, but he replied to the whole, collectively, as follows :—

I sincerely thank you for the Addresses presented to me, and for the hearty welcome received from you all on my landing on the shores of this the earliest colonial possession of the British Crown. I trust you will not think me regardless of your zealous loyalty if I acknowledge these Addresses collectively. It will afford me the greatest satisfaction to report to the Queen the devotion to her Crown and person unmistakeably evinced by the reception of her son, and so eloquently expressed in the Addresses from various bodies in this town and Harbor Grace. I am charged by the Queen to convey to you the assurance of the deep concern she has ever felt in this interesting portion of her dominions. I shall carry back a lively recollection of this day's proceedings and of your kindness to myself personally, but above all, of those hearty demonstrations of patriotism which prove your deep-rooted attachment to the great and free country of which we all glory to be called the sons.

He afterwards rode out to view the town, unattended.

A superb dinner and a grand ball were given in his honour during the evening.

The ball was given at the Colonial House, which was beautifully decorated with flags, banners, and appropriate devices for the occasion. Thousands of persons attended, and the Prince danced until half-past one, opening the ball with Lady Brady, and dancing afterwards with Miss Grant, Mrs. Major Bailly, Hon. Mrs. Kent, Miss E. Carter, Mrs. Ridley, Miss Mackarrol, Mrs. Young, Miss Robertson, Mrs. E. D. Shea, Miss C. Jarvis, and Miss Tobin. The following is the list of dances :—

1. Quadrille.
2. Quadrille.
3. Waltz.
4. Polka.
5. Quadrille.
6. Schottische.
7. Galop.
8. Lancers.
9. Mazourka.
10. Waltz.
11. Quadrille.
12. Polka.
13. Waltz and Galop.
14. Lancers.
15. Varsovienne.
16. Schottische.
17. Quadrille.
18. Polka.
19. Galop.
20. Contra Dance.

His Royal Highness remained in the room until three o'clock next morning. He seems to have pleased all parties (wherever he has visited), not only by his good looks, but by his affableness, unostentatious bearing, and good humour.

The Duke of Newcastle and Earl of St. Germains, as on subsequent occasions, did not mingle in the festivities of the dance. They, as well as His Royal Highness, and the rest of the suite, were dressed in full uniform.

During the day, a magnificent Newfoundland dog was presented by the Newfoundlanders to His Royal Highness, together with a collar of massive silver, and a steel chain. The collar is beautifully wrought in silver, with the Prince's crest and motto, &c., and bears the following inscription :—

" Presented to His Royal Highness, the Prince of Wales, from the inhabitants of Newfoundland."

The name given the dog by the Prince is " Cabot," after the celebrated Sebastian Cabot, the discoverer of the Island, and, if tradition is to be credited, the continent of North America before Columbus had visited any part of the main land.

On Wednesday the 25th, the Royal party attended the Regatta, on the Lake Quidi Vidi near the city, and appeared to be well pleased with the entertainment.

At ten o'clock on the morning of the 26th, the Prince and suite took their departure from Newfoundland, riding on horseback to the wharf. The same procession escorted him away that welcomed him; but, on this occasion, they wore very different faces from those when he landed: then all was joy; now all was regret at losing him so soon. The streets were decorated as before, the bells rang forth a right merry peal, cannons roared, and the cheers of the multitude rang forth, far and near, as on his arrival. Every place was crowded; every one appeared in his best. The soldiers lined the wharf and streets, and the National Societies appeared in the procession in full regalia.

Every ship in harbour also did honour by displaying its bunting to the best advantage, and by their men cheering heartily.

The embarkation took place at the Queen's Wharf, where the state barge was lying. The wharf was crowded as before with the fashionable and beautiful, as well as the chief functionaries of the Island, the Trade processions and the school children, all there to have a last look at their future sovereign, to shew their loyalty and to pray for his welfare.

His Royal Highness uncovered as he alighted from his horse, took leave of His Excellency, Lady Bannerman, and the Cabinet, and then, accompanied by his suite, stepped into the barge and was immediately rowed to the *Hero*.

Again the Citadel and Her Majesty's ships thundered forth a royal salute, completely drowning the great and lusty cheers of the people, the yards were manned, and the sailors and the people hurrahed together as no one ever hurrahed before.

The French war-vessel *Sesostris* also did honour, having displayed all her colours and manned her yards.

The Prince stepped on deck, showed his grateful acknowledgments by gracefully bowing to the people on shore, and then retired.

The squadron shortly after sailed for Halifax.

Before his final departure, His Royal Highness presented Lady Bannerman with a magnificent set of jewels, in commemoration of his visit to the Island.

It is almost needless to say that the people of Newfoundland were perfectly enraptured with the Prince; such devoted loyalty never was witnessed except in the other portions of his tour, and it has been admirably tested. Her Majesty may be assured of the loyalty of her great and warm-hearted Colonists.

25

RECEPTION AT NOVA SCOTIA.

The Royal Squadron arrived at Halifax on the morning of the 30th July, at 10 o'clock.

The weather was anything but agreeable; the sky being cloudy and the rain coming down in drizzling showers.

Nevertheless, the whole population turned out to welcome the Prince, and the greatest hilarity prevailed. Everything shewed that some unusual event was about to take place, and everybody determined to participate in it.

As the squadron neared the city, numerous small craft laden with passengers, went out to welcome it. They cheered as the *Hero* passed, and the Prince, who was on deck, acknowledged the compliment by bowing. The batteries fired royal salutes; there were minor ones from merchant vessels, &c.

H. M. S. *Nile* (flagship of Rear Admiral Sir Alexander Milne), then in port, manned her yards, and the men cheered right loyally.

As the squadron anchored in front of the city, thousands of persons gave thrilling and vociferous cheers, which rang loud and long.

The Prince and suite landed, near noon, at the dockyard, which was crowded with the chief dignitaries of the Province, and the ladies of Halifax.

He was met on the landing-steps by His Excellency the Earl of Mulgrave, Lieutenant Governor of Nova Scotia, who was introduced to His Royal Highness by the Duke of Newcastle, and with whom he shook hands, displaying that coolness and self-possession, and withal that courtesy, urbanity, and good breeding, for which his royal mother, and the royal family of England, are so justly celebrated.

The 63rd Regiment acted as a Guard of Honour and presented arms, their band playing the National Anthem.

The Mayor and City Council were next introduced, by the Lieutenant Governor, when the following Address was presented him, by them :—

To His Royal Highness Albert Edward Prince of Wales :—

MAY IT PLEASE YOUR ROYAL HIGHNESS,—We, the Mayor and Aldermen of the city of Halifax, in Nova Scotia, in the name of our citizens, do most cordially welcome your Royal Highness. We rejoice that our city should be thus highly honoured by the presence of the son of our revered and beloved Queen, the grandson of that illustrious Duke whose memory is gratefully cherished as the warm and constant friend of Nova Scotia, and the Heir Apparent to the powerful and glorious empire over which Her Majesty has for many years so wisely and beneficently ruled. We venture to approach Your Royal Highness with the expression of an earnest hope that your sojourn in our city and on this side the Atlantic, will be attended with much pleasure. We are fully persuaded that the reception which awaits your Royal Highness in every section of Her Majesty's North American dominions, will only impress you with the conviction, that devotion to the British throne and attachment to the British institutions are abiding elements in the minds of the inhabitants, and that the lustre which has been shed on the crown by the Christian and domestic virtnes of our most gracious Sovereign, is justly and gratefully appreciated by all her subjects. We earnestly implore the Giver of all good to guard and protect you, and restore you in safety to the parent land, and to that illustrious family circle of which we regard you as the ornament and pride, and that He may be graciously pleased long to spare your Royal Highness to fulfil those distinguished destinies to which your high position points.

The following was his reply :—

GENTLEMEN,—I have been led to expect that the loyalty and attachment to the British Crown which exists among the inhabitants of Halifax would insure for me a kind reception in your city, but the scene which I have witnessed this morning proves that my expectations are more than realized. For your welcome to myself, I feel, I assure you, sincere gratitude; but it is still more satisfactory to me as a son, and as an Englishman, to witness your affectionate attachment to the Queen, and to the laws and institutions of our common country. Your allusion to my illustrious grandfather is also most grateful to my feelings, and I rejoice to find that his memory is cherished amongst you. In your harbour the navies of Great Britain can ride in safety, whilst you prosecute that commercial activity which, under their protection, would seem destined to make Halifax one of the most important cities of the Western World, and to raise her inhabitants to a high prosperity. That such may be the fate reserved for it by Providence, is my very earnest hope. I request you to convey to the citizens of whom you are the representatives, my cordial thanks for the greeting they have given me.

He was then conducted to a fine high-mettled charger, upon which he mounted; the Duke of Newcastle, General Bruce, Earl of Mulgrave, &c., also taking horse. The Prince took his place in the centre, and the cavalcade joined the procession, amidst the cheers of the assembled thousands.

The procession proceeded in the following order :—

> The Union Engine and Axe Fire Companies.
> The North British and Highland Societies.
> The Charitable Irish Society.
> The St. George's Society.
> The Carpenters' Charitable Society.
> The African Society.
> The Sons of Temperance.
> The Volunteer Artillery and Rifle Companies.
> Her Majesty's Forces.

The streets were lined by the regular soldiers and volunteers, and were beautifully decorated with arches, transparencies, and evergreens. Of arches there were many,—one on Water Street; the Cunard dock with a model of a steamship and a motto; the Volunteer Artillery, composed of military trophies, and surmounted by a gun; three arches in the burnt district; * four in Brunswick Street; two opposite the parade-ground; one by the Roman Catholic Archbishop; a Masonic one; also one by the Governor; one by the General; and one at the Nuns' Convent.

The public and many private buildings presented also a fine appearance, being beautifully and artistically adorned with flags, banners, &c.; and to crown all, the people continually cheered His Royal Highness, as the procession passed on, a compliment he acknowledged by continually bowing.

On the parade, a pleasing sight was observed among the firemen, who carried a trophy fifty feet high, surmounted by a colossal figure holding a hose-pipe; but a still more pleasing one was the turning out of thirty-five hundred school children, dressed in white and blue, who sang the National Anthem.

Arrived at the Government House, the Prince was conducted into the drawing-room by the Earl Mulgrave.

In a few minutes after, the Members of the Legislature were announced, and, having been presented, the Premier (Hon. Mr.

---

* The scene of a late dreadful fire.

Young, now Chief Justice) presented the following Address of the two Houses of Parliament:—

To the Most High, Puissant, and Illustrious Prince Albert Edward, Prince of the United Kingdom of Great Britain and Ireland, Prince of Wales, Duke of Saxony, Prince of Cobourg and Gotha, Great Steward of Scotland, Duke of Cornwall and Rothsay, Earl of Chester, Carrick and Dublin, Baron of Renfrew, and Lord of the Isles, K. G.

The Members of the Executive Government, on behalf of the Legislature and people of Nova Scotia, tender to you, the son of their Sovereign, and Heir Apparent to her throne, the respectful homage of a loyal and united population, and cordially bid Your Royal Highness welcome to this continent.

Founded by the British races, and for more than a century, amidst the vicissitudes and temptations of that period, preserving unsullied her attachment alike to the throne, to the people, and to the institutions of the Mother Country, this Province has grown with a steady growth; and we trust that Your Royal Highness will observe in it some evidences of public spirit and material prosperity, some faint traces of the civilization you have left at home, some indications of a desire to combine commercial activity and industrial development with the enjoyment of rational freedom.

To the members of Your Royal House who visited Nova Scotia in her infant state, our country was deeply indebted for the patronage which enabled many of her sons to distinguish themselves abroad; and during the reign of Your Illustrious Mother the blessings of self-government and of unrestricted intercourse with all the world have been graciously conferred upon the Province.

With pride, we saw during the Crimean and Indian wars, Nova Scotians winning laurels beneath the Imperial flag; and Your Royal Highness has seen as you passed to your temporary residence what honour we pay to the memory of our countrymen who fall in defence of the Empire.

We trust that Your Royal Highness will also observe in the discipline of our Volunteers a determination to foster the martial spirit inherited from our ancestors, and energetically to defend, if need be, this portion of Her Majesty's dominions.

To the loyal welcome which we tender to Your Royal Highness, we beg to add our fervent prayer that the blessings of Divine providence may be freely showered upon you, and that you may be long spared in the high sphere in which you are called to move, to illustrate the virtue which have enshrined Your Royal Mother in the hearts of our people.

WILLIAM YOUNG.
JOSEPH HOWE.
ADAMS G. ARCHIBALD.
JONATHAN MCCULLY.
JOHN H. ANDERSON.
WILLIAM ANNAND.
JOHN LOCKE.
BENJAMIN WIER.

To which the Prince gave the following reply :—

GENTLEMEN,—I am deeply touched with the warmth and cordiality with which I have been welcomed to this colony, and thank you most heartily for your Address. It will be my duty, and it will be no less a pleasure to me, to inform Her Majesty of the proof which you have given me of your feelings of loyalty and devotion to Her Throne, and of your gratitude for those blessings, which it is her happiness to reflect, have during Her Reign been bestowed upon you and so many others of Her Subjects in all parts of the world. Most heartily do I sympathize in the pride with which you regard the laurels won by sons of Nova Scotia, and the affection with which you honor the memory of those who have fallen in the service of my country and yours. The monument you refer to will kindle the flame of patriotism in the breasts of those Volunteers whom I have passed to-day, and who, in this and the colony which I have lately quitted, are emulating the zeal and gallant spirit which have been exhibited throughout the Mother Country. One hundred years have now elapsed since the international struggles which retarded the prosperity of this country were brought to a close. May peace and harmony amongst yourselves complete the good work which then commenced, and increase the happiness and contentment of a loyal and united people.

He then bowed to the members, who retired.

The report goes that in the afternoon His Royal Highness rode out on horseback, and received a thorough drenching from a sudden shower; but he sat on his horse nobly and never flinched.

In the evening a grand state dinner was given by the Lieutenant Governor, where a party of forty-six ladies and gentlemen dined with the Prince.

On the 31st, he reviewed the troops of the garrison, consisting of the 62nd and 63rd Regiments of Foot, and a company of Engineers; and the Volunteers of Halifax, which consisted of five companies of Infantry, and one of Artillery.

When the whole had formed into line, His Royal Highness, accompanied by his suite, the Lieutenant Governor and his suite, all mounted, rode past and reviewed them, and afterwards through the lines; the multitude assembled cheering, which the Prince acknowledged. He then rode up to the flag-staff from which floated the royal standard.

The troops then filed past in excellent style. The Prince appeared in good spirits, and well pleased with the manner in which they had gone through the several evolutions.

At twenty minutes to two, he retired from the field, when the Artillery fired a royal salute. Subsequently he inspected the Citadel, and returned to Government House for luncheon.

Shortly afterwards, he again left for the Common to witness the Indian Games, &c., which consisted of a war-dance, foot-races, &c., and which amused him very much, he laughing heartily at the ludicrous scene, i. e. the war-dance. The Indians were equipped in their national costume, and paid great deference to His Royal Highness, styling him their " Great Brother." A vast multitude of people were gathered on the field while he was there, constantly using their stentorian powers in cheering.

In the evening the whole city and harbour were illuminated— one vast flood of light, nearly every house in the city and every ship in the harbour being lit up. The whole presented one of the most magnificent scenes imaginable.

A grand ball took place at the Provincial Building, which was, as well as the other public buildings, handsomely decorated. It was attended by three thousand persons; suffice it to say, the *elite* of Halifax and its neighbourhood. The Prince and suite, accompanied by the Earl of Mulgrave, &c., entered the ball-room at ten o'clock, the Prince leading Lady Mulgrave. His Royal Highness was dressed in full uniform, as also were the members of his suite. He received those present in the ball-room, who passed him in "single file."

He mingled in the festivities of the room with a great zest, dancing several times, opening the ball with Miss Young (niece of the Hon. Mr. Young, Premier), and danced afterwards with Miss Pilsbury, daughter of the U. S. Consul.

The following was the programme of dances:—

1. Quadrille............Lurline.	11. Quadrille.......Don Pasquale.
2. Waltz..............Rosebud.	12. Waltz..............Lurline.
3. Galop.............Charivari.	13. Galop..........Ever of Thee.
4. Lancers............First Set.	14. Lancers...........Third Set.
5. Polka.........Great Eastern.	15. Polka................Bertha.
6. Quadrille..........Satanella.	16. Quadrille..Off to Charlestown.
7. Waltz..Kathleen Mavourneen.	17. Waltz.......Reigning Beauty.
8. Galop..........Love Dream.	18. Galop..............Neptune.
9. Lancers..........Second Set.	19. Quadrille.............Zurich.
10. Polka...............Zelpher.	20. Waltz...............Martha.

Early on the morning of the next day (August 1st), he embarked on board H. M. S. *Valorous*, and steamed up the bay, and visited 'his illustrious grandfather's (the late Duke of Kent) farm, or rather the ruins of it, situated three miles from the city. He returned and witnessed the grand regatta. The boats running consisted of yachts, fishing-vessels, the boats of the different men-of-war, canoes, and whale-boats. He appeared to relish exceedingly this rather novel display.

At noon, a levee was held at Government House, when an immense number of gentlemen was presented.

In the evening, the volunteer officers were entertained at the same place by His Royal Highness. A grand display of fireworks also took place, and the fleet was illuminated; the latter presenting a spectacle of grandeur most beautiful to witness from the shore.

The Prince, accompanied by his suite, took his departure from Halifax at seven o'clock on the morning of the 2nd August, by special railway train *en route* for St. John, N. B., after a most auspicious entertainment.

His Royal Highness was accompanied by the Lieutenant Governor, General Trollope, the Ministry, and both branches of the Legislature.

An immense concourse of people collected to witness his departure; all exhibiting regret at the circumstance, but not forgetting to cheer loyally and loudly. Royal salutes were thundered from the ships and batteries as the iron-horse gently but swiftly bore its precious freight away.

At Windsor, an Address was presented to him, by the town authorities, to which he replied, and partook of a collation prepared by order of the Earl of Mulgrave. The usual loyal toasts of the Queen, Prince Consort, and Prince of Wales, were proposed by that nobleman, and drank with all the honours; the Prince acknowledging his by bowing.

After which the whole party entered carriages in waiting, and proceeded to Hantsport; the people cheering with ardour and enthusiasm.

They arrived there at half-past eleven a. m., which was, as well as Windsor, handsomely decorated. Here an Address was presented, and replied to, and the Royal party embarked on board H. M. S. *Styx* for St. John, N. B.; a royal salute being fired, and every evidence given of the loyalty of the Nova Scotians by their truly loyal and heartfelt cheers, which rang again and again, until the steamer was out of sight.

RECEPTION AT NEW BRUNSWICK.

The *Styx*, with His Royal Highness the Prince of Wales and suite on board, arrived at St. John, N. B., at ten o'clock on the evening of August 2nd. It not being customary to salute men-of-war vessels at night, the arrival was not noticed; but at daylight next morning, the batteries gave His Royal Highness a grand salute. The inhabitants arose a little surprised to find the Prince *awaiting them;* but hastily getting everything prepared for the reception, in a few minutes all was in readiness.

The landing took place at half-past ten, and a royal salute was fired by the *Styx*, as well as by the batteries.

The Prince was received at the wharf by the Honorable J. Manners Sutton, Lieutenant Governor of New Brunswick, and suite. Also by General Trollope, the Judges, &c., the Members of the Executive Council, the Mayor and Councilmen, the Mayors of Montreal and Boston, and the most prominent citizens of St. John.

The wharves and all around the landing-place were crowded with people dressed in their best, anxious to show their loyalty, and get a glimpse of their future monarch.

The Prince was conducted up the steps leading from the water, by the Lieutenant Governor, the band of the 63rd Regiment playing " God save the Queen." People cheered, and cannon roared enough to deafen any one.

The Prince was continually bowing to the people's homage, both when he was led to the Governor's carriage, and during the entire route to Government House.

The streets were lined by the Volunteers and Societies, a few arches spanned them, and the houses were decorated very nicely; but the whole affair was not so general as at Halifax, or as at St. Johns, Newfoundland.

The procession was organized as follows :—

     The Mayor and Corporation.
      The Town Major.
   Field Officers of the Militia in uniform.
 His Excellency the Lieutenant Governor's Aides-de-Camp,
  Lieut. Col. Drury and Lieut. Col. Hayne (mounted).
 The Officer commanding her Majesty's troops in New Brunswick.
  First Carriage—His Royal Highness Prince of Wales,
The Duke of Newcastle and His Excellency the Lieutenant-Governor.
 Second Carriage—His Royal Highness' Equerries: the Earl of
   St. Germains and Major General Bruce.
 Third Carriage—The remainder of His Royal Highness' suite.
 The Chief Justice, Judges, and Members of the Executive Council.
  The President and Members of the Legislative Council.
  The Speaker and Members of the House of Assembly.
    The Mayors of other Cities.
    High Sheriff and Coroner.
   Stipendiary and other Magistrates.
Heads of Civil Departments, and Office-Bearers of the National Societies.

The procession formed, and escorted His Royal Highness to " the Duke of Kent's Lodge," lately occupied and owned by the Hon. Mrs. Chipman, and which had been handsomely furnished by the Provincial Government for the Prince's use. Inside the grounds were assembled five thousand school-children fancifully dressed, and decorated with flowers.

As the procession with the Prince in his carriage passed up to the house, these little creatures threw bouquets, and sang the National Anthem, with the following verses added :

   Through ev'ry charming scene,
   O Lord ! preserve the Queen,

In health to reign.
Her heart inspire and move
With wisdom from above,
And in a nation's love
Her throne maintain.

Thy choicest gifts in store,
On her be pleased to pour;
Long may she reign.
May she defend our laws,
And ever give us cause
With heart and voice to sing
God save the Queen.

Hail! Prince of Brunswick's line,
New Brunswick shall be thine;
Firm has she been.
Still loyal, true, and brave,
Here England's flag shall wave,
And Britons pray to save
A nation's heir.

Soon after twelve His Royal Highness proceeded to the Court House, a fine-looking cut-stone building, and stood on the steps, while the National and Trade Societies, and Volunteers, passed before him. There was a great number of them, and they were certainly a fine-looking body of men.

After which he held a levee in the same building. A goodly number of gentlemen were presented, also two Indian chiefs. Two Addresses were presented, one by the Magistrates, the other by the Mayor and Corporation, of which latter the following is a copy :—

To His Royal Highness Albert Edward Prince of Wales, Duke of Cornwall and Rothsay, Earl of Dublin, Baron of Renfrew, Knight of the most noble Order of the Garter, &c., &c.

We, the Mayor, Aldermen, and Commonalty of the city of St. John, hasten to approach your Royal Highness for the purpose of welcoming to New Brunswick the Heir Apparent to the throne, and the future sovereign of this great empire, of which it is our pride to form a portion, and over which the beneficent sway of our beloved Queen, day by day, strengthens those ties which happily unite us with the mother country. Among us is still found a remnant of those who in the last century witnessed and partook of the joy and enthusiasm with which your Royal Highness' grandfather, the Duke of Kent, was received on his visit to the infant city, upon the founder of which, in token of royal approbation, great benefits had been recently conferred by the royal charter of his Majesty George the Third ; and with just pride we declare to your Royal Highness, that the feelings of loyalty and attachment which led to these shores the founders of this city, still eminently characterize the entire population of this colony. It is our prayer, that your Royal Highness will have a propitious termination to the tour through her Majesty's North American dominions, in which you are now engaged ; and we hope that you will vouchsafe to assure our gracious Queen, that peace and contentment are found among us under her rule, and that love and attachment to her person and crown is the common sentiment of her devoted subjects in this the commercial capital of her province of New Brunswick.

The Prince received the Address personally from W. R. M. Brutis, to whom it was handed by the Recorder, and returned the following answer direct, instead of through the Duke :—

GENTLEMEN,—I thank you with all sincerity for the Address which you have just presented to me, and for the welcome which it conveys to the colony of New Brunswick, and the important city of which you are the municipal representatives. When my grandfather, the Duke of Kent, paid to this place the visit to which you make so gratifying a reference, he found it but little more than a village. It is my good fortune to receive on the same spot from a city—which affords a striking example of what may be effected under the influence of free institutions by the spirit and energy of the British race—these demonstrations of love and loyalty unto me. Your commercial enterprise has made this port the emporium of the trade of New Brunswick ; and as the noble river which flows into it brings down for export the products of your soil, so I trust the vessels which crowd its piers will reward your successful industry with the wealth of other lands. I am not unmindful of the origin of this city, and it will be a subject of pride and pleasure to me to report to the Queen that the descendants of its founders have not departed from their first attachment to the crown of England, which brought them to these shores.

Returning to his residence, he partook of luncheon, and then drove over the Suspension Bridge (680 feet long, and under which are the Falls of St. John), to the small but beautiful suburb of Carleton, opposite, where the whole population turned out to welcome him.

In the evening, the whole city of St. John was beautifully illuminated, and perfectly eclipsed either Halifax, or St. Johns, Newfoundland. Everything was gotten up on a gorgeous scale, and was well calculated to give a good effect.

The Prince and suite bade farewell to this rather quiet but very pretty city on the following morning, Saturday, 4th August. Taking the cars for Rothsay Station (named after him) on the Kennebecasis; at which place they took the steamer *Forest Queen* for the capital of New Brunswick, Fredericton, where they arrived at six o'clock p.m., after passing up the fine river St. John. The Prince had an excellent opportunity, and no doubt availed himself of it, to view the delightful scenery that adorns this river, as also of witnessing the agricultural proclivities of the New Brunswickers.

The entire population was out to greet His Royal Highness, and crowded the wharves and fields, all exhibiting the greatest joy at the visit.

The bells rang forth merrily; guns fired everywhere, the reverberation sounding through hill and dale. Everything and every person seemed delighted on that day in that beautiful little place.

A troop of Volunteers lined the wharf, and presented arms to the youthful scion of royalty as he passed from the landing-place. A terrace was crowded with ladies, who waved their handkerchiefs to him, and the river was covered with small craft, which had gone out to meet the steamer.

While the steamer was nearing the wharf, and until she was moored, the Prince and suite stood on deck quietly surveying the scene, the Prince now and then acknowledging the cheers by bowing.

The Mayor and City officials conducted His Royal Highness to a carriage, and then joined the procession, which escorted him through the principal street to Government House.

The street was very nicely adorned by a few simple arches, characteristic of the city, and was lined by the Volunteers and Police. They had quite enough to do to keep the people back, who, no doubt, in their loyal enthusiasm, would have drawn the Prince themselves.

In the evening a grand torch-light procession was organized by the firemen and citizens generally, who paraded the streets. Bonfires were lit and other tokens of the loyalty of the inhabitants shown.

On Sunday morning His Royal Highness and suite attended Divine Service at the Anglican Cathedral, which was crowded to its utmost capacity by the people of the city and neighbourhood, long before the hour of service. This was the first time he had attended Divine Service on land since leaving England.

He was met at the door of the Cathedral by the Lord Bishop of Fredricton, who escorted him to his pew.

The Rev. J. B. Medley (son of the Bishop) read the Prayers; and the Rev. Chas. S. Medley, the Lessons and Litany. The Rev. Dr. Coster (of Carleton) read the Epistle; and the Rev. H. Pollard (of St. Stephen's), the Gospel. And His Lordship the Bishop read the ante-communion service, and preached the following:—

SERMON.

His Lordship took his text from the 12th verse of the fourteenth chapter of Romans,—" So, then, every one of us shall give an account of himself to God." We are assembled to worship God to-day on an occasion which possesses singular interest, and has also this feature of importance, that we have never all met in this church before, and it is wholly improbable that we shall ever meet here again. Apart, then, from these topics, on which there is no necessity for me to dwell, because your minds are full of them, there is another of unspeakable moment which claims your earnest attention. Pardon me, then, my brethren, if the subject be not what you expected. You may have thought that I would hasten to express (as well as my feeble abilities would allow) the language of congratulation and loyalty, and be the mouth-piece of those feelings which not only exist, but overflow, in all your hearts. If I adopt a different course, it is not that I do not share with you in the common joy. I rejoice with you heartily and loyally. But I have a higher mission to discharge. Can I, dare I forget that you are all, from the highest to the lowest, immortal souls?—sinners redeemed by the blood of a common Saviour—Christians, united by a common hope, placed for a few moments under my special charge. Can I forget how much may depend upon one soul even in this half-hour? Can I, above all, forget that if every one shall give an account for himself to God, I shall myself give an account for what I shall deliver to you this day. And, as I probably address many of you for the first and last time, can I, in justice to you, dwell on any other topics than those momentous truths in which alike all have a common interest, in regard to which the bonds of temporal polity, political action, and even national welfare, great as they are, are as nothing compared with the salvation of your souls through eternity. I beseech you to unite with me at once on this stupendous theme, and pray to God that by His help the words which He has spoken may take deep root in your hearts, that with no light, no momentary impression, the truths may dwell there and abide in you all your life long : and become the rule of your actions, filling you with those high and holy principles which will carry you safely through life, and enable you to give up your account, at the last day, with joy, and not with grief. The points which the text lays down for our consideration are two. 1st. That we shall all personally, and face to face, appear before God. 2nd. That this appearance will not be as a matter of choice, curiosity, or joint consent, but that God will summon each separate soul to give an account of itself to Him, the maker and judge of all souls. From these two topics we shall do well and wisely to infer what influence this truth shall have, not only on our feelings but on our daily habits of life. Glance, my brethren, for it is only a glance time will allow us at these two stupendous truths. Have you considered what it is to appear personally before God? Every one knows that it is an affair of some moment to make an appearance before an earthly potentate. Uneducated men are very brave and boastful on these subjects till they are brought into the presence of the court ; but the splendour of the ceremony, and the gravity and respectful behaviour of those who know how to conduct themselves, awe and impress the boldest. But if this court be sitting on questions of life and death, if the monarch be invested with absolute power, if on his fiat hang all your temporal interests, few men are to be found who do not feel some apprehension. But what court of the earth can furnish you with an image of the throne of God, seated in judgment. This is no question of earthly prudence, superior dignity, profit, or place, or emolument : the prize (if one may so term it) is your own soul ; the question, your own salvation. The demand is whether you are fit to enjoy what Christ has prepared for them that love him. With whom are you to meet? Not with a fellow-sinner who knows little of you ; but that which your own actions reveal. He who meets you face to face, being to being, he whom you will then for the first time look upon, is your Maker, Sovereign, Benefactor, Saviour, and omniscient Judge. He looks not into your eyes, but into your soul. He sees all is and ever has been there, and reads you off at a glance, what you have been and what you have made yourself, or what His grace has made you. There you stand with all your imperfections on your head, alone with God—alone with God! O, merciful Father, what a sight will this be of ourselves and of Thee. How will our poor knees tremble at this interview, and upon what can the best and holiest of us cast ourselves but on Thy mercy and the merits of our Redeemer for salvation! The good we have done is nothing; the errors we have committed are numberless. Thy power is infinite, Thy justice terrible, and the very sight of Thee is sufficient to destroy us, but for that merciful assurance. This our God we have waited for, and he will serve us. Now if the sight of God is so awful, what shall we say when we consider these sacred truths here laid down, that each soul will have to give its own separate account at the day of that meeting. We all know what sight-seeing is. Men run together to great sights from mixed feelings : some from curiosity, some from respect and loyalty, many from both these motives. Our curiosity will find no place there. It is to give account that you are summoned there. Giving account is not a pleasant duty when the accounts are complicated, the interests many and serious, and the penalties of breach of trust are heavy, and we are glad to be rid of the duty, and in no kind of action is the penalty or imperfection of human nature more abundantly displayed than in giving account. What efforts are made to make the best of a bad business, what evasive answers! What positive deception is practised! what immense ingenuity in avoiding the plain naked truth. Nay, take the highest standard of duty and the holiest life to be found amongst us, still there is an abatement required, there is a reserve, there is a secret chamber of the soul into which we never admit one human being besides ourselves. In some particulars we stand alone ; our dearest friends are not admitted into the sanctuary of the heart beyond a certain point. No soul stained by sin can bear that it should be looked at throughout even by a fellow sinner. Yet this account, so painful to all honest, humble Christians; so terrible to the holy Patriarch Job, that he said, "I abhor myself;" so awful to Abraham when he came face to face with God, that he said, "Behold I have taken upon me, yet am but dust ;" so fearful to St. Peter, that he cried, "Depart from me for I am a sinful man, O Lord;" so agonizing to Daniel, that he could eat nothing for many days ; so terrible to John that he fell at Christ's feet as dead—this account, so full of terror and of fear to the greatest and holiest of mankind, you, my brethren, and I must encounter. What is it that we are to render up? What is it that we can correct, evade, or fly from ? What is it that must all be made known. The life of our souls, the posture of our hearts towards God, the life of Christ as manifested in our mortal body, the use we have made of our baptismal privileges, the benefits we have derived from Sacred Scriptures, the union and communion we have had with our risen Lord, the prayers we have offered, the faith to which we have held fast, the example we have set in all the various hours of life, in all the companies we have been brought, in all the relations and capacities in which Providence has placed us, as subjects, as rulers, as citizens or freemen, as electors, as elected, as judges, as, magistrates, as pastors, as flocks, as hearers, as preachers, as tradesmen as mechanics, as rich, as poor, as gifted with powerful intellect or moderate abilities, as physicians, as merchants, as lawyers, as soldiers, as men of science, as handicrafts even of all kinds, as husbands, wives, brothers, sisters, children, masters, servants, as those for whom Christ died, and for whom He intercedes, and reigns in glory. Surely when you all think of this complicated, manifold, tremendous account, you must see the dignity of common things, the momentous issues of ordinary life,—the risk we run in living our common every-day life. Surely you must see how judgment and eternity mingle with the daily occurrences which seem too trifling to be remembered, and that your daily prayer, and daily fear, and daily honesty, and daily living to the Lord, are the threads which hold your life together. Every hour the word or action passes on to judgment. The word is spoken, the action done, and in one instant it has left the world, and it cannot be undone for ever, and another line is written on the face of eternity that cannot be blotted out. Surely I have said enough, though but little to show what holy principles should guide us, in consideration of these great truths. May God stamp them indelibly upon our hearts.

1st. The subject here set before us should lead us to a holy, yet, if I may so express myself, a cheerful fear. We are here presented certainly with a grave view of life, yet it is far from being a gloomy, discontented, or repining view. The God who sent His blessed Son to save us, who underwent toil and privation, ignominy, and death for our sakes, is also the God of boundless might. This God rejoices in the happiness of His meanest creatures, and denies not to us, at all fit seasons, the enjoyments with which His works supply us, in the paths of science, in the glories of art, in the splendour of the fields, in the recreation proper to youth, and animal spirits, and high health, and virtuous cheerfulness. We neither please nor worship Him by refusing to our fellow creatures those innocent joys which lighten the common burdens of humanity and cheer our saddened spirits for those graver duties which we have to discharge. So that whilst we fear Him we may rejoice in our Maker always, and may lawfully partake in those sports and recreations which are suitable to our character, which contain nothing sinful in them, provided we bear about with us everywhere a strict sense of our duty to God and to each other, and are ever ready to fulfil it. I have called this feeling by a compound name—a cheerful fear—because, under any system of theology which absolutely forbids general recreation or which denounces as sinful particular kinds of recreation whilst it tolerates others, the mind is led to assume the look of fear of God, rather than to feel it, or to feel abject terror in the thought of meeting our God rather than the holy and loving one which become a Christian. The proper medium would seem to be to remember that God denies us nothing which is really good for our body, that we must serve him with our hearts and rejoice with trembling, and that a cheerful, hopeful, large-hearted and thankful spirit is that which best enables us to discharge each duty as it comes, looking for the merciful allowance and being confident in the justice of God.

2nd. This account should also be a motive for perpetual love and thankfulness for the vast amount of our present mercies. Now, independently of those which personally belong to each of us, and on whom want of time forbids me to dwell, I may properly call your attention to-day to those which belong to us all as citizens. When we look round among the nations of the earth and consider the past and present condition of countries favoured with a fruitful soil and a more genial climate than our own, how inestimable is the price of our manly, rational, and constitutional freedom, how deeply should we cherish, how diligently should we guard and preserve, the integrity of our limited monarchy, the nice balance of our respective estates and realms, the just and merciful administration of our laws, and the various expressions of freedom and safe-guards against license with which a gracious Providence has endowed us! Our monarchy, our language, our religion, are rich in all the associations of the past; our progress in the useful arts and sciences has been widening and deepening every year; our deliverances from civil war and religious thraldom have been unexampled in the history of the world; our colonial possessions have in them all the seeds of a great future, and want only a higher education and a more potent development of natural resources to give them birth. A gracious Providence everywhere unites us by successful though calamitous war and by the nobler arts of peace. Our sufferings and our joys are the common property of the empire. One year our bosoms throb with fear and sorrow at the massacre of Cawnpore, in another we hail the coming of a Prince, not, like his great ancestor, reaping his youthful harvest of renown and blood inflicted upon a foreign land, but sent forth by the love of the Mother of our country, to consolidate the affections of a distant empire and to bring nearer in loyalty, love, and friendship the claims which science and commercial action have already united. Truly we shall have to give an account of these unnumbered blessings. This good measure heaped together and running over, which God has given into our bosoms, calling for no narrow gratitude in return, demands of us this day more thankfulness in our hearts, more fervour in our prayers, more charity towards each other, more virtue and holiness as a nation, than we have yet exhibited. And here the context to the passage before us leads me to notice that the whole argument of Paul on the subject is brought to bear on the great duty of a wise and charitable forbearance towards each other. The question which he discusses in this chapter concerning different kinds of food and religious observances, are questions which in principle are continually brought forward, and he brings in the solemn judgment of God to show how we should deal with them. Why dost thou judge thy brother—or why dost thou set at nought thy brother?—for we must all stand before the judgment seat of Christ. So then every one of us must give account of himself to God; let us not therefore judge one another any more. A judgment indeed we must form upon men and things with a view to our own Christian discrimination; but let it not necessarily be a judgment to condemnation; let it not, above all, be a heart of uncharitable judgment; but let the severity of your condemnation be directed to this point, that none of you put an occasion to fall in your brother's way, or cause him to fall by an unwise and careless use of your liberty. Here, then, you see another important principle arising out of the solemn subject of an appearance before God in judgment. If all of us will be judged, and if it be so hard and difficult for us to meet that judgment of ourselves, how strongly does this urge on us the principle of mutual amity, forbearance, gentleness, consideration, abstinence from boasting, arrogance, from envy, railing, evil surmisings, and uncharitableness? This is the special argument of the Apostle, and I wish there were not sufficient reasons for pressing it upon you. Much allowance is to be made for the excitement of men's minds; but let us recollect one thing, —we owe it to our Sovereign, we owe it to our Province, we owe it to ourselves, to let no ill-feeling mingle with or follow the gracious visit, if I may so speak, of our common friend. Let us charitably suppose that every one has done his best to welcome him. Differences of opinion are ensured by our freedom of thought; but we have too many points of union, too many subjects of devout and glowing thankfulness, to allow the envious, ill-natured, or uncharitable thought to have a lodgment in our hearts. Why should we set at nought our brother in Christ, when we shall meet together as sinners before a common tribunal hereafter? Let us remember that the unbounded liberty we enjoy of saying or printing all we feel, should be a check against, rather than a guarantee for license; for the greater our freedom the heavier must be our account. And now, addressing for the moment my dear friends and brethren of the Church of England specially, ought not this thought of your personal appearance before God to lead you to value more highly, and be more fervent in the use of your own holy and common prayer. You have sometimes perhaps looked upon what are called State prayers, as if they did not nearly concern you; you have repeated them without personal interest; no fervent Amen has come from the depths of your hearts. Our good Sovereign has now sent to you one of the dearest members of her family to remind you that she is not an abstraction, a fragment of the State,—a court ceremony, that stripped of its external comes to nought; but a living, personal, responsible being, an anointed Queen, a Christian ruler, fully alive to all the responsibilities of her exalted station, desirous to glorify God in it, depending upon the mercy of God in Christ Jesus the Saviour of us all, looking forward with you to His just and glorious advocate, and solicitous, nay deeply, tenderly solicitous, for the benefit of her people's prayers. And will you deny that profitable, motherly, natural pious request? Surely when we meet together in the church, the thought of this day's assemblage will sometimes infuse fresh fervour into that petition, which I presume, in your name, once more to offer. Endue her plenteously with heavenly gifts, grant her in health and wealth long to live, strengthen her that she may vanquish and overcome all her enemies, and finally, after this life, may she obtain everlasting joy and felicity through Jesus Christ our Lord. Amen.

Thus it may be seen, the remembrance that we shall all have to appear before God in judgment, has a directly practical bearing upon our whole lives. It may serve to correct our view of human life, to sanctify and soothe our sorrows, to dignify every common action, and to lessen the importance of worldly honour and gain; it may elevate the honest and humble the richest among us, by abasing all upon the foot-stool of one common Father, Benefactor, Saviour, and Judge.

But the subject cannot properly be closed without the suggestion of that holy and comfortable hope connected with it. Awful as is the subject to those who, like Felix, tremble at the judgment to come, the humble believer in Christ will remember with a trembling joy that it is not only judgment but salvation, if he is ready to be revealed at the last time. Of ourselves, indeed, we must speak less confidently; but we have all loved many dear ones gone before us, the reality of whose faith, the fervour of whose charity, the faithfulness of whose good works, supply us with the best foundations for a lively and comfortable hope. When we recollect the unfeigned faith that was in them, their gentleness and brotherly tenderness, their pious munificence, their fervent prayers, their humble and devout resignation, and how they passed through the gate of death supported by the peace of the Comforter, and, in a Father's arms, contented died away, we can even contemplate the judgment-seat of Christ with lively hope. On that seat is our Redeemer, our brother, and our friend; in that sacred name we acknowledge the marks of his sacred passion; in that majestic presence we recognize that gracious, awful Being, to whom all our prayers are offered; on whom all our faith is fixed, the author and guardian of our life, the Rock of Ages, in whom is everlasting strength. If I mistake not I speak to some who will recognize in this portrait the features of those much-loved friends whose memory I cherish daily with themselves. Their works abide with us, for our comfort. Let us, then, ever bear about with us this holy principle of duty, this two-fold remembrance of the account we shall have to give. He to whom we give it has promised to receive us to Himself. Let this principle awe and terrify the impenitent, awaken the slumberer, dry the mourner's tears, quicken every good resolution, moderate every joy, hallow every motive, form our shield against temptation, our hope and solace in that hour in which neither princes, physicians, nor friend, can grant us any longer their protection, succour, or control. In that hour, by Thy cross and passion, good Lord, deliver us. In that hour suffer us, not for any pains of death to fall from Thee. Above all, when God ariseth to shake terribly the earth, when the judgment is set, and the books are opened, good Lord, deliver us!

On Monday morning the Government of New Brunswick presented the following Address to His Royal Highness:—

The Members of the Executive Council, for themselves, the Legislature, and the people of New Brunswick, offer to you, the Son of their beloved Sovereign, and the Heir Apparent to the Throne, their respectful homage, and heartily welcome Your Royal Highness to this Province. The inhabitants of New Brunswick are the descendants of the Loyalists who, in the war of the American Revolution, adhered to the royal standard, and of emigrants from Europe and the British Isles; are ardently attached to British institutions; contented and happy in the enjoyment of that large measure of rational liberty which our mixed form of government secures. They have, with patience and industry, devoted themselves to the development of the resources of the country, and the advancement of its material interests; and ever since the organization of the Province in 1817, it has steadily advanced in all the elements of progress. The visit of Your Royal Highness brings to the recollection of many of the old inhabitants the time when your illustrious grandfather visited this Province, and they refer with pleasure to his benignity and courtesy. In forming the colony, it was the design of the Imperial Government that the constitution should be settled upon the model of its great original in the parent State; but it was not until the reign of Your August Mother, Her Most Gracious Majesty Queen Victoria, that the principles of self-government were fully established with ample power to regulate our trade, consistently with the general policy of the nation. Although in this portion of the Empire Your Royal Highness will not discover evidences of the great wealth and refinement of the Old World, we believe that you will be pleased with the energy of the people and their success, and that Your Royal Highness will receive new proof of their fitness for self-government, of their loyalty to the Queen, and of their attachment to the institutions of the fatherland. We hope that in witnessing the discipline of our Volunteers, Your Royal Highness will be assured that the patriotic spirit which animates the people of the parent State also pervades this portion of the Empire; and that if the necessity should ever arrive, all the available resources of New Brunswick will be freely offered for the defence of Imperial interests and the maintenance of national honour. In again tendering to Your Royal Highness our unfeigned congratulations, we would invoke the continuance of the Divine blessing upon your illustrious house, and most fervently pray that Your Royal Highness may long enjoy the high position to which Divine Providence has called you; ever the pride of Your August Mother and the hope of our common country.

The Prince replied as follows:—

GENTLEMEN,—I receive with much gratification an Address which, whilst it breathes a spirit of loyalty to the Queen, and affectionate attachment to Her Family, which animate the whole people of this Province, does not fail to remind me of the claim of your ancestors, to live in the memories of Your Sovereign, and of the British nation. The commercial activity of St. John, the thriving agriculture on the rich banks of the river which I have traversed; the smiling aspect of this city, the capital of New Brunswick, all tend to convince me, even apart from your gratifying assurances, of the prosperity and happiness which you enjoy under the Constitution of the parent State and the free institutions which you possess. Every visitor to your shores, but more especially the son of your Queen, must earnestly pray that your peaceful avocations may never be disturbed; but in case such a misfortune should await the Empire, I rejoice to observe in this, as well as the Provinces which I have lately visited, the self-relying spirit of patriotism which prevails; and I see in the discipline of your Volunteers the determination to protect the national honour which is manifested in every portion of the Queen's dominions. I beg you to accept my thanks for your congratulations, and for your earnest prayers for my present and future happiness.

Two other Addresses were delivered, one from the City of Fredericton and one from the Clergy. The Address from the Mayor and Corporation was as follows:—

To His Royal Highness Albert Edward, Prince of Wales:—

The Mayor and City Council of the city of Fredericton most respectfully greet your Royal Highness with a right hearty welcome to the metropolis of New Brunswick. From the affection we entertain for Your Royal Mother, our beloved Queen, we bid you welcome. From our regard to yourself, as the son of such a Mother and the Heir Apparent to the Throne, we bid you welcome. From our attachment to the Constitution which admits of such a benign and maternal sovereignty in the person of Your Beloved Mother, we bid you welcome. In obedience to the universal heart-throb of our Empire of perpetual sunlight, we bid you welcome. Victoria's son must be everywhere welcome throughout Victoria's dominions. Your Royal Highness, during your provincial tour, will visit larger cities and see greater developments of wealth and art than we present, but nowhere can there be found a people more devoted to the Throne than in and around the *Silvæfilia nobilis*. May the King of Kings graciously protect Your Royal Highness during your prospective tour, and bring you safely home again to the land of our fathers and the sunshine of the royal domestic circle.

To this Address he read the following reply :—

GENTLEMEN,—Your hearty reiterations of welcome demand my warmest thanks. In the name of the Queen I thank you for the expressions of your loyalty, and for the just tribute which you pay to the acts of her reign, and the sentiments which have always animated her. In my own name, also, I thank you for the warm reception I have met with in the city which you represent, and for the earnest wishes for my welfare which you have expressed. Your city, no doubt, is small in comparison with many others which I am about to visit; but the enthusiasm with which you so loudly greeted me on Saturday, and the devotional quiet which prevailed yesterday in your streets, prove to me that this community know how to fear God as well as to pay due honor to its earthly sovereign. I sincerely trust that these virtues may never diminish amongst you, while your limits enlarge and your wealth increases in proportion to the local advantages which Providence has bestowed upon you.

Afterwards His Royal Highness held a levee at Government House, when the principal gentlemen of the city and neighbourhood were presented. He then inaugurated a public park. He attended in the evening a grand ball given in his honour, where the following ladies were his partners: Hon. Mrs. Manners Sutton (Governor's lady), Miss Florence Parker (daughter of Judge Parker), Miss Fisher (sister of the Attorney General), Miss Lizzy Hazen, Miss Medley (daughter of the Bishop), Mrs. Justice Ritchey, Mrs. Bayard, and Miss Robinson.

His Royal Highness took his departure from the city of Fredericton on the next day (Tuesday the 7th), taking the *Forest Queen* to Indiantown, adjacent to St. John, where a hearty ovation greeted him. Thence he crossed the Suspension Bridge in a carriage to Carleton. On leaving this delightful locality, a party of stalwart, though gentle, firemen unharnessed the horses from his carriage, and drove "their dear prince," as they delighted to call him, across the bridge to the wharf, the whole populace cheering loudly. There he embarked on board the *Styx* for Windsor.

He arrived back again at Hantsport at 7 o'clock on the morning of the 8th; arrived at Windsor at eight, remaining an hour; arrived at Truro at half-past eleven, remaining an hour; and arrived at Pictou at half-past five p. m.

At all these places he was received with an enthusiasm which knew no bounds. At Truro, an Address was presented by the county member (Mr. Archibald), on behalf of the inhabitants of the place, to which the Prince replied. This place was beautifully decorated, and the school-children sang the National Anthem. The Prince was much pleased, and spoke a few words to the little folks.

He also accepted a slight collation, prepared by a party of ladies, who also waited upon him.

From Truro to Pictou, he, as well as his suite, travelled in post chaises.

At Pictou, the Prince was received with demonstrations of regard, and, in fact, perfect veneration. He immediately embarked on board the *Hero*, which, with the other ships of the squadron, sailed for Charlottetown, Prince Edward's Island.

RECEPTION AT PRINCE EDWARD'S ISLAND.

His Royal Highness arrived at Charlottetown about half-past eight on the morning of the 9th August, and landed from the *Hero* at one o'clock.

H. M. S. *Nile, Ariadne, Cossack, Valorous,* and *Flying Fish,* the Government surveying-vessel *Margaretta Stephenson,* and the French war-vessel *Pomene,* commanded by the Marquis de Montignæ, accompanied it. The Royal Squadron, on nearing the town, was met by the Micmac Indians in canoes, who welcomed the Prince. Salutes were fired from the batteries.

As, in many of the other places visited, the weather was very disagreeable, raining continually, yet thousands upon thousands came forth to welcome His Royal Highness. The city was crowded with visitors, and accommodation was a "scarce commodity."

The Prince landed at the Queen's Wharf, under eight royal

salutes, the *Pomene* also saluting, and was received by His Excellency Lieutenant Governor Dundas, and the high dignitaries of the Island, among whom were: Chief Justice Hodgson; Justice Peters; The Premier, Hon. Charles Palmer; Hon. Mr. Pope, Colonial Secretary; Hon. Mr. Hanraham, Attorney General; Hon. Charles Young, President of Legislative Council; Hon. Donald Montgomery, Speaker of the Assembly; the Archdeacon, Dr. Reid, Dr. McIntyre, Roman Catholic Bishop and other clergymen, Hon. T. H. Howland, Mayor, and Councillors; Lieutenant Colonel Longworth, Commandant, &c.

The Marquis de Montignæ and the officers of the *Pomene* were also on the wharf, and a Guard of Honor of the 62nd Regiment from Halifax, and the Militia.

The Prince was conducted to the Governor's carriage, by His Excellency, and was escorted to Government House by the Volunteer Cavalry.

The streets, as in the other cities visited, presented a fine appearance, being tastefully ornamented; the streets with graceful and well-made arches,&c., and lined by Volunteers; the houses with flags, banners, &c.

The able correspondent of the Toronto *Globe*, speaking of them, says:—

"The arch placed at the street-end of the wharf was built of evergreens, surmounted by a picture of Britannia sitting on a sea-horse, in the act of ruling the waves, and by two large carved lions. The motto it bore was, "Welcome to Prince Edward Isle." On a second arch festoons of roses were suspended from the hands of lovely-looking ladies in wood, who were, from the trumpets at their mouths, supposed to proclaim the words written underneath—"Welcome, our future King." Another arch still in Queen Street, bore figures of two volunteers, with guns and knapsacks all complete, and I think it was upon this erection that the words "May thy visit prove, Great Britain's heir, a closer bond with home," occurred. Opposite Queen's Square, in which are the Provincial buildings, images of two Scotch grenadiers appeared, also surmounting an arch. The circular-pointed market-house, an ugly building, had been planted round with spruce trees, and so hidden with bunting and flowers, that I scarcely knew it again. The post-office too had been decorated with equal success. In the square was the tent of an Indian chief, who, I should have previously mentioned, with his warriors and squaws paddled out to meet the Prince, and joined his voice with that of the applauding throng. Soon after passing the square, the procession moved down Kent Street to Government House. The arch immediately opposite Government House was the most beautiful of the whole. From the hands of two dancing girls flowers were suspended; and stars formed of bayonets, pikes, and swords were inserted in the pillars. His Royal Highness upon alighting immediately entered the house, and was seen no more that day, save by the Governor and his immediate attendants.

So far, in speaking of the decorations, I have confined myself to one class alone. Charlottetown showed a full compliment of bunting, of floral crowns, of evergreen decorations, of spruce trees, of mottoes, and of those hundreds of little things which go towards making a great display. The Chief Justice had a very nice little motto—" In hoc signo spes mea,"—the sign being the Prince's plume. The scene from the wharf was grand. Union Street is very wide, and rises gradually from the water, so that for upwards of a mile the mass of people could be seen, the narrow lane preserved by the militia being distinctly visible all the way up."

Every place was crowded by the people, eager to gaze upon the Prince, and to do homage to him; everywhere were cheers and cries of joy.

The school-children, to the number of two thousand, sang the National Anthem in Cochrane Square, as he passed, and afterwards cheered gallantly.

In the evening, there was a general illumination and fireworks, which were completely destroyed by the immense deluge of rain that fell.

It was on this evening, we believe, that Mrs. Macready, the celebrated actress, had the honour to read from the English Poets, to His Royal Highness and suite at Government House.

At eleven o'clock on the morning of the 10th August, a levee was held by the Prince at Government House. This was a most select affair, for only the highest personages of the Island were presented; and mainly through an inadvertence as to the time, it being understood that the hour for holding it was two p. m., whereas it took place at eleven. This mistake must have been rather pleasing than otherwise to the parties most interested.

At one o'clock, he reviewed the Volunteers of the Island, before the Government House, and seemed much pleased with their efficiency.

D

Shortly after, he received the Addresses* from the Corporation and the Provincial authorities, on the balcony in front of the Provincial Building; nearly the whole populace gazing on the interesting ceremony.

The following are the replies:

To the Provincial one, the following:—

GENTLEMEN,—It affords me great pleasure to receive this from an Island which, though the smallest of the British Colonies of North America, has strong claims upon the kindly recollection of the family of the Queen. Its name commemorates the performance of public duties in these regions by my grandfather. Its name is also borne by his descendant, who now visits your shores by desire of your Sovereign, not indeed to command her troops, or to hold any authority amongst you, but to assure all her subjects of the deep interest which she has ever taken in those who are extending British civilization and power in these distant possessions. With this, my visit to the lower Provinces is brought to a close; and even if I were not about to visit the St. Lawrence, and become acquainted with the magnificent country which lies upon its banks, I should carry back with me to England a grateful recollection of all the kindness I have received, and an endearing regard and sympathy for a people in whom the love of freedom is combined with a deep-rooted attachment to the mother country, and the institutions in which we have all been nurtured.

And to the Corporation:—

GENTLEMEN,—I thank you sincerely for the Address which you have just presented to me, and I avail myself of this occasion to request you to express to the citizens, whose municipal councillors you are, my warm acknowledgements for the hearty welcome with which they greeted me yesterday. That loyalty to the Queen, and attachment to the British crown are the characteristics of the population of Charlottetown, I never doubted. You have given proofs of those feelings which it will be my happiness to convey to Her Majesty, and to assure her that you share largely in the sentiment which I may now pronounce to be universal in these colonies. Your expression of affectionate interest in all that concerns my future welfare and usefulness in the career which, by God's will, may be before me, are such as to demand a no less cordial response on my part. I assure you they will not be forgotten.

---

* We regret that we have been unable to procure copies of the Addresses.

In the evening a grand ball was given at the Provincial Building, which the Prince and suite attended. The room was tastefully and elaborately decorated. Many beautiful devices graced it, and caught the eye. The inscriptions were many and good. Among them was the following:—

" Thy grandsire's name distinguishes this isle ;
We love thy mother's sway, and court her smile."

And:—

" Heaven, favoured Prince, bestow on thee
A people's love, a glorious destiny."

And again :—

" The gorgeous sun, as on his course he wends
On Britain's realm, in darkness ne'er descends."

The Prince opened the ball with Mrs. Dundas (the Lieutenant Governor's lady), dancing afterwards with Miss Wright (Treasurer's daughter), and continued to dance until three o'clock next morning.

His Royal Highness left Charlottetown on the morning of the 11th.

He was attended to the wharf by the Lieutenant Governor and Cabinet, Mayor and Councillors, and the people generally, all regretting that the happy moments had passed so quickly, and cherishing a hope that one day they might see him again.

His Royal Highness embarked on board the *Hero*, the usual salutes were fired, and the fleet sailed for the ancient city of Quebec (Lower Canada).

RECEPTION IN CANADA.

The squadron first sighted the shores of Canada on Sunday, 12th August, at noon. The scenery along this place (the Gulf) is regarded as very enchanting, from the variety which is continually exposed to view. In one place you have the grand and rugged promontories of rocks, while here and there dark shoals appear out of the water; in another, you have a delightful plain, verdant and fragrant, quiet vales running down to the water's edge, while ever and anon, you see a smiling milk-white cottage peeping out from amidst the rich foliage; and so the panorama is continually changing, each scene you fancy more beautiful than the ones you have just passed.

The fleet entered Gaspé Bay at sunset, which must have added additional lustre to the magnificent natural beauties of the place.

Here the Provincial Government steamers *Victoria* and *Lady Head* were anchored, having on board the Governor General, His Excellency the Right Honorable Sir Edmund W. Head, and the Ministry of Canada, they having come down from Quebec to meet the Prince, and welcome him to Canada.

His Excellency had chosen this delightful spot for the first reception in Canada, so that the impression made on His Royal Highness might prove favorable to us.

As the *Hero* and the other vessels of the squadron passed, the *Victoria* and *Lady Head* dipped their colours, and the *Hero* returned the compliment. Soon after the *Hero* sang out, "Is the Governor General on board?" The *Victoria* replied, "He is on board." They immediately dropped their anchors, and no other words were passed. Everything on board the ships was still for the night; but not so on shore, where the people, in their own peculiar way, were celebrating the Heir Apparent's arrival, by a grand illumination, popping of guns, and by continual shouts of joy and welcome.

At half-past eight on Monday morning (13th), His Excellency the Governor General went on board the *Hero*. He was received by a salute, by a Guard of Honour of the Royal Marines, and by His Royal Highness the Prince of Wales and suite.

His Excellency welcomed the Prince to Canada, and the whole squadron proceeded into Gaspé Basin. The houses along the shore were beautifully decorated with flags and evergreens, &c. They were as white as snow, having been whitewashed for the occasion. Everything had a holiday appearance. Every house displayed a flag.

Previous to the arrival of His Royal Highness, His Excellency was presented with an Address from the inhabitants of the district of Gaspé, thanking him and the Ministry for their wise administration, &c. His Excellency and the Ministry were afterwards entertained at a dinner by the Town Council.

The fleet, when opposite the residence of Mr. LeBoutillier

(M.P.P. for Gaspé), received a royal salute, from a battery situated in front of it.

The people here cheered tremendously, as indeed they did all along the shore.

Near this the *Hero* ran aground upon the end of a long spit which runs out from the shore. The *Lady Head* went to her assistance, but she preferred that of her stout ally the *Ariadne*. A hawser was conveyed to that vessel by the *Flying Fish*. The *Ariadne* gave one tremendous jerk. The hawser broke, but the *Hero* was liberated, and again floated on the water as stately and majestically as ever.

This circumstance had scarcely taken place, when a deputation, consisting of the Sheriff, and other officials of the crown, &c., for the district, arrived in several boats. They presented an Address to His Royal Highness; and a Petition, praying him to allow Gaspé in future to be called Port Albert, in commemoration of the visit. The Prince replied that he was sorry he was unable to comply with their request: it remained with the Provincial authorities.

Shortly afterwards the Canadian Ministry, with the exception of Mr. Vankoughnet, absent at the Seat of Government, proceeded on board the *Hero*, and were presented to the Prince, by the Duke of Newcastle, as follows:—

Hon. John Ross, President Executive Council and Minister of Agriculture.
" G. E. Cartier, Attorney General East, (Premier).
" John A. Macdonald, Attorney General West.
" A. T. Galt, Minister of Finance.
" John Rose, Commissioner of Public Works.
" N. F. Belleau, Speaker Legislative Council.
" Charles Alleyn, Provincial Secretary.
" Sidney Smith, Postmaster General.
" Geo. Sherwood, Receiver General.
" J. C. Morrison, Solicitor General West.
" L. S. Morin, Solicitor General East.

They then lunched with him, and returned to the *Victoria* with His Excellency the Governor General. The whole fleet then started for the Saguenay River, on the St. Lawrence, the Provincial steamers leading the way.

Owing to a slight accident, the *Ariadne* did not come up to the other vessels, which were lying at the mouth of that river, till the following morning.

We cannot do better than avail ourselves of the following excellent sketch of the trip up the Saguenay, published in the Quebec *Chronicle*, and written by a gentleman of that place :—

THE PRINCE'S VISIT TO THE RIVERS SAGUENAY AND STE. MARGUERITE.

(From a Local Correspondent.)

TADOUSAC, Friday, Aug. 17.

Without trenching upon the duties of your faithful chronicler, allow me to give a few additional details of His Royal Highness's excursion up the Rivers Saguenay and Ste. Marguerite. This account, though scarcely forming a page in the grand tour, is a glimpse at one of the pleasant bye-paths along the formal highway of the state progress.

Early on Wednesday morning, the fleet was descried off the Saguenay, and the watchers on the rocks looked with anxious eyes as the *Hero* seemed to steer so much higher westward, in entering the estuary, than local navigators consider safe. The *Ariadne* entered farther towards the east. The *Flying Fish*, and the *Queen Victoria* with His Excellency the Governor General and staff, and the Members of the Executive Council, on board, soon joined the *Ariadne*. The steamer *Tadousac*, having on board Mr. D. E. Price, M.P.P., and several experienced Saguenay pilots for distribution amongst the fleet, had been waiting outside since daylight. Meanwhile, a St. Lawrence pilot, taken by the *Hero* from the South Shore, had attempted to push through the channel flanked on either side by well-known reefs. In delightful contempt of Commander Bayfield's Chart and Sailing Directions, he managed to ground the ship within one hundred feet of the chequered buoy which marks Bar Patch, off Lark Islet. She struck with a rending jar; but the strong ebb-tide, the prevailing calm, and her own easy rate of motion, probably saved her from material damage. Under any other circumstances this accident might have proved very serious. After remaining aground some three hours, her consort moved her from the dangerous situation at young flood, and, by request of the Commodore, the Captain of the *Tadousac*, Mr. E. Tremblay, took charge and conveyed the vessel into safe anchorage off Moulin à Baude. This untoward incident, and consequent detention, completely frustrated the arrangements which, with loyal spirit and admirable taste, had been organized by the inhabitants of Saguenay and Grand Bay. The fleet also was deterred thereby from proceeding further inwards, and remained at anchor outside. About noon, however, His Royal Highness and suite embarked on board the *Victoria* with His Excellency, and the party proceeded up the magnificent Saguenay. Passing L'Ance a l'Eau the consular flags of Norway and Sweden, and the United States, with the British Union flying between, were dipped in honor of the illustrious visitor, and a royal salute was fired in good style from the small battery of three guns provided there at Mr. Price's establishment. The salute was promptly acknowledged by Captain Pouliotte, and the *Queen Victoria* was scarce out of sight when the cannon reports were mingling with a hundred echoes startled from the surrounding mountains. Notwithstanding the day was gloomy, and a drizzling rain and chill wind swept down the great gorge of the Saguenay, the scenery of that noble stream stood out, in grim relief, against the murky background. Each point of interest was eagerly scanned by His Royal Highness and attendants, until the steamer reached the spacious bay between the lofty cliffs of Eternity and Trinity. Here she passed close under the almost perpendicular rocks, and fired a gun, the reverberations from which seemed fairly to make the rugged mountains around to tremble. The afternoon was far spent ere they reached L'Ance aux Arables, and the stiff headwind and strong ebb-current rendered it impossible to reach Grand Bay and return in time to pass the night on board His Royal Highness's vessel. Great preparations had been made at Ha-ha Bay for the Prince's reception, and a loyal Address was to have been presented, through Mr. Kane, on behalf of the civic authorities. The disappointment is the more to be regretted, since the enthusiastic welcome which awaited His Royal Highness was such as will not be exceeded in hearty earnestness at any reception throughout the Province. The municipalities, backed by Mr. Price, and cordially assisted by the inhabitants, had erected beautiful arches, ornamented with appropriate devices, along the whole line of procession, which was carpeted and decorated in sumptuous fashion—a staging had been built—batteries arranged for firing salutes—and a concourse of upwards of 8000 people eagerly waited the opportunity of expressing their loyalty and respect. Words cannot depict the disappointment felt at their non-arrival; and we learn with satisfaction that His Royal Highness and suite express themselves very much disappointed on account of being unable to accept the gratifying homage of the people of Grand Bay and the valley of the Saguenay. A copy of the Address intended was presented and read, on board, to His Royal Highness by Mr. Price, who, on behalf of the Municipal authorities and the inhabitants of the County of Chicoutimi, expressed the extreme regret which would be felt from their inability to deliver the same and enjoy the anticipated honour of welcoming His Royal Highness in person.

It was after dark, when the *Victoria* anchored alongside the *Hero*, and left His Royal Highness and suite again on board.

The weather having cleared up during the night-time, yesterday (Thursday) morning dawned bright and genial. After partaking of an early breakfast, His Royal Highness, from the *Victoria*, accompanied by their Excellencies Sir Edmund Head and the Earl of Mulgrave, the Duke of Newcastle, Major General Bruce, Commodore Seymour, Dr. Auckland, Captain Grey, Major Teesdale, Mr. Engleheart, Mr. Ellis, Mr. Stapleton, Captain Retallack, Hon. Messrs. Macdonald, Cartier, Galt, Morrison, Ross, Smith and Morin, landed at the River Ste. Marguerite, some six leagues within the Saguenay. The forenoon grew finer and more enjoyable—abrupt contrasts after the mist and misery of the preceding day. As the sun climbed up behind the still dripping hills and shone out warmly upon the opposite banks of the Saguenay, where huge patches of moist moss-covered plateaux flecked with various shades of green lent a soft richness to the beauty of the surrounding scenery, the sight was worthy to be seen by princely eyes. The morn was lovely and the scene delightful as the heart could wish. At landing, His Royal Highness was escorted by some twenty birch canoes manned by Indians. The camping ground had been fixed at a grassy plot on the west side of Ste. Marguerite's Bay, where eight tents had been pitched. From that designed for His Royal Highness floated the Royal Standard, flanked on either side by the Union Jack. A platform was also run out into the tide-way, at the end of which waved another flag, and a pavement of boulders made dry the way up to the base of the hillock on which the white tents stood half concealed by green trees and overshadowed by the high mountains around the rear. Everything here was arranged with the utmost forethought and good taste. The Prince's tent was certainly a model of simple elegance,—carpeted by sweet smelling boughs of young sapins, and furnished, even to the minutest details of camp comfort, with seats, lounges, bed, tables, toilet, &c., each and all neatly constructed of osier twigs and white birch bark. The effect was most *apropos*. A lunch-table was set and supplied in a similarly handsome manner,—indeed, all of these preparations reflect great credit upon Mr. Price, and Messrs. Rubridge, Maguire and Carman, who acted for Mr. Blackwell, the lessee of the premises. When His Royal Highness first landed from Mr. Price's boat, he was welcomed by that gentleman as at the earliest landing upon Canadian soil, and a cheer went up from the flotilla of canoes and boats that made the old hills ring again. His Royal Highness being soon equipped for sea trout fishing was taken by Mr. Price to the most favorite spots; and after the rest of the party had been fitted out from the abundance of His Excellency Sir Edmund Head's supply, and the inexhaustible fly-book of Mr. Galt, they were soon dispersed over the beach, trying each his luck.

The season is too late for this description of fishing, and the recent rains had so swollen and discolored the stream that the anglers plied their art with but indifferent success. The Prince here first essayed the angle' and killed several fine fish. Practice alone is needed to make His Roya Highness as expert in fishing as he already is at fowling.

The rising tide in all tributaries of the Saguenay flows in with imperceptible speed, and creeps around through hidden inlets and by countless rivulets with such treacherous stealth that a busy fisher may find himself surrounded ere he is even aware of the impending isolation. This peculiarity occasioned a very amusing incident. His Royal Highness, apparently absorbed in the sport, stood upon a large rock where gullied banks on either side threatened to cut him off from the mainland should the flowing tide surround it unperceived. We watched it from the shore behind. As if by previous concert the flood eddies gathered stealthily here and there in rear, and soon came pouring down along every watercourse so fast that the canoes could not get round in time to be available. Whilst wondering how the Prince would extricate himself from the encroaching streams, we espied Mr. Price knee-deep in the gully carrying across His Royal Highness upon his back with the utmost *sang froid*. Trout fishing over, the Prince and party repaired to the encampment, and partook of a sumptuous lunch provided at the royal tent, preparatory to ascending the rapids of the river Ste. Marguerite to fish for salmon near the falls. The steamer *Tadousac* had, through the kind consent of her owner, Mr. Price, brought up from Tadousac a party of ladies and gentlemen with the intention of enjoying a sight of the Prince *en passant* at the place of disembarkation. Through the polite attentions of His Excellency the Governor General and others of the royal suite, they were invited to the camps; and His Royal Highness consented in the most affable manner to this impromptu presentation. As Mr. Price officiated beside His Royal Highness, the writer glanced about the semicircle of introducees, and read in their faces something more than fashionable curiosity abundantly gratified, as their eyes spoke a mute welcome to the youthful Prince more eloquent than words. We might not, as King Richard bade his courtiers, " throw away all formal respect and ceremonious duty," but we feel sure that the quiet heartfelt welcome (with only so much ceremony as is consistent) that greeted His Royal Highness at Ste. Marguerite, will not be deemed less true and worthy of remembrance when compared with noisier and more enthusiastic greetings in crowded thoroughfares and " busy haunts of men." The writer perhaps exceeds their wishes in mentioning the names of those who were so favored by the honour of an informal presentation :

Mrs. J. Radford, of L'Anse à l'Eau ; Mrs. F. Whitcher, of Quebec, Misses White and Norwood, of Tadousac ; Miss Urquhart, of Montreal ; Messrs. Radford, Rubridge, Maguire, Carman, Barrie, and your Correspondent.

In commemoration of His Royal Highness's visit, it is proposed to give the place of encampment, &c., the name of Prince of Wales' Bay. A stone will be there erected, cut from the rock upon which he alighted at landing, and will have thereon a suitable inscription.

A brigade of eleven canoes started after luncheon to ascend the rapids. His Royal Highness led in one of Mr. Price's canoes, at the bow of which streamed a miniature standard. His Excellency Sir Edmund Head, the Earl of Mulgrave, the Duke of Newcastle, Mr. Price, Major General Bruce, Commodore Seymour, Dr. Auckland, Mr. Engleheart, Captain Grey, and the writer, followed, each in separate canoes. The river was very much swollen and turbid, and even the usual rest of dead water between each rapid was now converted into fierce currents, so that it took above three hours to accomplish the ascent with setting poles. The canoes went some six miles up the stream. It was late when the salmon pools were reached, and, the water being very high and muddy, gave little hope of catching salmon. Several fish were, however, tempted to rise, and one was hooked, which His Royal Highness played for a considerable time, but, in one of his vigorous leaps, the hook gave way and he was lost, much to the Prince's surprise and disappointment. The time being so limited, and the day far spent, no other opportunity of striking a fish could be had. The pools were full of salmon; and had His Royal Highness been able to pass the night there, fishing for his own and three other rods could have been certainly found. In the novelty and excitement of mounting and returning through the rapids, and viewing the wild scenery on every side, any comparative disappointment on the score of fishing was fully compensated. As the long line of frail canoes in Indian file came bounding with their precious freight down the boiling rapids, the passengers were delighted; and whenever they drew nearer to each other, expressions of wonder and delight were heard—wonder how these tiny barks could withstand the tumbling waters, and delight at the buoyant swiftness and quick-varying views of their descent. The reader can form a vague idea of the passage from the fact that about 40 minutes only were covered in returning over the ground it had just taken three toilsome hours to pass upwards. The Prince and entire party were delighted with this novel excursion. After revisiting the encampment, the Royal party returned on board the *Victoria*, and repaired to dine on board the *Hero*, next day fulfilling the passage up to Quebec. We have but one parting wish to add to our earnest welcome, and that is, that His Royal Highness, and other distinguished visitors, may sometimes look back towards this Saguenay visit with one tithe of the pleasurable feeling with which we shall ever remember his manly affability and princely bearing, and their noble courtesy.

After passing up the rest of the noble river St. Lawrence, the fleet anchored at a short distance from Quebec on Friday night,

August 17th ; the Provincial steamers, with the Governor General and Ministry on board, returning thither.

We copy the following from the correspondence of the New York *Tribune;* but we, of course, cannot vouch for the veracity of the correspondent:—

" The short trip around Prince Edward Island had given needed rest to the royal party. It was not an eventful voyage, although a very agreeable one. Minor excitements were afforded in a variety of ways. The *Hero*, with the Prince on board, ran aground twice, to the particular dissatisfaction of the officers.

At one point a man fell overboard, and was rescued with a promptness that delighted everybody, himself included.

The *Ariadne* was detained a while by a troublesome bit of machinery, which got hot, and melted, and was repaired so speedily that all the mischief was taken out of it before any knew the difference.

The night before the second ascension of the Saguenay, the Prince, on turning in at, or possibly a little after midnight, was challenged to be up and on deck at the end of the middle watch. A bet of a sovereign was ventured. The Prince would be up at any hazard—even that of repudiating his berth altogether. This, however, was not needed ; his friends would look to his interests. So, just before 4 o'clock the summons came to him. Sleep was dear at that moment, but the disgrace of forefeiting the wager had to be averted. In some malicious way his clothes had been tampered with, and his stockings evaded all search. But without stockings, and, on the whole, imperfectly clad, the Prince found his way up in the dark, and just won his sovereign by dropping on deck exactly at the moment that eight bells struck. * * *

The last night upon the St. Lawrence was celebrated by a merry gathering on board the *Hero*. The scene toward 9 o'clock was utterly void of stately or ceremonious conditions. Grouped together on the main deck, the Prince and his party, officers from other ships, and visitors from the halls of Canadian Governments, smoked and sang and frolicked in a manner calculated to quite dispel the doubts, which everybody knows have always existed, as to the capacity of gentlemen with large titles and severe responsibilities to participate in human and natural enjoyment. At the close, a minister high in Provincial fame, impelled solely by melodious instinct, stepped to the centre and broke out in a very earnest Canadian song, of emphatic accent and tender purport.* A

---

* The following is the song above alluded to :—

A LA CLAIRE FONTAINE.

FROM THE FRENCH.

As by the crystal fount I strayed,
On which the dancing moonbeams played,

circle encompassed Mr. Cartier and listened approvingly. The chorus was found to be attainable with little effort—a chorus some might say that fitted to perfection at the first trying on. Now a few voices chimed in, the Prince leading, then others' maturer, the Duke's beyond a doubt, among them. Afterwards others' not less distinct, then everybody's, the contagion leaving none unconcerned. As each verse

---

  The water seemed so clear and bright
  I bathed myself in its delight—
   I loved thee from the hour we met,
   And never can that love forget.

  The water seemed so clear and bright,
  I bathed myself in its delight;
  The nightingale above my head,
  As sweet a stream of music shed—
   I loved thee from the hour we met,
   And never can that love forget.

  The nightingale above my head,
  As sweet a stream of music shed,
  Sing, nightingale! thy heart is glad!
  But I could weep, for mine is sad!
   I loved thee from the hour we met,
   And never can that love forget.

  Sing, nightingale! thy heart is glad!
  But I could weep, for mine is sad!
  For I have lost my lady fair,
  And she has left me to despair!
   I loved thee from the hour we met,
   And never can that love forget.

  For I have lost my lady fair,
  And she has left me to despair;
  For that I gave not, when she spoke,
  The rose that from its tree I broke—
   I loved thee from the hour we met,
   And never can that love forget.

  For that I gave not, when she spoke,
  The rose that from its tree I broke;
  I wish the rose were on its tree,
  And my beloved again with me!
   I loved thee from the hour we met,
   And never can that love forget.

ended, the refrain came clearly out; all that could turn a tune, and some perhaps that could not, uniting with determined ardor, and sending forth to the waves, which sang their own gentle song, the declaration—

"Jamais je ne t'oublierai;"

and it did seem extremely probable that no one there present and thus engaged would be likely to forget any member of the party, or any detail of the scene itself.

It was a good thing to see the Prince of Wales approaching this more than half French Province, and, while drawing near, joining so jovially in the chorus of a French song, sung by a French officer of the Government. But it lasted only a little while. At half-past 9 the lights vanished and the cigars were sacrificed, the Prince yielding to the regulations of the ship with greater readiness than some gentlemen of superior years, who were insubordinate to the extent of the inch or two of tobacco that remained unburned. Then the deck became dimmer, the listening sailors moved slowly forward, the sentries took up their positions, the big Newfoundland dog rattled his chain for good night, and curled himself away, and the guests mounted to the quarter-deck for an hour's stroll, or turned to their quarters, singing lightly, as they disappeared on all sides—

"Jamais je ne t'oublierai."

Saturday, August 18th, was an important day for Quebec, and the Quebecers, and not only for them, but for Canadians generally. Seeing that that was the day assigned for the Prince of Wales' first public entry into Canada, no wonder there was such a stir and excitement everywhere in the city. People got up by daylight and crowded the Terrace, to see if there were any signs of the royal fleet.

Preparations on a grand and great scale were going on, and had been going on for a length of time, in honour of that auspicious occasion; neat and well-made arches were erected everywhere along the Prince's route, every place was decorated, and flags appeared from all quarters.

The people were in a great state of enthusiam. Not only the British residents, but the French Canadians also, bore part in the general exultation.

At nine o'clock, a.m., a general fleet of first-class river steamers, composed of the *Victoria, Napoleon, Bowmanville* (with excursionists from Toronto, more than 500 miles distant), *Jacques*

Cartier, Saguenay, Caledonia, Columbia, Jenny Lind, Magnet, Voyageur, Mayflower, Providence, and *Muskrat,* left Quebec, laden with passengers, to meet the Prince's squadron and escort it to Quebec. They were all gaily dressed out with flags and evergreens, while some had bands of music on board; and, as each passed down the river, it presented a very brilliant appearance.

Unfortunately the weather was on a par with that of St. Johns, Nfld, Halifax, St. John, N.B., and Charlottetown; the sky was covered with mazy and ugly-looking clouds. The rain did not come down in a good and refreshing shower, but in little drizzling ones, making one feel more and more like a hypochondriac. Altogether the city would have appeared as dull as dulness could make it, but for the active preparations going on; and the people would have felt as miserable, but for the buoyancy of their spirits.

During the whole of the afternoon, and in fact during the whole day, the entire front of the city was crowded with persons, to catch the first glimpse of the *Hero.* At two o'clock, a huge black mass of smoke appeared directly over Point Levi, and as soon as it was seen, it was surmised that it must be from the royal vessels' funnels. And in this the people were not mistaken; for, upon patient watching and waiting for about an hour, they perceived that the black mass of smoke moved nearer and nearer, towards the point which the fleet was to round. At about three or half-past three o'clock, the *Hero* appeared round the Point. It was supported on either side by the fleet of river steamers. The *Ariadne* followed, and then the *Flying Fish*; but so hazy was the weather, or so much smoke obscured them, that it was not until they had gained the western extremity of the Island of Orleans, that the excited and enthusiastic multitude that crowded, and in fact covered, every available spot, could obtain a good view of them. Then what a sublime, what a splendid picture presented itself! The murky clouds which before had covered the entire horizon, had partially cleared away, and the sun appeared, lighting up the magnificent scene before them. The Gibraltar of America looming up to the sky, covered nearly everywhere with human beings; the city decorated gaily with evergreens and flags; the surrounding country dressed in its brightest hue; the river covered with large and small craft, displaying their various colours, and dipping them to the men-of-war; the British war-vessels *Nile*, *Valorous*, and *Styx*, (which had arrived a few days previously,) covered with flags, of all shades and colours ; and, above all, the enthusiastic and hearty cheers, and ringing of bells, that tolled in delightful melody who was monarch there ;—all this formed a scene which can never be forgotten.

Then came the thundering and deafening royal salutes from the three men-of-war, from the Citadel, the Durham Terrace, and the Grand Battery. (The guns of the latter had not been fired for thirty or forty years previously.) What a noise ! it fairly shook Quebec again and again.

Majestically came on the *Hero* and the other ships. How like a queen she looks in the excited fancy ! Telescopes and opera-glasses are brought to play. A red coat is discovered on deck. " It must be the Prince," cry all,—perhaps some poor marine on guard. At four o'clock the Prince entered his barge, accompanied by the Admiral, Sir Alexander Milne, (having gone on board when the *Hero* anchored,) the Duke of Newcastle, &c. Other boats conveyed the Earl of St. Germains, Governor Bruce, Major Teesdale, Capt. Grey, &c. Again the ships and batteries thundered forth a royal salute, reverberating from shore to shore, and echoing behind the mountains again and again. The smoke had cleared away, and behold Albert Edward had landed upon the shores of the most ancient city in North America. His Excellency the Governor General, the Right Honorable Sir Edward Walker Head, Bt., and suite, and the Canadian Ministry attired in their handsome uniforms of blue and gold, met His Royal Highness on the landing-steps and welcomed him, as also did Lord Lyons (British Ambassador at Washington, U. S.), Lieutenant General Sir W. Fenwick Williams, of Kars, Commander of the Forces, and his suite, Sir Allan N. McNab, and Sir E. P. Taché, Aids-de-Camp to the Queen, the various civil and military personages of Quebec, among them Mr. Mayor Langevin.

Then it was that the assembled multitude from the wharves, steamers, and the rocks above, gave the Prince cheers which can hardly ever be effaced from his memory, so intensely inspiring and truly loyal were they.

As the Prince passed to the pavilion to receive the Address of the Corporation, a Guard of Honour of the Royal Canadian Rifles presented arms, and then their band performed the National Anthem, the other bands taking it up, and the bag-pipes played some national air.

The handsome pavilion on the wharf was decked out with national banners and spruce trees. The Mayor, surrounded by the City Council, presented His Royal Highness with the following Address :—

MAY IT PLEASE YOUR ROYAL HIGHNESS,—

The Mayor, Councillors, and Citizens of Quebec, are happy on being the first among the Canadian subjects of Her Most Gracious Majesty the Queen, to present their respectful homage to Your Royal Highness. They will long continue to regard as a memorable epoch, the day on which they have been permited to receive, within the walls of their city, this visit from the eldest son of their beloved Sovereign, the Heir Apparent to the British Crown.

When we became aware that Her Majesty, finding it inconvenient or impracticable to proceed to so great a distance from the central seat of Government, had deigned to testify the regard which Her Majesty entertains toward Her Canadian subjects, by sending our future sovereign in her stead—we felt gratified and proud in receiving such a mark of distinction, from one whose public and private virtues command the admiration of the whole world. We feel assured that Our Most Gracious Queen was desirous to show, by this act of condescension, that she knows how to appreciate and honour in a special manner the most important of her colonial possessions.

In this Province, Your Royal Highness will find a free people, faithful and loyal, attached to their sovereign and to their country. In this the most ancient city of Canada, Your Royal Highness will be in the midst of a population devoted to your interests, testifying, by the heartiness of their acclamations and good wishes, that, though they derive their origin from various races, and may differ in language and religious denominations, yet they have but one voice and one heart in expressing loyalty to their sovereign, and in welcoming him who represents her on this occasion, and who is one day destined, according to the natural order of events, to become her successor.

The people of Quebec rejoice in beholding Your Royal Highness in the midst of them. They are happy because they have the opportunity of expressing in a direct manner their respect and attachment; happy because he will hereafter, in all human probability, wear the crown of this great empire ; will be enabled, during his brief sojourn in Canada, to judge for himself of the loyalty of the whole Canadian people in general, and of the citizens of Quebec in particular. Your Royal Highness will also enjoy the opportunity of forming an adequate opinion of the extent of the country, its productions, its resources, its progress, and the great future reserved for it; and will be enabled to perceive that Canada, with a population of three millions of inhabitants, though only an appendage of the United Kingdom, possesses institutions as free, and a territory three times as extensive.

In conclusion, we entreat Your Royal Highness favourably to accept, for Our Most Gracious Sovereign and Yourself, along with our loyal and respectful homage, the assurance of our sincere attachment; while we most heartily wish that this visit to Canada may prove as gratifying and agreeable to Yourself, as it is to the citizens of Quebec.

HECTOR L. LANGEVIN,
Mayor.

The Prince replied as follows :—

GENTLEMEN,—It is with no ordinary feelings of gratification and of interest in all around me that I find myself for the first time on the shores of Canada, and within the precincts of this its most ancient city.

I am deeply touched by the cordiality with which I have been welcomed by the inhabitants.

For the Address which you have just presented to me, I beg you to accept the hearty thanks which, in the name of the Queen, I offer you.

Be assured that Her Majesty will receive with no little satisfaction the account of my reception amongst you; proving, as it does, that Her feelings towards the people are met on their part by the most devoted and loyal attachment to Herself, her throne, and her family. Still more will she rejoice to learn, from your own lips, that all differences of origin, language, and religion, are lost in one universal spirit of patriotism, and that all classes are knit to each other and to the mother country by the common ties of equal liberty and free institutions.

For myself, I will only add, that I shall ever take a deep concern in all that tends to promote the prosperity of this beautiful and interesting city.

The Mayor then called for three cheers for His Royal Highness the Prince of Wales, which were loyally and heartily given.

The Prince and suite were then conducted to carriages; the Prince, the Duke of Newcastle, and Earl St. Germains to the Governor General's; Governor Bruce, Earl Mulgrave (who accompanied the royal party from Nova Scotia), Lord Lyons, and Sir W. F. Williams, to another; the Canadian Ministry to others; the Mayor and Corporation last.

E

The Clergy, the Judiciary, the National Societies, Mechanics, Indians, &c., and Volunteers, turned out in the procession, which was well organized.

The 17th Regiment and the Police lined the road from the wharf to Buade Street.

Everywhere a perfect ovation awaited the Prince; the men cheered and cried, to give vent to their surcharged feelings; and even women were found who cheered as lustily as the men, but the generality only smiled archly on the young Prince, and waved their handkerchiefs. On Buade St. and along St. John St., the Canadian Volunteer Militia Companies, under Colonel Sewell, lined the streets and presented arms.

The procession escorted His Royal Highness and the most important persons of his suite, to St. John's Toll-Gate, when, opening out in two lines, the Prince's carriage passed between them; the Quebec Volunteer Cavalry, under Col. Bell, alone escorting it to Cataraqui, the Governor General's temporary residence, situated outside the town, and where His Royal Highness arrived at about half-past five or six o'clock.

In the evening, although it rained, there was a very fine illumination. The rain did not put a damper on the people's enthusiasm, for nearly every house was lit up; the rich and poor alike did honour to their future sovereign. There was not a man or woman in Quebec, who, if he or she had but a half-penny, hastened to buy a "dip" to light up their humble dwelling, so as to add to the great glare, and show their loyalty to England. On the whole, the illumination in Quebec beat all the preceding ones in honour of the visit.

On Sunday morning (19th), H. R. H., together with the Governor General, the Duke of Newcastle, the Earl St. Germains, Governor Bruce, Lord Mulgrave, Sir Fenwick Williams, Admiral Sir A. Milne, and the suites of H. R. H., the Governor General, Lord Mulgrave, the General, and the Admiral; and most of the officers of the Army and Navy in town, attended Divine Service in the Anglican Cathedral.

His Royal Highness was met at the entrance by the Lord Bishop (G. J. Mountain), and the clergymen of the Cathedral, who graciously bowed. He was then conducted to the Governor

General's pew, which had been beautifully furnished for the occasion, the organ (under Mr. Carter) playing the Coronation Anthem.

Every part of the church was secured; every inch of ground that commanded a view of the Prince was crowded; people were standing during the whole of the service, but every one took example from the Prince, and gave it that attention which it so much deserves.

The Prayers were read by the Rev. Dr. Percy; the Lessons by the Rev. G. Vernon Houseman; the Epistle by the Rev. Dr. Adamson (Chaplain to the Legislature); the ante-communion service by His Lordship the Bishop, and the following sermon preached by the Rev. Mr. Houseman:—

SERMON.

TEXT, *Hebrews* II. 3, "How shall we escape if we neglect so great a salvation?"

It is to be feared that our very familiarity with many of the most important passages of Scripture produces in us a deadness to their otherwise striking character. The eye, we know, becomes so accustomed to the objects which, at first, elicited our unbounded admiration, that by degrees we lose the intensity of the first impression; and the ear too becomes so familiarized with sounds which, at one time, produced exquisite feelings of rapture, that they cease to be regarded with the same pleasure which attended their first utterance; and in a similar manner it happens that the most solemn and momentous statements of the Bible lose in our minds, by frequent repetition, much of their deep and pointed meaning. Does it not happen that the sinner who is conscious of being a violator of God's laws, can hear repeatedly the awful denunciation of the Bible against the impenitent, and yet feel no alarm, no remorse, and no anxiety for the future—can listen to the thrilling descripton of the bottomless pit, where the worm dieth not and the fire is not quenched, and yet be less alive to their condition than the devils who believe in the existence and know some of the attributes of God, and tremble? Nor can the ungodly be alone charged with failing to lay to heart and profit by the clear enunciation of the word of the living God. Even those who profess and call themselves Christians, and are traversing this narrow way which leadeth unto life eternal, too frequently do not recognize the beauty and the force of many of those passages which are mercifully intended to cheer, sustain, and console them in accomplishing the arduous and important task which they are called upon to perform. So earthly are our affections, so weak our faith, so languid our hope, that we can oftentimes hear of the sublime and glorious promises of God without allowing our hearts to be drawn out in the profoundest admiration and love towards Him, who not only hath given His life a ransom for many, but hath also purchased for his people an inheritance incorruptible and undefiled, and that fadeth not away.

And if what I have stated be correct, cannot we be charged with having frequently heard the earnest enquiry made by God himself, in the words of our text, without having weighed in our minds the full import of the question—without having arrived at any definite conclusion on the subject—without having returned an answer to our own hearts—an answer founded upon reason, and dictated by an enlightened conscience?

If this be the case—if the passage has never been viewed with the light which revelation throws upon it—if we have not hitherto pursued the enquiry with an earnest desire to profit by it, let us listen once again, and that, too, with seriousness and attention, to the all-important demand, "How shall we escape if we neglect so great salvation?"

In directing your attention to the words before us, I would speak of the exceeding excellency of the salvation offered to man—that salvation which the wicked reject—which few Christians duly appreciate—which none can adequately estimate.

To arrive at any just knowledge and understanding of the salvation offered to us in the Gospel, we should consider what man originally was—what is his present condition, what his future prospects. As Adam stood, at the first, in innocence before God, there was stamped upon his whole nature the likeness of his Maker. No breath of defilement had passed over him, no taint of evil had invaded his breast. So pure and holy was he, that he could with unabashed face look upon and hold converse with the Great Author of his being. And in this unsullied state it was his delight to obey the will of God, for there was a ready and active response to everything which emanated from the Lord God. But we well know how soon the glory of the Eternal Power and Godhead, which was reflected in all its brightness in the heart of the creature, ceased to be so exhibited. Man fell, and by his fall his mind lost its divine knowledge, his will its original uprightness, his affections their wonted subjection. And in Adam fell the whole human race, for from this corrupted stem has sprung the degenerate millions who have since peopled this earth. Thus, when we look around us and survey either men in general or ourselves in particular, we cannot but mark the utter absence of all inherent holiness, the inward workings of a heart deceitful above all things, and desperately wicked. Instead of loving and admiring God and rendering unto Him the homage which is His due, we naturally start aside from communion with him, we crave after the sordid pleasures of earth, and find ourselves too much engrossed with the things which are temporal. Even such a one as St. Paul, rescued by a miracle from his perilous position of persecuting the Church of Christ, and who afterwards exhibited a life of ardent devotion and deep-seated attachment to the Lord who had bought him, was compelled to write, with feelings of self-abasement and genuine humbleness of spirit, "The good which I would I do not; but the evil which I would not, that I do."

Nor does the future hold out any bright or cheering prospects to man in his natural condition. So clear and decisive are the threatenings of God against the impenitent, that we would, if we dared, draw a veil over all that is revealed upon the subject. But while we might naturally sink at the prospect of eternity, there is unfolded to us, in the Word of God, the blessed assurance that there is a way opened by which we can be delivered from the body of sin and brought into the glorious liberty of the children of God. A divine method is set before us by which iniquity is pardoned, the wrath of God appeased, mercy extended to the penitent, and a region of ineffable splendor and glory secured to the believer, as his rich inheritance in the world which is to come.

Surely, when we contemplate the salvation which is thus offered to us,—a salvation which accords with man's highest aspiration,—a salvation which satisfies his most enlarged desires, we cannot but acquiesce in the description given by the Apostle where he terms it *great*, and see the force of the enquiry "How shall we escape if we neglect so great salvation" by the redemption which is in Christ Jesus and through the sanctifying influence of the Holy Spirit? And I would have you further remember, that the Gospel which is in itself so excellent, *is revealed to us as the express will of God.*

To reject the offers of salvation, considered solely in reference to their own intrinsic merit, and to live without God in the world, is the height of folly and madness. But when we consider that the divine purposes have been conveyed to us by a special revelation, the sin of despising what has been designed for our spiritual and eternal welfare is enhanced a hundred fold. God, acting upon a principle of equity, has declared "unto whomsoever much is given, of him shall be much required;" so that if He has been pleased to unfold, in all its simplicity and clearness, the way of salvation—if He has ordained the terms upon which we are to be partakers of it—if He has bound us to the observance of it by the severest penalties, and encouraged us by most ample and glorious promises, how manifestly inexcusable are we, if we neglect all the overtures of mercy, and in the pride and rebellion of our hearts declare that "we will not have this man to reign over us." If the servant that *knew not* his Lord's will, was yet to be beaten with stripes (although only a few) because he did things worthy of stripes, must we not acknowledge (even although in the acknowledgment we may condemn ourselves) that he who lives in direct opposition to the will of God, conveyed to us even more clearly than by "disposition of angels," shall stand inexcusable both here and hereafter, and so be beaten with many stripes?

For it must be admitted by all, that the salvation which is made a special subject of revelation, is declared in such positive terms, and the manner in which it is to be secured is made so simple, that it is impossible for any to misunderstand, except those who are wilfully blind to God's overtures of reconciliation through Jesus Christ. We know that there were once times of ignorance which God winked at, but now, in terms which are written most legibly upon every page of the Bible, He commandeth all men everywhere to repent. Salvation was the theme of the prophets of old. It was the substance of all our Saviour's teaching. It is that for which He suffered and died. The cross of Christ was deemed by St. Paul and the other early preachers of Christianity as the power of God unto salvation. By this weapon their splendid triumphs were achieved. And in like manner " Christ and Him crucified" has been the one glorious topic upon which all the servants of the Lord have been subsequently delegated to expatiate; and thus the things which God, of old, declared by those who wrote under the immediate inspiration of the Spirit, have been sounded throughout the world as with a trumpet's blast. And, with regard to ourselves who live in a Christian country, it is our privilege to know with singular clearness the things which have been thus revealed. According to our knowlege then, and according to the manner in which that knowledge has been exercised, shall we be judged hereafter; and lest we should love darkness rather than light, and turn away from Him that now speaketh from Heaven, a voice from on high arrests our attention, and we hear the solemn enquiry "How shall we escape if we neglect so great salvation?"

But further, we must not lose sight of the dignity of Him by and through whom the great salvation is proposed, and hence aggravate the sin of those who neglect it.

You remember how, on one occasion, when the Apostle St. Paul was writing to Timothy, he uses this language, so expressive of the overwhelming grandeur of the Gospel Scheme of salvation: "without controversy great is the mystery of Godliness; God was manifest in the flesh, justified in the Spirit, seen of Angels, preached unto the Gentiles, believed on in the world, received up into glory."

The incarnation of the Son of God, and the glorious results which followed from his dwelling among men, filled the Apostle's mind with the stupendousness of the work and the blessedness of those who should believe in his name. And when we are led to contemplate the same subject, and remember that "God, who, at sundry times and in divers manners, spoke in time past unto the fathers by the prophets, hath in these last days spoken unto us by His Son," we cannot but acquiesce in the declarations of the Saviour, "if I had not come and spoken unto them they had not had sin, but now they have no cloke for their sin." We know indeed that the more prominent object for which the Saviour became incarnate was, by becoming a sacrifice for sin, to reconcile the sinner to God, to break the fetters with which Satan had bound the whole family of mankind, to bear, in his human nature, the curse of the law—in one word, to make possible the amazing combination of God being just and yet the justifier.

But this was not all; for what mean those miracles which astonished the multitude and convinced so many—those discourses which riveted the attention of the populace, and drew forth from their lips the almost involuntary acknowledgment of His divine power? Why were angels commissioned to announce His birth—why was the last trying scene attended with so many extraordinary incidents as to draw from the Gentile centurion, at the moment of the Saviour's dissolution, the truthful exclamation, " truly this was the Son of God."

Oh! was not all this allowed to transpire to impress upon the minds of those who witnessed these things, and of those who should subsequently hear of them, the importance of a salvation which divine wisdom saw fit to be achieved by such a sacrifice and promulgated with such extraordinary accompaniments? Are not the sayings and the doings of Christ, together with the wonders which transpired from the cradle to the grave, handed down to us and continually pressed upon our attention to remind us of the price which was paid for our deliverance from the grasp of Satan; and the fact that God will, in consideration of what Christ has endured for us, freely give us all things, and consequently that there is not only the voice of Divine Justice calling for retribution, but the whisperings of conscience confirming the sentence, if the facts connected with the incarnation of the Redeemer are regarded as a fictitious narrative and produce no saving effect upon our characters, —if, in one word, " we neglect so great salvation?"

Once the thunderings of Sinai accompanied the giving of the law, and he that despised Moses's law died without mercy; of how much severer punishment, justly argues the Apostle, shall he be thought worthy who hath trodden under foot the Son of God, and hath counted the blood of the covenant wherewith he was sanctified, an unholy thing, and hath done despite unto the Spirit of grace? Oh, let us not resemble the Jews of old who were condemned in the parable of the Householder; for the husbandmen not only ill-treated the servants who were sent to receive the fruits, but they killed the heir, that they might, as they supposed, seize on his inheritance; being, however, themselves miserably destroyed for such wicked and such unjustifiable conduct. And if we slight the Son of God and neglect the salvation which he offers us, shall we not likewise perish?

And then, again, consider the clearness and fullness of the evidence upon which rests our acceptance of the gospel covenant. It is in no dark or ambiguous manner that the salvation spoken of in our text is offered to us. As God has endowed man with reasoning powers, so, in the delivery of gospel truths, He has directed us to weigh well the evidence upon which this subject is presented. And then, if the proof be not unreasonable, but clear and ample, yea, undeniable, is there not additional ground for accepting all that has been revealed; and will not this conclusive evidence witness against those who neglect so great salvation?

And what are the facts upon which we may ground our belief in the Gospel Scheme of salvation?

May we not take the whole series of prophecy which is to be found in the Old Testament, and see how all are fulfilled under the New? And these prophecies (oftentimes so improbable in themselves) were known to have been promulgated prior to the event, and yet received a palpable fulfilment; so that we feel convinced that God alone by His Holy Spirit could have instigated the writers, and that He was, by their utterance, not only preparing the minds of His ancient people for the things which should be hereafter, but also was establishing an evidence which should compel every mind open to conviction to receive the salvation introduced by the Son of God.

And then, again, consider how the truths of Christianity are recommended to us by that great variety of undeniable proofs which St. Paul calls "the power and demonstration of the Spirit." Thus, the Scripture narrative furnishes us with an account of the conception of our Lord by the miraculous operation of the Holy Ghost and the wonder which attended his birth,—the visible descent of the Spirit upon Him at His baptism, accompanied by a voice from heaven declaring Him to be the beloved Son of God—the miracles, both numerous and varied, which He performed during the course of His public ministry—His transfiguration on the Mount, witnessed by three chosen disciples—His agony in the garden—His crucifixion and the supernatural effects which followed —His resurrection—His ascension—and moreover the outpouring of the Holy Ghost on the day of Pentecost, according to His express promise: and all these circumstances handed down to us in the writings of those who were the chosen companions of our Lord, and testified by those who were eye-witnesses and ear-witnesses of the events concerning which they write, and which the enemies of our religion have never been able to disprove, form such an array of evidence that, if, in spite of these things, any presume to reject the Gospel as not being conveyed with sufficiently distinctive evidence to permit their acceptation of it, we cannot but say that Satan hath blinded their eyes and hardened their hearts, and that no other proof would satisfy them, even though one should rise from the dead and declare it.

Surely we, my brethren, give a hearty and ready assent to what the Bible has revealed; and if we thus yield the testimony of the understanding and of the mouth, should we not, acquiesce also with the heart? and can we not, with the accumulative evidence with which God in His wisdom and providence has favored us, clearly see that those cannot escape who neglect the great salvation.

The subject, then, we have now been considering is one which concerns us all most deeply. Our present life is one of probation. We are each living in preparation for one which shall know no termination. God, in His providence has shewn us what we *are*, what we *should* be, what we *must* be, if we would inherit the blessings of His Kingdom of Glory. By the words of our text, He would remind us of our privilege and the imminent peril to which we expose ourselves as long as we neglect the salvation, the great salvation, which is so freely, so lovingly offered to us in Christ. Daily and hourly does God plead with us. He appeals to us in the language of loving-kindness and entreaty. He warns us in terms expressive of his wrath and vengeance, which will descend upon those who make light of his proffered salvation.

Once again He proposes for our consideration the solemn enquiry of our text. Oh! let us argue the matter with ourselves, and that, too, carefully, candidly, truthfully, prayerfully, and scripturally, that God may not have to testify against any one present as He did against Ephraim of old : "I have written to him the great things of my law, but they were counted as a strange thing."

Rather let us accept (even readily, cheerfully, and gratefully) the offers of salvation, that we may be accounted worthy to enter in through the gates into the heavenly city.

There are many circumstances of a novel and interesting character which, at the present time, naturally engage our attention, gladden our hearts, and strengthen our loyalty. But while we welcome with enthusiasm, and a just enthusiasm, to this Province, one whom, in the Providence of God, we expect at some future day to reign over the British Empire; while we hail his arrival with joy, binding us, as it must do, with closer attachment to the land of our forefathers, and with many of us the land of our nativity—while we bid him good speed in his present visit, and pray that every blessing may abundantly rest upon him, let us never fail to remember, that, before the King of Kings and Lord of Lords, we must all one day appear, and " then shall the righteous shine forth as the sun in the kingdom of their Fathers." That such blessedness may be his, that such blessedness may be ours, may God of His infinite mercy grant, for Jesus Christ's sake.

On leaving Church, His Royal Highness was met at the entrance by a great crowd of persons, who all uncovered, but did not cheer, which augured well for their respect for the sacred day. The Prince took off his hat, smiled on all, and stepped into the carriage with the Duke of Newcastle, Earl St. Germains, and the Governor General, and was speedily out of sight.

On the Thursday following, His Royal Highness presented the Cathedral with a splendid and handsomely-bound copy of the Holy Bible, bearing the royal arms on the cover, with the following inscription in his own writing :—

TO THE CATHEDRAL OF QUEBEC,

in memory of

Sunday, August 19*th*, 1860.

ALBERT EDWARD.

On Sunday afternoon, the royal party paid a visit to Spencer Wood, where are the ruins of the Governor General's former residence. It commands a splendid view of the St. Lawrence, and is surrounded by some of the finest scenery in the country.

The weather on Monday (20th) was as unpropitious as on Saturday, we may say infinitely worse. Sunday had been a remarkably fine day, but Monday, the day on which the Prince was to see some of the natural beauties in and around the city, turned out a rainy day; which, after all the Quebecers' expectations, was too bad, and nearly every one you met made that exclamation, or some other very much akin to it. His Royal Highness remained at the Governor General's residence all the forenoon, until about two o'clock, when, the weather having cleared up a little, the Prince signified his intention of paying a visit to the Chaudière Falls, situated about five miles up, on the opposite side of the river.

His Royal Highness, with his suite and the Governor General, went down to the place of embarkation in His Excellency's carriages, and at Cape Rouge took one of the *Valorous'* boats, and, with his suite, was speedily rowed across the stream to the village of St. Nicholas. Here, sixteen splendid horses * were awaiting the royal party. The Prince mounted a celebrated mare called "Lady Franklin;" and the noble manner in which he bestrode the animal, gave ample evidence of his equestrian skill.

After viewing the Falls, and one of the party taking a sketch of them, the Prince and suite returned to the village inn, where the stewart (Mr. Sanderson, of New York) had laid out a sump-

---

* Purchased by the Provincial Government.

tuous luncheon, to which the royal party did ample justice. They then returned by a small steamer to the city.

On Tuesday (August 21st) His Royal Highness proceeded to take possession of the Palace (late Parliament Buildings), and hold a levee there. The whole building had, under the judicious superintendence of the Board of Works, been entirely refitted and renovated. The new furniture was the costliest and most elegant that could be obtained. Rooms were provided for the whole suite, and guests; in a word, everything was conducted on a most satisfactory footing.

We take from the Toronto *Globe* the following description of the interior portion of the building :—

But to come to particulars. In the first place, the whole building has been painted from top to bottom, every hole and corner cleaned, every cobweb abolished, every spot of dirt scrupulously wiped out. Entering by the broad staircase, we find that the walls have been hung with light-coloured satin-paper, divided into panels by dark broad borderings. The staircase and the corridors have all been carpeted; and placed along the latter are large couches and chairs for the resting of the attendants who will be in waiting night and day. The principal corridor runs the entire length of the building, and has windows at each end—which windows have been coloured with coats of arms Royal and Princely, with maple-leaves, with roses, shamrocks, and thistles, fruits and flowers all combined. The Council Chamber, in accordance with the original designs, has been fitted out as a reception-room, in which the levee is to be held. A velvet carpet covers the floor; a costly affair. Upon a white ground, are worked groups of flowers in many brilliant colours, purple and yellow predominating. The Speaker's gilded chair stands upon its accustomed scarlet dais; the walls of the room are hung with the pictures once occupying similar positions in Toronto. The six large windows in the room are hung with double curtains of scarlet and white, falling in graceful folds from the large gilt cornices above. The polished brass railings, with their numerous lamps, have not been removed. And it was not needed that they should be. Reflecting back with increased brilliancy the sun's rays as they pass the windows, they add much to the adornment of the room. The chandelier, with its many lights and small glass globes, is the one used last session, but it has been carefully cleaned, and looks "as good as new.". The Speaker's rooms leading from the Chamber have been fitted up for the use of His Royal Highness. The carpet is velvet, dark flowers upon white ground, looking exceedingly rich. A French bedstead of black walnut, with sheets of finest linen, has been provided for the repose of our illustrious visitor.

The posts are square, and, if it is allowable to use such language, in the Italian style. The foot-board is adorned with a well-executed carved crest of His Royal Highness. There are no hangings yet, but there are going to be—they will be attached immediately the Prince arrives. Two tables, one with a large mirror, the other with a marble top, are beautiful specimens of cabinet-work. The chairs are of the same material as the rest of the furniture,—black walnut, with covers of crimson silk. The sitting-room has a carpet of the same pattern, and is papered in the same way as the bedroom. A side-board of the description used for the holding of plate—not being either a cabinet-maker or an auctioneer, I forget the technical term for it—is placed in this apartment. From the side-board itself rises a large mirror, a row of semicircular shelves being attached to each side. Along the top is a carved cornice, with the Prince of Wales crest and a crown in the centre. At one end is a shield bearing a sheaf of wheat. Over it are small banners; underneath it is the word " Toronto." At the opposite end is a similar shield, but bearing an anchor, inscribed below with the word, " Quebec." The centre-table is rather plain; but between the pieces of which the top is composed, there is no perceptible difference. A large piano also of walnut, one of Chickering's, is placed in the room. Five nearly straight-backed chairs, richly carved, complete the equipment of this apartment. Next to it is the bath-room. By means of the appliances provided there, His Royal Highness may have either a hot, a cold, or a lukewarm bath as he pleases. It is very nicely fitted up. But, though the Prince is to be thus magnificently lodged, His Grace the Duke of Newcastle has the greater space and more costly furniture. The sitting-room intended for his use is supplied with a beautiful Brussels carpet, hung with satin paper, bordered with green and gold. On one side stands a walnut sofa, of a very large size, with much carving upon it. In the centre is the head of a huntsman, on each side is a large eagle, with wings spread and neck stretched as though just about to swoop down upon its prey. A book-case, so large that it covers one end of the room, stands opposite a Chickering piano. The centre is occupied with a beautiful centre-table, while between the windows are two small side-tables, and a writing-desk. Then, there is a stuffed arm-chair, so soft that a feather-bed is as a board to it, two library chairs, and two cane-seated chairs. The three windows are hung with scarlet curtains suspended from large gilt cornices, richly ornamented with bunches of grapes, the centre bunch being coloured to represent the luscious fruit when in full bloom. From the ceiling descend two chandeliers, each with three burners. On the wall, over the sofa already mentioned, is a portrait of the Prince, a copy from Winterhalter, decidedly the best I have yet seen. The bed and dressing-room of the Duke are on the opposite side of the narrow corridor, and are fitted up with a mahogany suite of furniture. The

House of Assembly has been converted for the time being into a dining-room. But little alteration has been made in it—except that the floor has been raised, and everything reburnished or repainted. Three sideboards have been added. One of them, occupying the place generally devoted to the exhibition of Mr. Speaker Smith, is of oak, and similar in design to that exhibited, I believe, by Messrs. Jacques and Hay in Toronto last October. The carvings are very rich, and display a great deal of artistic skill. They consist of representations of game, fish, and fruit upon the panels and along the mouldings of the side-board. The portrait of Her Majesty, formerly in the library in Toronto, is placed over the chair, and the portraits of Provincial celebrities are suspended in the neighbourhood. General Sir W. F. Williams is to occupy the Speaker's apartments, which, like the rest, have been completely refitted for his accommodation. All the committee-rooms, leading from [the corridors, have been furnished in a less costly, though not less complete manner than those intended for the gentlemen already noticed. The bed-rooms are all on one side—the sitting rooms on the other. Each bed-room is furnished in the same style as the sitting-room opposite to it—but no pair of rooms is like to another pair. The suites in some are of maple, in others of mahogany, in others of walnut. In some the carpets are light, in others dark. Take the first we come to. The bed-room has a carpet of dark flowers upon a white ground. The paper is light-flowered satin, pannelled with deep borders of blue and green. A French bedstead, a chest of drawers, a sofa covered with crimson silk damask, a large rocking-chair, two other chairs covered with the like material, and a marble-topped washing-table, all of dark maple, stand in the room. The window is lined with white muslin curtains, a three-light bronze chandelier is suspended from the ceiling; and to the wall two small gas-branches are affixed. The furniture in the sitting-room opposite is also of walnut, and consists of a sofa, four chairs, a centre-table richly carved, with representations of the rose, shamrock, and thistle, a card-table, and a small book-case. The white satin-paper has a border of dark blue and gold, and there are two chandeliers, instead of one as in the bed-room. The toilet service is generally of white china with blue bands, ornamented in places with the Prince's crest. But there is great variety. Each room is supplied with a bell-pull, and wires in the corridors will enable any of the servants in attendance to summon those of their fellows whose assistance they may desire. The doors are all numbered, as in an hotel, and a registry of the occupants of the rooms will be kept for reference. The kitchen I told you of has been erected, and is in full blast; for wending my way into the lower regions, I came across a strong smell of roast and boiled. Its mysteries I did not further seek to penetrate.

A Guard of Honour of the 17th Regiment was in front of the

building with their band, and a portion of them lined the street through which the Governor's carriage was to pass. They presented arms, the band played the National Anthem, and a royal salute was fired from Durham Terrace when His Royal Highness arrived, who was received at the entrance by Lord Lyons, General Sir W. F. Williams of Kars, Admiral Sir Alex. Milne, Col. Sir A. N. MacNab, Col. Sir E. P. Taché, the Ministry, Col. Irvine, A.D.C., Major Teesdale, Capt. Grey, and Capt. Retallack, A.D.C., &c. They escorted him to his suit of apartments, and shortly after to the Reception Chamber (the Assembly room), where the levee was held.

There he took his seat upon the throne, surrounded by high Civil, Military, and Naval Personages, all in uniform.

The first party presented, was the Roman Catholic Hierarchy, composed of all the Roman Catholic bishops of the Province, attired in purple robes, with gold crucifixes. They were separately introduced by one of the party. Then came the Judges of the Superior Court, and the Legislative Council of Canada (to the number of about forty-three, some being absent). The Usher of the Black Rod announced them by three bows; then followed the Speaker, and then the Sergeant-at-Arms, with the mace. All the members were attired in suits of superfine black. The Speaker (Hon. N. F. Belleau) advanced, and, on behalf of the Legislative Council, presented the following Address, reading it first in English and then in French:—

To His Royal Highness, &c., &c.

MAY IT PLEASE YOUR ROYAL HIGHNESS,—

We, the Legislative Council of Canada, in Parliament assembled, approach Your Royal Highness with renewed assurances of our attachment and devotion to the person and Crown of Your Royal Mother, our beloved Queen.

While we regret that the duties of State should have prevented our Sovereign from visiting this extensive portion of Her vast dominions, we loyally and warmly appreciate the interest which Her Majesty manifests by deputing to us Your Royal Highness as her representative; and we rejoice, in common with all Her subjects in this Province, at the presence among us of Him who at some future, but, we hope, distant day, will reign over the realm, wearing with undiminished lustre the Crown which will descend to Him.

Though the formal opening of that work, the Victoria Bridge, known throughout the world as the most gigantic effort in modern centuries of engineering skill, has been made a special occasion of Your Royal Highness's visit, and proud as are Canadians of it, we yet venture to hope that you will find in Canada many other evidences of greatness and progress to interest you in the welfare and advancement of your future subjects.

Enjoying under the institutions guaranteed to us all freedom in the management of our own affairs, and, as British subjects, having a common feeling and interest in the fortunes of the Empire, its glories and successes, we trust, as we believe, that the visit of Your Royal Highness will strengthen the ties which bind together the Sovereign and the Canadian people.

The following was His Royal Highness's reply :—

GENTLEMEN,—From my heart, I thank you for this address, breathing a spirit of love and devotion to your Queen, and of kindly interest in me as Her Representative on this occasion.

At every step of my progress through the British Colonies, and now more forcibly in Canada, I am impressed with the conviction that I owe the overpowering cordiality of my reception to my connection with Her to whom, under Providence, I owe everything, my Sovereign and Parent.

To Her, I shall with pride convey the expressions of your loyal sentiments; and if at some future period—so remote, I trust, that I may allude to it with less pain—it shall please God to place me in that closer relation to you which you contemplate, I cannot hope for any more honorable distinction, than to earn for myself such expressions of generous attachment as I now owe to your appreciation of the virtues of the Queen.

Few as have yet been the days which I have spent in this country, I have seen much to indicate the rapid progress and future greatness of United Canada. The infancy of this Province has resembled in some respects that of my native Island, and as in centuries gone by the mother country combined the several virtues of the Norman and Anglo-Saxon races, so I may venture to anticipate in the matured character of Canada, the united excellencies of her double ancestry.

Most heartily I respond to your desire that the ties which bind together the Sovereign and the Canadian people may be strong and enduring.

Now followed the knighting of Mr. Belleau, the first knighthood conferred by the Prince, and the first conferred in Canada. No one was certain that this great event was really going to take place, and those assembled were somewhat surprised when the Duke of Newcastle advanced and intimated that it was His Royal Highness's pleasure to confer a knighthood on the Speaker of the Legislative Council.

Mr. Belleau knelt, and the Prince, drawing forth his sword, touched him upon both shoulders, saying, "Rise Sir Narcisse Belleau;" and by this act, and his subsequent one, Albert Edward, in honoring Canada, insures a country's regard and fondest love.

The members of the Legislative Council were then presented separately, and retired.

The Legislative Assembly now appeared, headed by the Speaker (Hon. Henry Smith), and followed by the Sergeant-at-Arms and about one hundred and twenty members.

Their Address was as follows :—

MAY IT PLEASE YOUR ROYAL HIGHNESS,—

We, the Legislative Assembly of Canada in Parliament assembled, approach your Royal Highness with assurances of our devoted attachment and loyalty to the Person and Crown of our most Gracious Sovereign.

The Queen's loyal subjects in this Province would have rejoiced had the duties of State permitted their august Sovereign to have herself visited their country, and to have received in person, the expression of their devotion to Her, and of the admiration with which they regard the manner in which she administers the affairs of the vast empire over which it has pleased Divine Providence to place Her.

But while we cannot refrain from expressing our unfeigned regret that it has proved impossible for our Queen to visit her possessions in Canada, we are deeply sensible of Her gracious desire to meet the wishes of her subjects, by having permitted them the opportunity of welcoming, in this part of her dominions, the Heir Apparent of the Throne, our future Sovereign.

We desire to congratulate your Royal Highness on your arrival in Canada, an event to be long remembered as manifesting the deep interest felt by the Queen for the welfare of Her colonial subjects.

On the auspicious occasion, when for the first time the Colonies have been honoured by the presence of the Heir Apparent, we receive an earnest of the determination of our Most Gracious Sovereign to knit yet more closely the ties of affection and duty which unite us to the British Empire, and enable us to share in its liberties, its glories, and its great historical associations.

The approaching opening of the Victoria Bridge by Your Royal Highness has been the more immediate cause of your present visit to Canada; and we trust that you will find on that stupendous work the most striking evidence in which the capital and skill of the Mother Country have united with the energy and enterprise of this Province in overcoming natural obstacles of the most formidable character ; but, we trust that in your further progress, Your Royal Highness will find, in the peace and prosperity of the people and in their attachment to their Sovereign, the best proof of the strength of the ties which unite Canada to the Mother Country, and of the mutual advantages to the Empire and to the Colony from the perpetuation of a connection which has been fraught with such great and beneficial results.

We pray that Your Royal Highness may be pleased to convey to our Most Gracious Queen the feelings of love and gratitude with which we regard Her rule, and especially of Her condescension in affording us the occasion of welcoming Your Royal Highness to the Province of Canada.

His Royal Highness replied as follows:—

GENTLEMEN,—No answer that I can return to your Address will sufficiently convey my thanks to you, or express the pleasure which I have derived from the manifestations of loyalty and affection to the Queen, my mother, by which I have been met upon my arrival in this Province.

As an Englishman, I recognize with pride, in those manifestations, your sympathy with the great nation from which so many of you trace your origin, and with which you share the honors of a glorious history.

In addressing you however as an Englishman, I do not forget that some of my fellow-subjects here, are not of my own blood. To them also an especial acknowledgment is due, and I receive with peculiar grasification the proofs of their attachment to the Crown of England. They are evidence of their satisfaction with the equal laws under which they live, and of their just confidence that, whatever be their origin, all Canadians are alike objects of interest to their Sovereign and Her people.

Canada may be proud that within her limits two races of different language and habits are united in the same Legislature by a common loyalty, and are bound to the same Constitution by a common patriotism.

But to all of you and to the three millions of British subjects of whom you are the Representatives, I am heartily thankful for your demonstration of good-will, and I shall not readily forget the mode in which I have been received amongst you.

With you I regret that the Queen has been unable to comply with your anxious desire that she would visit this portion of Her Empire,— I have already had proofs of the affectionate devotion which would have attended her progress,—but I shall make it my first, as it will be my most pleasing duty, upon my return to England, to convey to her the feelings of love and gratitude to her person and her rule, which you have expressed on this occasion, and the sentiment of hearty welcome which you have offered to me her son.

Then the Honorable Henry Smith, after the same preliminaries had been gone through as with Sir N. F. Belleau, knelt and was also knighted.

Numbers of gentlemen and many Addresses were presented afterwards, and at half-past one the levee broke up.

At three o'clock in the afternoon, a number of gentlemen of the Ministry, and both houses of the Legislature, partook of a *dejeuner* at the Palace.

Later, the royal party paid a visit to the Montmorenci Falls, situated a few miles from the city in the beautiful valley of the St. Charles. Dorchester Bridge which they had to cross, and in fact the whole road, was nicely ornamented with arches, flags, and evergreens, and the people came out and cheered the Prince as the carriage passed by.

The Falls of Montmorenci are celebrated for their grand natural beauty, being the highest in British America, and for the beautiful scenery and interesting places which abound around them ; for instance, the natural steps, &c. The Prince and suite returned highly delighted with the excursion.

In the evening, the Prince and suite attended the grand ball given in his honour at the Music Hall. He arrived at about ten o'clock, and was received by a Guard of Honour of the Royal Canadian Rifles, their band playing the National Anthem ; and by the hearty and loyal cheers of a large concourse of people outside.

After visiting his dressing-room, the Prince and suite repaired immediately to the ball-room, one of the finest in North America, but on this occasion deserving of something more than a mere passing notice, which we are sorry space will not allow us to give. Suffice it to say, that the entire building had been entirely renovated a few days before, and the ball-room presented a most beautiful appearance, being decorated in an elaborate manner with flowers of every hue, flags, banners, &c., and crowded with the cream of Quebec society.

The Prince opened the ball with Madame Langevin (the Lady Mayoress), and danced secondly with Miss Irvine (daughter of

Lieutenant Colonel Irvine, A.D.C.), and afterwards with the following ladies:—
Madame Cartier (wife of the Premier), Miss Price, Miss Le Mesurier, Miss Derbishire, Miss Sewell, Miss Caron (daughter of Judge Caron), Lady Milne, Miss Napier, Mrs. Serecold (daughter of Judge Duval), Miss Dunscomb, Miss Fisher (sister of the Attorney General of New Brunswick), Miss Mountain (daughter of the Bishop), Miss Anderson, Mrs. Ross, Mrs. Bell, Miss Tilley (daughter of the Provincial Secretary of New Brunswick), and Mrs. R. H. Smith.

The following was the Programme of dances, the Prince dancing nearly every one :—

1. Quadrille......Bonnie Dundee.
2. Polka................Cupid.
3. Galop........The Reception.
4. Quadrille...Queen's Canadian.
5. Valse..............Dinorah.
6. Polka Mazurka...Fairy Queen.
7. Lancers............Original.
8. Galop.............Pellisier.
9. Schottische..........Lenora.
10. Quadrille..........Palermo.
11. Polka..............Ariadne.
12. Galop ....Hero.
13. Quadrille....Berliner Couplet.
14. Valse...........Il Trovatore.
15. Polka Mazurka......Rigoletto.
16. Lancers.............Duval's.
17. Galop............Charivari.
18. Polka..............Selinen.
19. Quadrille......Don Pasquale.
20. Valse..... Dream of the Roses.
21. Galop............ Strothfield.
22. Lancers............English.
23. Valse.................Sybil.
24. Galop........... Night Bell.
25. Sir Roger De Coverley.

On the following day he visited the Laval University,* situated on the Grand Battery not far from his residence, and which is a large, fine-looking cut-stone building, erected by the Seminary, and supported chiefly by the Roman Catholic portion of the population.†

His Royal Highness was met at the door by two gentlemen of the Institution and escorted to the Hall, where the following Addresses were presented to him; that from the Roman Catholic Hierarchy by Bishop Horan of Kingston, C. W.—

To His Royal Highness the Prince of Wales.

MAY IT PLEASE YOUR ROYAL HIGHNESS,—

We, the Catholic Bishops of the Province of Canada assembled at

---

* Named after the first Bishop of Quebec.
† The corner-stone of which was laid by the Earl of Elgin, while Governor General.

Quebec to take part in the universal joy caused by the visit of Your Royal Highness to this portion of the British Empire, hasten to express, in our own name, and in behalf of our Clergy, the feeling of happiness we experience in seeing in our midst the Heir Apparent to the Crown of England, the son of our August and Dearly-Beloved Queen, who, by her virtues, adds a fresh lustre to the throne of one of the most powerful monarchies in the world.

Charged with the sacred mission of preaching to the people confided to our care the duties as well as the dogmas of Christianity, we are ever careful to teach them that it is " by God Kings reign ;" and that, therefore, entire submission is due to the authority they have received from on High, for the happiness of their subjects. We feel convinced it is to the traditional respect for the high moral principle of legitimate authority, which constitutes the strength of all society, that Canada has long enjoyed a peace and tranquillity which promise to be of uninterrupted duration.

We are happy in giving Your Royal Highness the assurance that the Catholics of this Colony partake of our sentiments of gratitude to Divine Providence for the many advantages which they possess, under the protection of the British Government, especially as regards the free exercise of their religion. We have a firm conviction that the presence of Your Royal Highness amongst us will tend to develop and to strengthen still more these feelings of attachment and loyal devotion which bind them to the mother country.

In conclusion, we pray Your Royal Highness to accept our warmest and most ardent wishes for the prosperity of the vast Empire, the destinies of which you will one day be called to rule. Happy in forming a part of an Empire under which this, our own beloved country, has made such rapid progress, we shall not cease to offer up our prayers to Almighty God, to beg of him that they who wield authority may ever be guarded by the unvarying laws of Justice and Equity, that they may labor with constantly-increasing success for the happiness of the people subjected to their rule, and that they may thus perpetuate before the eyes of other nations the glory of the British Crown.

The Address of the Laval University was as follows:—

MAY IT PLEASE YOUR ROYAL HIGHNESS,—

It is with feelings of the greatest respect that the members of the Laval University beg leave to lay at the foot of Your Royal Highness their homage, and the expression of their liveliest gratitude.

They are happy to see within these walls the Heir Apparent of a vast empire, the eldest son of a noble Queen, whose domestic and public virtues the world acknowledges and loudly proclaims ; the worthy Representative of that gracious Queen to whom the University is indebted for the charter of its erection. Charged with the mission of receiving in the name of our August Sovereign the homage of Her faithful subjects, Your Royal Highness will, we fondly hope, deign to accept the expression of the deep gratitude with which we are filled towards Her Majesty.

Actuated by this feeling, we pray Your Royal Highness to believe that the Professors and Alumni of this Institution will make it their constant endeavor to prove themselves worthy of the royal favor. This, the first and only French Canadian University thus honored with the royal protection, will be a lasting monument of the desire of Her Majesty to provide for the happiness of all Her subjects, while it will form a new tie between their fellow-subjects of French origin and the mother-country to whose care we have been committed by Divine Providence.

It is true that, unlike the *Alma Mater*, Oxford, where Your Highness has been pleased to matriculate, our existence cannot be counted by centuries—our alumni are but few, our libraries, our museums, our collections, offer nothing to excite the curiosity of Your Royal Highness, accustomed to visit the great and antique Institutions of Europe ; our beginning is but humble—our hopes are in the future.

We trust in the future destinies of this colony, which, under the protection of England, is in the enjoyment of peace and abundance, whilst other countries are distracted by violent convulsions.

We trust in the future of that glorious metropolis whose influence is so weighty in controlling the destinies of the civilized world.

We place our trust in the protection and justice of the August Queen, to whom we are indebted for so signal a mark of benevolence.

We also place our trust in the young Prince whom Providence will call one day to give on the throne the example of all those royal virtues he has inherited from the most gracious of Sovereigns, the noblest of mothers.

The Prince replied to both these Addresses as follows :—

I accept with the greatest satisfaction the welcome which you offer me in your own name as the Catholic Bishops of the Province of Canada, and on behalf of your clergy, and I assure you that I feel deeply the expression of your loyalty and affection for the Queen.

I rejoice to think that obedience to the laws and submission to authority, which form the bond of all society and the condition of all civilization, are supported and enforced by your teaching and example.

The assurance that you enjoy the free exercise of your religion, and that you partake in the benefits and protection of the British Constitution, is a pledge that your hearts, and those of your fellow-subjects, of whatever origin they may be, will ever be united in the feelings you now express, of attachment to the Crown of Great Britain.

I acknowledge with gratitude the earnest prayers which you offer to

Almighty God in my behalf; and I trust that my future course may be such as will best promote the welfare of this great Province and of its inhabitants.

To you, Gentlemen, who are engaged within the walls of this building, in the education of the youth of the country, I also tender my thanks. I trust that your University may continue to prosper, and that, in future years, its sons may look back upon the days they have spent under your instruction, with the same gratitude and sense of the benefits they have enjoyed, as I and others feel towards the more ancient Institutions of my own land.

As he concluded the reply, the audience, composed of the *elite* of Quebec, cheered heartily and clapped their hands, and the Seminary band played " God save the Queen."

After having been shown through the several departments of the institution, with which he expressed himself much pleased, the Prince and suite were escorted to their carriages, and proceeded to the Ursuline Convent, which was beautifully decorated for the occasion, and where the following Address was presented to him by Miss Stuart (daughter of Judge Stuart) :—

QU'IL PLAISE A VOTRE ALTESSE ROYALE,—

Les Religieuses Ursulines regarderont toujours comme un honneur signalé, la visite de Votre Altesse Royale dans leur antique monastère et elles demandent humblement, qu'il leur soit permis de déposer à ses pieds, en cette circonstance solennelle, l'hommage de leur respect et de leur dévouement.

Bien que vivant dans le cloître, elles ne sont indifférentes à rien de ce qui intéresse leur patrie ; elles ont toujours pris la plus large part à la reconnaissance et à l'attachement des plus fidèles sujets de Sa Majesté, dans l'Amérique Anglaise ; comment ne partageraient-elles pas, aujourd'hui, la joie publique à l'occasion de l'heureuse arrivée de Votre Altesse Royale en cette province.

Deux fois déjà, des princes de la glorieuse maison de Brunswick ont visité ce pays, et même cet établissement d'éducation, le plus ancien de l'Amérique Britannique, et les annales du Monastère en font mention avec bonheur comme d'événements du meilleur augure : avec quel enthousiasme désormais n'ajouterons-nous pas aux noms illustres de ces princes, celui de Son Altesse Royale, Albert Edouard, Prince de Galles.

Il serait inutile de vouloir redire, en ce moment, ce que publie la Renommée de la bonté de votre Altesse Royale, et de toutes les autres qualités qui l'appellent à s'asseoir, un jour, sur un des plus beaux trônes de l'univers ; mais les Religieuses Ursulines conserveront intacts, et transmettront à celles qui doivent leur succéder, le souvenir et les impressions de cette gracieuse visite.

Que le ciel continue à prodiguer ses faveurs à notre auguste Souveraine et que la prospérité toujours croissante de son règne soit un heureux présage de la gloire que l'avenir prépare à l'héritier présomptif de sa brillante couronne.

His Royal Highness thus replied :—

MADAME,—I thank you for these expressions of kindly interest in my visit to the city of Quebec, and the personal good wishes which this Address manifests.

Your exertions in the cause of education are well known, and I trust they may long continue to exert a beneficial influence upon the population of this interesting country.

After which the young ladies attending the Convent sang "The Prince's Welcome," an ode composed for the occasion. They were accompanied by a Miss Blackiston on the harp, and acquitted themselves admirably. The following is the piece in question :—

>   Hark ! hark ! a merry, merry peal
>   Rings out o'er all the land ;
>   Its echoes through the cloister steal—
>   It fires our youthful band.
>   Bring harp and song ! let melody,
>   Let joy, gush forth in numbers free,
>   Thy welcome, 'tis that merry peal
>   Of joy o'er all the land !

>   SOLO.

>   'Tis gladness all, thy welcoming,
>   From Albion's Isle afar :
>   And loyal hearts their homage bring,
>   To hail thy rising star ;
>   And joyous youth its promise tell,
>   While tuneful notes of triumph swell ;
>   Lo ! Britain's Heir deigns here to rest ;
>   Oh ! haste to greet our Royal Guest !

>   2ND CHORUS.

>   Wake ! wake ! another merry peal,
>   And let it echo long,

> While wishes for the Prince's weal
> Are mingled with our song.
> May ev'ry blessing on thee rest;
> Thus rings the merry peal :
> And thus we hail thee, Royal Guest,
> Thus pray we for thy weal,
> While still that merry peal
> Rings loud, and echoes long!

His Royal Highness then retired.

At two o'clock p. m., he visited the Citadel.

In the evening, a grand display of fireworks took place on the Esplanade. Many beautiful devices in a variety of colours were given, among them the Prince's arms, the royal arms, " God save the Queen, " Duke of Newcastle's and Earl St. Germains' arms, &c. The Prince was present, with a part of his suite, during the whole of the display.

On the following morning at 11 o'clock, His Royal Highness, accompanied by his suite, the Governor General, General Williams, Admiral Milne, Sir A. N. MacNab, Sir E. P. Taché, Hon. Mr. Cartier (Premier), &c., took leave of Quebec and embarked on board the splendid steamer *Kingston* (chartered by the Provincial Government, and beautifully furnished) for Montreal.

The procession which escorted him to the wharf was the same that had welcomed him there. The 17th Regiment and Royal Canadian Rifles lined the streets from his residence to the wharf, where the Volunteer Artillery, as the Guard of Honour, presented arms as he passed, and the band played the National Anthem.

Royal salutes were fired by all the batteries, and by Her Majesty's ships in port; and as the *Kingston* steamed out, cheers, long and loud, from the excited and enthusiastic multitude, greeted the ear of the Heir Apparent to the British Throne.

The sailors of the fleet manned the yards, and, as the *Kingston* steamed round the harbour, they cheered lustily, heartily, and with a British will, the band on board her playing " Rule Britannia " until out of sight.

The trip up to the city of Three Rivers, about half-way between Quebec and Montreal, at the mouth of the River St. Maurice, and which was reached at three o'clock p.m., was a delightful one; the weather was beautiful,—all that a person could wish. The sun shone in his gorgeous attire, and the rich, varied, and magnificent scenery of the noble river showed itself to much advantage. No wonder that the Prince and his party were in high glee, and delighted.

A royal salute was fired by the Field Battery of the place ; and the entire population of the town, and the people from the surrounding country (entirely French), crowded the wharves, which, as well as the town, was handsomely decorated, and cheered the Prince loudly.

A Company of Light Infantry from Montreal was on the wharf, and, when the Prince landed, presented arms.

An Address was presented him by the Mayor (J. E. Turcotte, Esq., M. P. P.), to which His Royal Highness gave a suitable reply. The royal party then returned to the steamer, it being their intention to lie there until the morning, which they did.

In the evening (mainly through the instrumentality of the Mayor) the entire town was illuminated, and looked extremely well.

During the night, the steamer *Quebec*, (the largest, oldest, and swiftest boat in Canada,) came in from the ancient capital, Quebec, carrying the Members of the Legislature, and some of the chief government officers. A meeting was called of the Members, when a deputation, consisting of the Hon. Messrs. De Blaquière and Drummond, was despatched to wait upon His Royal Highness praying him to allow the *Quebec*, with the Members, to escort him to Montreal. The Prince was graciously pleased to acquiesce to this.

So the *Quebec* lay at Three Rivers all night, with the *Kingston* ; but, alas, the next morning broke in with bad weather, miserable, foggy, drizzling—Prince's weather ; nevertheless, the royal party amused themselves in the ample and comfortable cabins of the *Kingston*, and the Members of the Legislature in the commodious, but, on that occasion, somewhat crowded ones of the *Quebec*.

Both boats left Three Rivers in the morning. In Lake St. Peter they came up with the steamer *St. Lawrence*, with members of the Trinity House on board, who had come down to escort the Prince to Montreal. It fell in the wake of the *Kingston*, with the *Quebec*.

All along shore the *habitans* came out and welcomed the Prince, and even when the rain came down in the worst manner, there were people found on the shore doing homage to the son of our beloved Queen.

Near Montreal, the three steamers came up with a regular fleet of vessels, which were gaily and beautifully dressed with flags and evergreens, and perfectly crowded with passengers. They were the *Victoria, Passport, Mayflower, L'Assomption, Terrebonne, Hochelaga, Topsy, Napoleon, James McKenzie, Redpath, L'Aigle, Caledonia,* &c., &c.

As the *Kingston* passed them, their passengers gave the Prince " three times three ;" a regular downright loyal British cheer, and the bands on all of them struck up " God save the Queen." Nothing could be more sublime, nothing more beautiful. But for the rain, every one would have been in the greatest hilarity of spirits.

At Montreal it was thought better, on account of the rain, to postpone the landing; and in the emergency, that indefatigable Minister of the Crown, Mr. Rose, chartered a steamer and went down to meet His Royal Highness on behalf of the Reception Committee, and acquaint him with their request; which the Prince graciously complied with, the *Kingston* anchoring shortly after for the night below St. Helen's Island.

Nine o'clock on Saturday morning was the hour named for the Prince's entrance into the metropolitan city of British America. Long before that hour, however, every conceivable nook in and around the piers from which a sight of the landing could be obtained, was densely crowded by over 40,000 people.

The weather had been very boisterous during the night, and raining incessantly; but before nine it cleared up, the sun shone forth, and the weather was at once delightful.

Near that hour the *Kingston* was perceived, preceded by the same fleet of steamers that had gone down to meet it the day before, steaming up the river, her colours, as well as those from the others, flying from her masts, while flowers and evergreens decked her sides.

The battery on St. Helen's Island fired a royal salute as she passed, the people along the river cheered loudly, and the bells from all the city churches rang forth gaily.

Shortly after nine the noble vessel made the landing-place, which was handsomely and gorgeously decorated. A massive pavilion stood near the edge, which, although made of wood, was gilded and painted in a neat, masterly style. It was surmounted on the four sides by groups of flags, while at the top floated the royal standard. It looked really grand, contrasting with the wharf, which was laid out with trees, and carpeted where the Prince was to walk. The regular lines of soldiers, and the gay uniforms of the officers gathered there, gave the affair quite a festive appearance.

On the wharf were the chief civil and military personages of Montreal; the Metropolitan Bishop of Canada (Dr. Fulford); the Moderator of the Church of Scotland; the Clergy of the Church of Rome; the Members of the Ministry; the Members of the Legislature; the Mayor, Aldermen, and Councillors, the officers of the Corporation, &c., &c. The entire Volunteer Force of Montreal, composed of Infantry, Rifles, Cavalry, and Artillery, were also there. The Rifles acted in conjunction with the Royal Canadian Rifles as Guard of Honour.

The Prince and his suite stood on the upper deck until the steamer was safely moored, when they descended, and His Royal Highness stepped on the shore of Montreal. Then did the cheers of the people ring forth in one continued cry of joy, and the cannons of the Field Battery thundered forth a salute, accompanied by H. M. S. *Valorous*, *Styx*, and *Flying-Fish*, the men manning the yards and cheering vociferously. The Volunteer Rifles presented arms and the bands played the National Anthem.

The Mayor (C. S. Rodier, Esq.), in his robes of office, then conducted His Royal Highness to a rich scarlet dais, under the handsome pavilion, and presented him with the following Address:—

MAY IT PLEASE YOUR ROYAL HIGHNESS,—

We, the Mayor, Aldermen, and citizens of the City of Montreal, respectfully beg leave to approach Your Royal Highness, to felicitate you on behalf of the citizens of Montreal on your safe arrival in this Province, and to offer to Your Royal Highness our most cordial and hearty welcome to this city. We avail ourselves of this propitious occasion of a visit from the Heir Apparent of the British throne, to express to Your Royal Highness our devoted loyalty and attachment to the Person and Government of our most Gracious Sovereign, your illustrious mother; and to declare our humble but fervent admiration of her wisdom, moderation, and justice as our Sovereign, and our love and veneration of the virtues and graces which adorn her private life. As circumstances do not permit our beloved Queen to honour this distant but important section of her Empire with a personal visit, Her Majesty has been graciously pleased to confer on her faithful Canadian subjects the next dearest boon it was in her power to bestow, by authorising this most welcome visit of Your Royal Highness. This gracious manifestation of Her Majesty's consideration and regard is hailed with thankfulness and joy by all her loyal and devoted subjects in these Provinces; but we beg most respectfully to assure Your Royal Highness, that by none amongst the millions who compose their number, is it more highly esteemed, more fully appreciated, and more enthusiastically felt and acknowledged, than by Her Majesty's devoted and loyal subjects, the citizens of Montreal. The immediate object of Your Royal Highness's most gratifying visit to Canada is to open the Victoria Bridge; that magnificent monument of enterprise and skill with which the fame and prosperity of this city will evermore be intimately connected and most permanently identified.

In this stupendous work, Your Royal Highness will not fail to observe how natural obstacles, almost insurmountable in their ponderous strength and complicated variety, have been triumphantly overcome by the combined power of British enterprise and capital, and of Canadian energy and skill. And we beg to assure Your Royal Highness, that this wonderful achievement of engineering and mechanical perfection will henceforth possess a new claim on our interests and regards, associated as it must evermore be in our memories and affections with this auspicious visit of Your Royal Highness, and the interesting ceremony of its perfect consummation by Your Royal Highness's hands. We earnestly hope that Your Royal Highness's visit to this city will be one of unmixed satisfaction and delight; and we pledge ourselves, for the citizens of Montreal, that they will one and all esteem it the highest gratification and honour to use every means in their power to render your too-short stay amongst them agreeable, happy, and comfortable. We pray that Your Royal Highness will be pleased to communicate to our Most Gracious Queen, your royal and beloved mother, our feelings of ardent loyalty and devotion to her royal person and crown, and our lively gratitude and acknowledgments for this last gracious evidence of her royal condescension and favour, Your Royal Highness's most welcome and grateful visit to this city and province.

To which His Royal Highness replied :—

GENTLEMEN,—The Address you have just presented to me, in which you proclaim your loyalty to the Queen and attachment to the British Crown, demands my warmest acknowledgments. The impression made upon me by the kind and cordial reception which has been accorded to me on this first visit to Canada, can never fade from my mind; and deeply will the Queen be gratified by the proof which it affords that the interest which she takes in the welfare of this portion of her Empire, and which she has been anxious to mark by my presence amongst you, is met, on their part, by feelings of affectionate devotion to herself and her family.

For myself, I rejoice at the opportunity which has been afforded me of visiting this City, a great emporium of the Trade of Canada, and whose growing prosperity offers so striking an example of what may be effected by energy and enterprise, under the influence of free institutions. That this prosperity may be still further enlarged is my earnest hope; and there can be little doubt that by the completion of that stupendous monument of engineering skill and labor which I have come in the name of the Queen to inaugurate, new sources of wealth will be opened to your citizens, and to the country new elements of power developed, and new links forged to bind together in peaceful co-operation the exertions of a wide-spread and rapidly-increasing population.

His Royal Highness was then conducted to the Governor General's carriage, as also were the Duke of Newcastle, Earl St. Germains, and the Governor General; the different Societies fell in, the bands struck up joyful airs, and the procession advanced.

A finer procession was hardly ever witnessed. The members of the various Societies attired in their best, wearing their insignia and carrying their colours, the many different uniforms of the military companies present, the Rifles so steady and so efficient in their movements, the Cavalry mounted on good chargers and looking so erect and soldier-like, the Members of the Ministry in their new Windsor uniforms looking the *beau idéal* of courtly diplomatists, the Mayor in his scarlet robe like a second Lord Mayor of London and preserving the dignity of one —all joining in the hearty demonstration of the people in favour of the Prince of Wales.

Montreal is to Canada what London is to Great Britain,—the metropolis; and not only because she possesses an overflow of population or commerce, but because she has earned that name by her fair reputation, her wealth, and her stability in advancing towards greatness, and, being the centre of trade in Canada, doing in one year more perfected work, and more commerce and ready-money business, than is done in five years in any other city in British America.

No wonder, then, that, as the richest city in British North America, she should give the Heir Apparent to the British Throne a reception so magnificent, which cannot but be always remembered, by, not only the Prince himself, but all that had the good fortune to witness it.

Montreal sustained her good name on that auspicious occasion; and her citizens deserve to be ever honoured for showing their devoted loyalty to the Throne in such a substantial and commendable manner.

The whole city was beautifully ornamented with flags, banners, trees, flowers, evergreens, transparencies, and arches, which, for taste, skill, architecture, and varied beauty, can hardly be excelled; they appeared so very neat, beautiful, and substantial, and were adorned and painted so very elaborately.

We regret that we are unable, from want of space, to give a full and separate description of the arches. In all there were about eight, at the following places:—Jacques Cartier Square; Dalhousie Square; Place d'Armes; Victoria Square; St. Catherine Street; St. Lawrence Street; Griffintown; and Simpson Street.

His Royal Highness was escorted through nearly all these arches to the Crystal Palace (which he was to inaugurate),—a new building, built somewhat after the London one of 1851, but of course on a much smaller scale,—where he arrived at a quarter to eleven, and was received by a Guard of Honour of the Montreal Infantry and by a royal salute from the Field Battery, and at the grand entrance by the President, Secretary, and members of the Sub-Committee of the Board of Arts and Manufactures of Lower Canada, who conducted him to the retiring-room, and, after remaining there a few minutes, led the way to the main building, where he took his seat on the central dais. The organ pealed forth, and the Oratorio Society sang with good effect the National Anthem. The floor and galleries were crowded with the *elite* of Montreal, and a great number of visitors from other places. The Members of the Legislature were also there.

The interior portion of the building looked excellently, being very prettily adorned with flags, &c.

On His Royal Highness's right stood the Governor General, Major Teesdale, and Captain Grey; on his left, the Duke of

Newcastle, Earl St. Germains, General Sir W. F. Williams, &c. The military and naval officers also were there, and the Members of the Executive Council. The Marquis and Marchioness of Chandos, Lady Franklin, Lady Georgiana Fane, Lord Hinchin brooke, and the Hon. Mr. Elliot, attended as spectators.

The Governor General, at the conclusion of the National Anthem, stepped to the foot of the dais, and presented the following Address to His Royal Highness :—

MAY IT PLEASE YOUR ROYAL HIGHNESS,—

The people of this Province are aware of the interest with which Her Most Gracious Majesty and the Prince Consort honoured the Exhibitions of 1851 and 1855. They know that among the objects which excited attention on these occasions, the productions of Canada held an important place ; and they venture to hope that Your Royal Highness will on the present occasion condescend to meet their wishes by opening the Exhibition which is to take place in this building. They believe that Your Royal Highness may find that the objects submitted to your notice will afford some evidence of the industry and progress of Canada, and some promise of her future success. On the part therefore of the Provincial Government, I pray Your Royal Highness to do us the honor of opening in the city of Montreal this Exhibition ; and we trust that such condescension on your part may stimulate our people to greater exertions, and may be long remembered among the gracious acts which are destined to mark the visit of the Heir Apparent of the Throne of Great Britain.

To this His Royal Highness replied as follows :—

GENTLEMEN,—Most readily I consent to the request you have made ; a request the more agreeable, because it is conveyed to me by my kind friend Your Excellency the Governor General. I am not ignorant of the high position obtained by Canada in the Great Exhibition of 1851, which was opened under the happy auspices of the Queen and the Prince Consort; and carrying out the design of the memorable undertaking, this smaller, but to Canada most interesting, collection of the products of your land, and of works of art and industry, has my entire sympathy, and claims my best wishes for its success. I hope and believe it will realize all the objects for which it has been designed.

The Governor then took his place at the right hand of His Royal Highness, and Bishop Fulford offered up the following prayer :—

Almighty God, the Creator and Giver of the Universe, we Thy

creatures desire humbly to approach Thy throne of Grace, confessing Thee as the Author of our being, and the Giver of all good gifts, by whose mercy alone it is that we are enabled to think or to do anything that is acceptable to Thee. We acknowledge with grateful hearts all Thy past mercies to us, and specially Thy goodness manifested in the abundance of the fruits of the earth, now awaiting the ingathering of the harvest. We also bless Thee, O Lord, for that continued public tranquility in the land which has given us the opportunity of pursuing with any measure of success, those enterprises which belong to peace, and promote the prosperity of the people. We beseech Thee now to look favorably upon this work of our hands; and while we give Thee hearty thanks that we have been allowed thus far to carry forward the execution of our designs, we beg Thy blessing on the undertaking which we are this day assembled to inaugurate. Let us not rest with pride or self-complaceny upon the results of human intellect and human ingenuity, but make us always to remember that whatever is of the earth is earthly and perishable, and that all flesh is as grass, and the glory of man as the flower of grass, which withereth and fadeth away. And enable us also to exercise our several talents as shall best promote Thy glory and the edification and well-being of Thy creatures, that we may give account of the trust committed to us with joy and not with sorrow; and we beseech Thee, O Lord, so to guide and direct our hearts, and to overrule our purposes, that, while endeavouring to make known Thy power and wisdom in the works of creation, and to develop the gifts of Thy creatures in the advancement of science and art, we may allow no strife or vain-glory to disturb our unity of action or hinder our success; and in order thereto, may we be taught by Thy Spirit not to think too highly of ourselves, but, in lowliness of mind, each to esteem others better than themselves. Grant that this mind may be in us which was also in Jesus Christ; for which we pray in His name, who died for us that we might live unto Him, and who now liveth and reigneth with Thee and the Holy Ghost, in the unity of the Godhead, Thy only Son Our Lord. Amen.

The Grace of our Lord Jesus Christ, the love of God, and the fellowship of the Holy Ghost, be with us all, evermore. Amen.

A procession was then organized to conduct His Royal Highness through the building, and the several departments in it. Mr. Chamberlin, the Secretary of the Sub-Committee of the Board of Arts and Manufactures, and the Equerries in Waiting, leading the way, the party passed through the most interesting parts. Whilst in the Mineralogical Department, His Royal Highness entered into conversation with Dr. Dawson, the President of the Board, relative to the Canadian specimens. In the Fine Arts

Department, his Lordship Bishop Fulford, President of the Art Association, said that the Council were desirous of presenting him with a Canadian picture from the collection, and praying His Royal Highness to select one. The Prince good naturedly selected Mr. Way's water-colour painting, "The Prince's Squadron at Anchor at Gaspé Basin." When passing along the St. Catherine Street end of the building, he stepped out on the balcony, and the immense crowd gathered outside cheered immediately. The whole party then returned to the dais, when the Governor General said, "By command of His Royal Highness, I declare this Exhibition opened." The Hallelujah Chorus was then sung by the Oratorio Society, under the direction of Professor Fowler; and the Prince and suite retired to his room, whence they left shortly afterwards for the Victoria Bridge (which he was also to inaugurate).

We copy the following from the Montreal *Herald*. It refers to the preparations at the Bridge, and to the people assembled prior to the arrival of the Prince :—

But before his arrival a large company had assembled. There was first of all a number of what may be called *ex officio* visitors—among them the Executive Committee of the Citizens' Fund, and the Special Committee of the City Council. The former all wore a plume on a blue ribbon. The arrangements at the Point had all been made under the superintendence of Mr. Scott, the architect usually employed by the Grand Trunk Company, and he had done his business well; for, with a crowd of several hundred persons all pressing forward, there was not the slightest confusion. Except a little pressure at the doors, everything passed off with the most perfect order, each man finding his seat on the cars, and afterwards on the scaffolding of the Bridge, with the greatest ease and comfort. By about 1 o'clock all were seated in the following manner. A space formed by the walls of the Bridge at the commencement of the tube had been enclosed so as to form an oblong pit, having one end closed at the top by the first pier, and at the bottom of which ran the rails, of course passing under the pier. At the southern end of this enclosure, and against the pier, a scaffold was erected almost at the level of the top of the pier, reached by a stair from the level on which the rails are laid. On each side of the rails were seats appropriated to the Members of the Legislature. Upon the walls were galleries; and the top of the pier itself, the last stone of which was to be laid, was appropriated to members of the press, Canadian and Foreign. The gallery was hung with red baize. Over the pier there was an arched board with the royal arms, and below it the words "Finis coronat opus." This board served to conceal the wheel-crank and other

G

machinery which were intended to lift the stone from its wooden supports preparatory to its being deposited on its bed. The whole of the gallery was erected under the direction and at the desire and expense of Mr. James Hodges, who wished to give his Canadian friends this last token of his regard. To that part of the structure, therefore, they were admitted by his invitation. The company who came at the invitation of the Manager were accommodated on the embankment in two rows of seats, one on each side of the track. Every place on all parts of the Bridge were numbered, and, as we have said before, all the visitors had found their places before H. R. H. arrived. In the interval some flags, with appropriate designs, had been handed to the ladies, who seemed well pleased with these pretty toys."

The Prince and suite arrived at the Victoria Bridge station, at about one o'clock. He was met by the Hon. John Ross, President of the Executive Council, and President of the Grand Trunk Railway; T. E. Blackwell, Esq., Vice-President, G. T. R., and the Members of the Executive Council.

Mr. Ross presented him with the following Address:—

To His Royal Highness Albert Edward, Prince of Wales, &c., &c.

MAY IT PLEASE YOUR ROYAL HIGHNESS,—

The Directors of the Grand Trunk Railway Company of Canada beg leave to offer to your Royal Highness a respectful welcome to the Province.

The Canadian Parliament has made the completion of the Victoria Bridge the occasion on which to invite our most gracious Sovereign to visit her Canadian possessions; and, in welcoming your Royal Highness to Canada as her representative, they have referred, with just pride, to this great work as evidence of the results achieved through the union of British capital and skill with Canadian enterprise and progress.

The Victoria Bridge, as your Royal Highness is aware, has been constructed in the face of the greatest engineering difficulties. It is the connecting link of eleven hundred miles of railway, extending from the extreme western limits of Canada nearly to its eastern boundary, and also affording an outlet to Provincial trade to the Atlantic when the rigour of our climate closes the natural channel by the St. Lawrence.

This great national highway has been carried through by a vast outlay of British capital, fostered by the most wise policy and generous aid of the Canadian Parliament; and, as now completed, will develop and promote not only the interchange of commerce and intercourse between the various districts of this widely-extended Province, but will also secure to it a large share of the rapidly-increasing trade of the West.

Canada now possesses a complete system of railway communication, combined with an internal navigation of unrivalled extent; and, in your future progress to the West, your Royal Highness will observe the best evidence of the wisdom and energy which have thus been applied to the development of the resources of this great Province.

The Directors have now to express their profound gratitude to their most gracious Sovereign, and to your Royal Highness for your consideration in honoring this enterprise with your presence ; and they pray that your Royal Highness will now be pleased finally to inaugurate the completion of the Victoria Bridge, and thus to permit the greatest engineering work of modern days to be associated with the auspicious occasion of the first visit of the Heir Apparent of the Throne to Her Majesty's loyal Province of Canada.

To which His Royal Highness made the following reply :—

GENTLEMEN,—It is with mingled feelings of gratification at the duty which I am called upon to undertake, and admiration of the magnificent spectacle of successful science which is before me, that I proceed to comply with your invitation, and, in the name of the Queen, to inaugurate a work as unsurpassed by the grandeur of Egypt or of Rome, as it is unrivalled by the inventive genius of these days of ever-active enterprise.

I regret that the great man, whose name is now doubly enrolled in that page of my country's history in which its worthies are inscribed, has not lived to see this day. I regret that ill-health prevents the presence of another who labored with him to plan and execute this vast design ; but to them, and to the eminent firm and those employed by them in carrying out the works, no less than to your countrymen, whose energetic exertions first gave birth to the scheme of which this Bridge is the consummation, the thanks of the great community of North America are due.

Your Sovereign has testified her appreciation of the magnitude and importance of the enterprise, by deputing me to come so far to commemorate on the spot, on her behalf, the completion of a monument of engineering skill, which will, henceforth, bear Her name, and convey to future generations, another proof, in addition to the many which exist, of the successful industry of the great people committed by Providence to Her rule.

May this ceremony be auspicious to all concerned. May the Railway, and this Bridge, which is its connecting link, realize all the expectations of its promoters, and continue throughout the great future of this Province a source of permanent and ever-increasing prosperity.

His Royal Highness arrived at the Bridge from the Station at half-past one precisely, in a beautiful carriage lined with crimson velvet, and the outside ornamented in an elegant manner.

He immediately ascended the stairs of the scaffold, to the platform above, the Hon. John Ross leading the way, while the following noblemen and gentlemen accompanied him:—

The Duke of Newcastle, Lord St. Germains, the Governor General, General Bruce, Admiral Milne, Captain Hope of the *Flying Fish*, Major Teesdale, Captain Grey, Lord Lyons, Commodore Seymour, His Lordship the Bishop of Montreal, Dr. Mathieson, the Hon. John Young, most of the Members of the Executive Council, Dr. Auckland, Mr. Engleheart, Secretary to the Prince; Sir Allan MacNab, Mr. Blackwell, most of the Directors of the Grand Trunk Railway; Mr. Shanly, Mr. Trembinski, Sir W. Logan, Sir H. Smith, the Speaker, the commanders of the *Styx* and *Valorous*, and several other gentlemen.

The Prince was received by James Hodges, Esq., the builder of the Bridge, who handed him a wooden mallet and silver trowe the Prince bowing and uncovering as he received them.

The trowel bore on the inside the following inscription:—

TO COMMEMORATE
The completion of the Victoria Bridge by His Royal Highness
Albert Edward, Prince of Wales.
MONTREAL, 1860.

On the reverse was an engraving of the Bridge. The handle was wrought into the form of a Beaver, which was attached to the blade by a Prince of Wales' plume, the edges of the blade being decorated with a border of the Rose, Shamrock, Thistle, and Maple Leaf.

His Royal Highness took the trowel, and with a few dexterous strokes levelled the mortar, previously roughly spread. The stone was then lowered under the directions of Mr. Hodges' foreman. While the tackle was being adjusted, H. R. H. looked with evident interest on the broad river-scenery before him, and made smiling observations to the Duke of Newcastle and the Governor General. At length the large mass was lowered to its permanent resting-place. It was a stone 10 feet long by six broad and two deep, weighing several tons. The Prince concluded this part of the ceremony by giving one or two formal taps with the masonic gavel, and the Bridge was completed, to be henceforth known by the name of Victoria Bridge.

" The band of the Royal Canadian Rifles struck up the National Anthem as the ceremony was concluded.

The last stone having been laid, H. R. H., and a large number of the official gentlemen in attendance upon him, took the royal car and proceeded to the central arch, where the last rivet was still to be driven,— an operation which was executed by the Prince with great spirit and good-will. Three rivets were first driven by the men, the Prince having first selected the hole which he would fill. This happened to be a tolerably high one—about the level of his head, and some of the bystanders suggested that a more convenient one should be selected. But the Prince adhered to his own choice. Those who have seen the rivets driven, know that it is done with a very rapidly repeated stroke; and when H. R. H. observed the dexterity of the workmen, he observed that he was afraid he should prove only a bungling hand. However, the last rivet being pushed through, he took the small hammer, and, after giving two or three taps to steady the bolt, Mr. Hodges having applied the cupping-tool and given him a large hammer, of several pounds weight, he speedily completed this very last touch to the great structure.

The royal carriage then made its appearance, and H. R. H. speedily took his seat, and it drove away to the *déjeuner* at the Station, amidst the hearty cheers of those assembled.

Six hundred guests sat down to the *déjeuner* (given by the Grand Trunk Railway Co.), which was beautifully "laid out" for the occasion. At the head of the table was a dais, on which sat the Governor General, Sir E. W. Head. He had on his left, H. R. H. the Prince of Wales, Duke of Newcastle, Lord Lyons, General Bruce, Admiral Milne, Sir Basil Hall, Major Teesdale, Capt. Grey, Sir E. P. Taché, and Mr. Engleheart; and on his right, the Earl St. Germains, The Lord Bishop, Sir A. N. McNab, General Sir W. F. Williams, Sir Henry Smith, Commodore Seymour, the Mayor, Dr. Mathieson, &c., &c.

In about an hour's time, His Excellency rose and proposed the health of Her Majesty the Queen, which was enthusiastically responded to.

Shortly afterwards the Prince Consort's health was proposed and drank with all the honors.

Again His Excellency rose and proposed the health of His Royal Highness the Prince of Wales. Never can His Royal Highness forget the enthusiasm displayed, the cheering and the hurrahs on that occasion. They gave him the full assurance of Canada's love and loyalty.

After the cheering had somewhat subsided, His Royal Highness rose. Every one held their breath; a pin could not have fallen but the company would have heard it; every one was in expectation and suspense, and every one felt honoured.

At length they were most agreeably surprised when H. R. H. spoke, and their cheering was nearly as unbounded as it had been previously. "I propose," said the Prince, "the health of the Governor General, success to Canada, and prosperity to the Grand Trunk Railway." This of course "paved the way" for three times three.

Shortly afterwards, H. R. H. rose and retired; and, after paying a brief visit to the Grand Trunk works, where the following Address was presented to him by the workmen, took his departure for his residence:—

To His Royal Highness Albert Edward Prince of Wales.
MAY IT PLEASE YOUR ROYAL HIGHNESS,—

It is with feelings of unmingled gratification and pleasure that we, the Working Men and Artizans of the Grand Trunk Railway Company, cordially welcome to this portion of Her Majesty's Transatlantic Dominions, one so nearly connected with Our Gracious Sovereign as yourself.

Although separated by the wide Ocean from the land which gave birth to most of us, we yet bear in our hearts the warmest love towards it, and the deepest reverence and loyalty towards that Monarch whose presence here to-day Your Royal Highness represents.

The noble structure which Your Royal Highness has inaugurated, has been to many of us the scene of our daily toil; and whilst carrying out the gigantic conception of the designer, we have been able fully to estimate the difficulties which he had to contend with and overcome; and, now that he has passed away from this sphere of existence, we feel proud that we possess in these Her Majesty's Canadian dominions so magnificent a funeral monument of one who rose from our own class, and who shared with us the privilege of being a British subject.

Before Your Royal Highness departs from these shores, there will no doubt be many opportunities afforded you of judging of the loyal and devoted feelings of attachment general in these Provinces towards Your Royal Mother; and we are sure that whatever spot you may visit, you will find one feeling common (we are proud to say in every land where the English tongue is spoken, and in which we heartily join) of love and attachment towards that Lady whose virtues are known and acknowledged in every land and in every home,—Your Mother and Our Queen.

Wishing Your Royal Highness every pleasure and benefit from your sojourn amongst us, and a safe return to the parent land.

Signed *(in behalf of the Workmen of the G. T. R.)*,

J. CURTIS CLARKE.

103

His Royal Highness made the following reply :—

GENTLEMEN,—I accept with peculiar pleasure an Address of artizans and working-men who have, by the sweat of their brow and the skilled labour of many a hard day's toil, contributed to erect this monument to the greatness of their country—a structure scarcely less honorable to the hands which executed than to the minds which conceived it. I mourn with you the loss of Robert Stephenson. In your regrets you bring to mind that it was from your class that his eminent father sprung. Let me further remind you, that England opens to all her sons the same prospect of success to genius combined with honest industry. All cannot attain the prize, but all may strive for it, and in this race victory is not to the wealthy, or the powerful, but to him to whom God has given intellect, and has implanted in the heart the moral qualities which are required to constitute true greatness. I congratulate you upon the completion of your work. I earnestly hope it may prosper ; and to you who have raised it to its present grandeur, and to your families, I heartily wish every happiness.

His Royal Highness at the conclusion of his reply was enthusiastically cheered, as he was also on leaving the Station.

For the following lengthy description of His Royal Highness's residence we are indebted to the Montreal *Herald* :—

THE MONTREAL RESIDENCE OF HIS ROYAL HIGHNESS THE PRINCE OF WALES.

The mansion where H. R. H. is to reside during his stay in Montreal is that of the Hon. John Rose, the Commissioner of Public Works, who, in that capacity, has had charge of the arrangements for the Prince's reception, Mr. Rose being obliged to reside at the seat of government. However the house has recently been tenanted by Sir W. F. Williams, who volunteered to resign it for the Prince during H. R. H.'s stay in town. The house is finely situated on the lower plateau of the mountain, standing in about three acres of ground, which are beautifully decorated by ornamental trees, and parterres of flowers. The mountain rises up steeply behind it ; but the house itself is high enough to afford a prospect over the entire city, the river, and the country beyond. The house itself is about fifty feet square, with a wing, two stories high, with handsome porch and entrance, the whole being surmounted by a pediment. Being perfectly white, it forms a very pretty object among the dark trees, in which it is embowered. It is approached by two streets. The entrance gates have been renewed, and decorated with carved plumes of Prince of Wales' feathers. The exterior of the house has been newly decorated for the reception of the royal guest; and it would probably have been difficult to find a residence in the city, upon the whole, more agreeable. At the entrance are two handsome coloured lamps, and the outer door and vestibule door are in enamelled glass. The entrance-hall is papered with an imitation of a fine yellow marble; having, at the end, niches containing female figures bearing gas lights. On the left hand is the library. The room is fitted up with a paper of rich dark green, with perpendicular stripes of gold. The carpet is a new Brussels, the ground of a dark green colour, with the pattern formed of two devices, arranged in alternate rows. One of these consists of a number of short lines, crossed by others, all of various light colors, to give relief to the ground, and with colors changed alternately. The other and more conspicuous device consists of a light-coloured border enclosing a *fleur de lys;* the ground within the border alternately yellow and brown, and the *fleur de lys* alternately white and yellow. The curtains are of a green damask; and the sides are surrounded with books on rosewood shelves; other shelves with books standing out on the floor of the room.—On the other side of the passage is the dining-room. The carpet in this room has not been changed. It is a Brussels with a large pattern, in which red and white are the predominating colours. The mantle-piece is of black marble, and the room is hung with pictures. The paper is a rich red flock; and at the end farthest removed from the window, there is a large mirror. The table and side-board are of mahogany, and the chairs of the same wood, with black leather covers. We believe that all is exactly as it was when used by the proprietor. The curtains match the paper in tint.

The drawing-room is a very handsome apartment at the north-western corner of the house. It has two windows opening on to the Mountain, northwards, and a very large bow-window looking towards the west. The curtains here are of a fine grey chintz, having stripes formed by a pattern of moss-rose leaves and flowers; and they are trimmed with silk and lace. The curtain-rods are of wood, painted white and gilt. The mantle-piece is of white marble, with a fine mirror in an elegant but by no means florid frame; and there is a console-table and mirror between the windows. The carpet in this room is velvet, of a small flowered pattern, in which all the brightest colours seem to be confused, without giving to the eye any distinct conception of the design. The papering is very elegant. The ground represents a grey watered silk, with a few sprigs of gold. The bands of the panelling are of a very light pink, with gilt and light blue lines for borders. The furniture and knick-nacks are of the ordinary kind used for drawing rooms; but in simple taste, becoming the bachelor quality of the Prince. The whole of the furniture and decorations in this apartment are new. All the wood-work in the lower story, except the drawing-room, which is white and gold, is painted oak on the inside and mahogany outside. The stairs to ascend to the bed-chambers are lighted from the roof by two sky-lights, having below them stained glasses, flush with the ceilings, the chief decoration being two Prince of Wales' feathers, chiefly in ruby colour. These lights throw a fine mellow colour over the stairs. The stairs and the passage at the head of them are carpeted with dark green; the pattern black.

The Prince's bed-room is the south-eastern apartment of the upper story. Its furniture consists of a bed, wardrobe, washstand, writing-table, sofa, cheval-glass, easy chair, and four small chairs. All the furniture is of a clear bird's-eye maple. The bedstead is a four-poster without curtains; having the headboard raised a little above the footboard. All the posts are surmounted by carved crowns, and the pillars are fluted and otherwise carved. The headboard rises from the sides to the middle, where the peak terminates with a large crown. The royal arms are below, encircled with ivy; a little lower is an elegant fillet composed of the leaves of the rose, shamrock, thistle, and maple-leaf; and again below that, the Prince of Wales' feathers and motto, both of a very neat size. In the centre of the footboard, there is a carved oval, having within it the Prince of Wales' feathers and motto, surrounded by foliage. The wardrobe is surmounted by the Prince of Wales' feather and motto, below which there is a band of open work across the front, and two folding-doors with arched mouldings and carvings within them. The chairs and sofa are covered with green and gold damask; the small chairs having open worked backs. The cheval-glass has its frame decorated by a carved coat-of-arms and crown like the bed; and the washstand has a white marble top. All the rest of the furniture is of the same curled-maple as the bedstead—all in very simple taste. The carpet is a green Kidderminster, with a very small pattern, consisting of white and red spots arranged in diamond form. The paper has a light ground panelled with broad stripes of lilac, bordered with pink and white.

The dressing-room adjoining the bed-room is furnished in a still plainer manner than the bed-room. Its *meublement* consists merely of a sofa and four chairs, all of rosewood, with green and gold damask to match the furniture of the bed-room. The carpet is green with a small yellow spot.

The Duke of Newcastle's bed-room is situated on the side of the house opposite to that occupied by H. R. H. The general style of the furniture is the same; but it has been apparently chosen with a view to mark the gradation of rank by some slight difference in elegance. Thus the washstand, instead of a white marble top, has a black one; the bedstead has hardly any carving upon it, and is, as well as the other furniture, of what upholsterers call " white-wood," instead of maple; and the chairs, instead of damask, are of dark green " wrept." The paper is panelled with lines of gilt and white flowers and sprigs. The carpet is of a commoner description than that in the Prince's apartment, of a dark green ground, with a pattern consisting of small oblong spots of white, red, and yellow, arranged in groups diagonally. Another apartment intended for Lord St. Germains, and a very small one for the Governor General, with a single-sized bed, are both fitted up in the same style as the apartment intended for the Colonial Secretary. The decorations and the stained glass have been prepared by Messrs. McArthur and Spence; the furniture is from the factory of Jacques and Hay of Toronto, and the new gates, with the capital carving thereon, are the work of Mr. Maxwell. Mr. Baylis has furnished the carpets. The whole of the arrangements in the house and grounds have been under the superintendence of Mr. Lawford, of Lawford and Nelson.

In the evening, the city was most brilliantly illuminated, perfectly eclipsing anything of the kind ever seen on this continent. The city was one perfect blaze of light. In every street was to be seen beautiful transparencies; the arches were all illuminated and looked superb; and the crowded streets, until two o'clock on Sunday morning, showed how well the Montrealers' illumination was appreciated.

Besides all this, a large number of the ships in port were lit up with coloured lights, and set off rockets. There was a grand display of fireworks from the Victoria Bridge. His Royal Highness came down "incog" in his carriage to see the illumination, and was driven down Notre Dame Street. Now it so happened that a proclamation had been issued that day by the Mayor, prohibiting any vehicles from driving through the illuminated streets, and the consequence was that a constable, little imagining who was the occupant, soon seized the Prince's horses, and ordered the coachman to turn back. But the coachman would not return. He informed the constable that he was the Prince's coachman, and that the Prince himself was inside; but the constable replied by putting his finger to his proboscis. The crowd, hearing that the Prince was in the carriage, made a desperate push, and was about to take the horses out, and draw the Prince themselves; but the coachman perceiving this, drove hastily away.

On Sunday morning the 26th, His Royal Highness attended Divine Service at Christ Church Cathedral.

He arrived precisely at eleven o'clock, attended by his suite, and was met there by Sir Fenwick Williams, Sir A. Milne, and their respective suites. The whole party was met at the door by His Lordship Bishop Fulford, Metropolitan Bishop of Canada,

&c., who conducted the Prince to his seat, which was the Bishop's pew.

The prayers were read by the Venerable Archdeacon Gilson, as also the Litany; 1st Lesson by the Rev.Canon Townsend; 2nd Lesson by the Rev. Mr. Wood; Epistle by the Bishop of Rupert's Land (Dr. Anderson); and the Gospel by Bishop McCrosky of Michigan, U. S.

The Bishop of Montreal delivered the following—

SERMON.

1st Cor. 9th Chap. 25th v., "And every man that striveth for the mastery is temperate in all things. Now they do it to obtain a corruptible crown, but we an incorruptible."

We find various expressions and illustrations used in Scripture to explain to us the nature of the Gospel, and the condition of the Christian. These everywhere meet us, both in the Parables of the Lord, and in the Epistles of the Apostles. In the former (the Parables of Christ) we find perhaps more frequent allusions to the state of the Gospel Kingdom as a whole; in the Epistles we are for ever reminded of our relation to that Kingdom as individuals, and of our place and duty as members of it. To describe the unity of such members one with another, and their connection with, and dependence upon Christ, St. Paul speaks of Christians being living stones, built up into the spiritual Temple of God, forming together one great and complete edifice, dedicated to God, and in which He dwells, as He of old vouchsafed His visible presence in the glorious Temple of Solomon at Jerusalem; and all built upon Christ as the foundation and chief corner-stone, which gives strength and security to the whole. On other occasions the Apostle speaks of believers, under the figure of many members united in one body, and having different duties and offices, the head of which is Christ, the life, the intelligence, the wisdom, and the glory of all. So also to describe the difficulties we have to encounter, he likens the Christian to a soldier, carrying on a continuous warfare in an enemy's country; and in his Epistle to the Ephesians he enumerates the various portions of that spiritual armour,—by which he is to be secured from danger,—the breastplate of righteousness, the shield of faith, the helmet of salvation, and the sword of the Spirit. The Captain whom he follows is the Lord Jesus Christ; and the ensign around which he rallies, is the banner of the cross. In the chapter from which I have selected a verse for my text on this occasion, St. Paul in these latter verses compares the Christian to those persons who used to enter the list as competitors for the prizes in the public games which were constantly being celebrated in different parts of Greece. And with great propriety and that skilful adaptation of his mode of argument (which is so remarkable in this

Apostle), does he allude to the subject of these games, when writing to the Corinthians, since the place where some of these were held, was in the neighbourhood of their own City of Corinth ; so that they all must immediately have understood the meaning, and must have felt the full force of his argument; and very probably, by themselves in their own persons, or in the persons of their intimate friends, had striven for the mastery in them. St. Paul reminds them, how that, when intending to enter the lists as a competitor for the prize in the race, or any of those energetic exertions that require a great display of bodily activity and endurance, they were used to train and discipline themselves with unwearied care, submitting to denials of many usual bodily gratifications, without hesitation and murmur, rising early, feeding themselves with moderation and exercising themselves by rule, that their wind might be good and lasting, their muscle strong and full, and no unhealthy action excited in their system such as might injure their strength and lessen their speed, and thus destroy all chance of their success. Such watchful care over themselves, such self-discipline, was absolutely necessary if they hoped to win the prize.—No man was ever foolish enough to expose himself to certain defeat and well merited ridicule without them. " Every man," (says the Apostle,) ye know it so to be. " Every man that striveth for the mastery is temperate in all things." And yet in these games, after all his care and pains, he may not succeed ; for again he writes : " Know ye not that those that run in a race, run all, but one only (the best among them) receiveth the prize." In this respect the comparison with the Christian no longer holds good, except by way of contrast. We as Christians have our race to run : we must, like the Corinthian competitors, keep our bodies under, and bring them into subjection ; we must not give a loose rein to self-indulgence, to sloth or luxurious living, and this not like them, that we may be able to perform great feats of bodily strength, but that, by mortifying the deeds of the body, we may give place and pre-eminence to our spiritual nature : not allowing the corruptible body to press down the soul, nor the earthly tabernacle to weigh down the mind ; which soul and mind in the Christian have been renewed again after the image of their Maker, and are capable of high and holy communion with Him. " Every man " (says the Apostle)—" Every man that striveth for the mastery is temperate in all things."—This holds good in the Christian, as well as in competition for victory in the Isthmian Games. Without exercising over ourselves something of the same watchful care and rule of life in our spiritual race, it is a contradiction in terms to say, that we are striving for the mastery at all in our spiritual race,—that we have entered the lists at all as Candidates for the heavenly prize ; " For they (says the Apostle, to the Romans) that are after the flesh do mind the things of the flesh ; and if ye live after the flesh, ye shall *die*." But as I said before, here the comparison ends: the rest is by way of contrast. *We* run not our race against each other. If one gets a prize, it is not to the loss or hindrance of his fellows, but rather to their gain. We have no need to guage and measure the successful progress of a brother, envying his swifter course, as if our chance of success was thereby endangered. For crowns there are awaiting every racer in the Christian race, be he first, or be he last, who, having striven manfully, and gained a victory over himself, his fallen nature, his evil passions, and the temptations of the enemy, shall arrive in due time at the goal, pressing towards the mark for the prize of the high calling of God in Christ Jesus. With this encouragement, then, " so run " with such care and such preparation, "that ye may obtain." "One star may differ from another star in glory," yet are they all bright, brilliant, and perfect, the handiwork of God, and have their appointed place in the firmament of Heaven. If we lose the prize, it cannot be because a brother's hand has snatched it from our grasp. Such is not the nature of our race; but rather every fresh successful combatant in the spiritual contest is another witness added to the great cloud of saints already gathered together in Jesus, who testify to us of the excellence of His grace, and have left the prints of their foot-marks along the narrow course of life, as tokens and waymarks, and warnings to us, lest we err from the appointed track, and lose ourselves in the wide wilderness beyond. No, if *we* fail, it is because we have *never really* striven for the mastery; we have *not* been temperate in *all things*, we have *not* kept our bodies under and brought them into subjection: but we have preferred present ease to future glory, and have bartered away our birthright of an eternal inheritance, for such pleasure, gratification, or self-willed indulgence, as we may chance to fall in with on this perishable earth. And this brings us to the particular consideration of those words which are contained in our text, and in which St. Paul reminds Christians of the greatness of the prize proposed for their reward, who are successful in that great spiritual race in which we are all called to engage. They, the competitors of the Grecian games, strove earnestly for the mastery, were temperate in all things, and kept their bodies under, in order to win the prize proposed, which, after all was but a corruptible crown, a perishable honour in itself of most trifling value. *We* do it, or as Christians ought to do it, in order to obtain an *incorruptible crown*, a never-fading glory, an enduring substance.

And upon this I would remark, that, however excellent virtue may be in itself, and however real the satisfaction arising from a consciousness of submission to the law and will of God, and however perfect and pure the requirements of *such* a state of grace as shall enable us to bring under dominion the lusts of the flesh, and place them under subjection, that we may walk in the liberty of the children of God,—yet as this is not now our natural state, not one that we are capable of appreciating or understanding until we *have* been *already under* discipline, but one that, in order to its attainment and perfection, requires that moral training which the Apostle is here enforcing, and which, in its various forms, and according as it thwarts our own wills and inclinations, is so often grievous, troublesome, and distasteful to us; *therefore*, in comparison to the weakness of our nature, God has been pleased, not merely to propose certain duties which we are required to perform, and for the performance of which he offers us sufficient help, but He is also for ever reminding us of the greatness of the rewards which, unworthy as we are of the least of His mercies, He yet has ready for our acceptance; and which are in His Divine economy, necessarily, as it were, connected with the performance of such duties.

" The soul of man (observes one of our great Divines) in all its choices is naturally apt to be determined by pleasure; and the sensitive and inferior appetites (which would draw it off from duty) are continually plying it with such suitable and taking pleasures; and doubtless there is no way for duty to prevail over them, but proposing greater inducements, and offering the soul greater gratification, bound up with an eternal reward." It is the declaration of St. Paul to the Corinthians, "that, if in this life we only have hope, we were of all men most miserable." And let us suppose that, when God bids us fast and pray, mortify our fleshly appetites, abstain from the allurements of sensual pleasures and deny ourselves; being smote upon one cheek to turn him the other; and lastly, to choose death rather than wilfully commit the least known sin;—suppose, I say, that God should command us all these severe precepts, merely as excellent actions in themselves, high degrees of virtue, most pleasing to God, and upon *that* ground both commanded by Him and to be performed by us: certainly these considerations (nothwithstanding all the reason and truth that are in them) would yet strike the will but very faintly; for men care not for suffering, while they think it is only for suffering's sake. But let us take our rule from Christ. "Blessed (says He to His disciples) are ye when men shall revile you, and persecute you, and speak all evil against you falsely for my sake; rejoice and be exceeding glad." But why? *Was it*, then, such matter of joy either to be reviled and trampled on, to be calumniated and abused, or crushed under the hard rule or power of men? No, certainly; but we have the reason given us for this in the next words,—" For great (says Christ) is your reward in Heaven." Again, we know how Christ, reading the state of his heart, and knowing the particular cure needed by one who had set his heart too much upon things below—we know how Christ answered the rich young heir who was enquiring of Him the way to Heaven. " Go (says He) and sell all that thou hast and give to the poor." Now certainly, had he stopped here, this would have been as severe a command as could have been passed upon any such enquirer. But, in fact, our Saviour did not require this young man here absolutely to quit his riches, but only to exchange them, and to part with a smaller estate in possession for one greater in reversion,—with a small enjoyment now, for an infinite hope hereafter: " Do this (says Christ) and thou shalt have treasure in Heaven."

And *further*, when our Saviour preached to the world the great evangelical duty of taking up the cross, we do not find that He made the mere burden of bearing it any argument for taking it up. And therefore He says " There is no man that hath left house, or brethren, or sister, or father, or mother, or wife, or children, or lands, for my sake and the gospel's, but he shall receive an hundred-fold now in this time, and in the world to come eternal life." So that we here see the duty and the reward walking hand in hand, the riches of the promise still surpassing the strictness of the precept, and (as it has been well observed, that it is the custom in the royal diadems of Christian kings) the Cross and the Crown put together. If our God, who knows whereof we are made and has compassion upon our weakness, has thought it right thus constantly to enforce our several duties, by reminding us of the greatness of the rewards proposed for us upon our submission to his precepts, it is surely intended that we should weigh and consider the value of those future rewards, and keep them in remembrance, as a due balance and counterpoise to set against the immediate temptations of sight and sense. And this is most certain, that no man's practice can rise higher than his hopes. It is seen in aqueducts that no pipe or conduit can force the current of the water higher than the level of the spring-head whence the water first descends; and in like manner it is not possible for a man who professes to himself only the rewards of this world, so to rule his life and conversation as to arrive at a better. And the reason is simply this, because, whoever makes these present enjoyments his whole object, must be reckoning them absolutely to be the best things he can have, and accordingly he looks no further, he expects no better. And if so, it is not to be imagined that he should never obtain what he never so much as cast a thought after. For no man will ever arrive at heaven by chance. When, therefore, we are called to take up a cross for Christ's sake, to mortify the deeds of the body, to deny ourselves, to be merciful, meek, patient, humble, chaste, and pure, let us not shrink from the call that is made upon us, but remember the great recompense of the reward, the incorruptible crown that awaits us, if found faithful and ready to endure hardness as good soldiers of Christ. It is these very duties that have reference to what St. Paul calls bringing the body under subjection which are most opposed to the natural and to the performance of which perhaps we require, if we may so say, the greatest encouragement. Speaking the truth, justice towards offenders, or rendering to every one his due, are virtues much more frequent in the world than temperance, sobriety, and chastity, and such other virtues as have a tendency to limit the enjoyments of the animal man, and which come more properly under what the Apostle calls "the lusts of the flesh, which war against the soul." But they do war against the soul, and therefore we must wage war against them. And it is that we can not only reach heaven, but, when admitted there, be capable of enjoying the purity and peace of heaven, that we must be temperate in all things and put ourselves under discipline and watchful rule. This is often no doubt, painful, irksome, and contrary to present ease and enjoyment; but for any worldly object of sufficient importance, what will not man undertake, what self-denial submit to, what patient endurance will he not practise? and "they do it to obtain a corruptible crown." And shall not we, as Christians, equal in our zeal and steadfastness these children of this world?—we, to whom is proposed an incorruptible crown? We have a sure promise of help in our task. And we shall find too that light will spring up around our onward path, and present satisfaction reward our ripening labours.

But when the task is over and the labour done, what tongue can tell, what heart conceive, those good things which God has in store for those that love him! Enduring treasures as contrasted with the perishable and uncertain treasures of this world,—enduring treasures *there*, where neither moth nor rust can corrupt, nor thieves break through and steal, where there is no canker-worm of care to corrode the heart, nor disturbance of sin to mar their joy; riches, honor, glory, peace, rest, knowledge, fellowship with the saints in Christ—communion with God, and whatever the imagination of man can shadow forth as excellent or desirable—these are the images, under which are detailed to us such descriptions of our heavenly inheritance as may excite our desires, and animate our hopes. Shall we forego the prize? We have been entered as candidates for heaven; as baptized Christians we have been put in trust with a great mystery. Shall we forfeit our adoption? Shall we not strive for the mastery? Shall we not, at the close of our earthly career, wish to die the death of the righteous? Then let us live the life of the righteous. Be thou faithful unto death (saith the Spirit) and I will give thee a crown of life.

The church was not uncomfortably filled, the admission having been by ticket from the Bishop.

A great crowd of persons assembled outside the Cathedral to witness His Royal Highness coming out, all uncovering as he entered his carriage. An attempt at a cheer was made, but speedily put down, it being known that the Prince is not in favour of these demonstrations on the Sabbath.

The Lord Bishop, received during the ensuing week, the following note from General Bruce, and the present accompanying it:

MONTREAL, Sept. 1, 1860.

MY DEAR LORD,—The Prince of Wales commands me to request your acceptance, on behalf of the Cathedral of Montreal, of the accompanying copy of the Holy Bible, as a slight memorial of his visit to that fine edifice and attendance on your service there.

The Bible contains on the fly-leaf the following inscription in His Royal Highness's hand-writing:—

Presented to the Cathedral of Montreal, in memory of the 26th of August, 1860.

ALBERT EDWARD,
Prince of Wales.

On Monday morning, at ten o'clock, His Royal Highness and suite witnessed the Indian Games on a field near the Mountain. The games consisted of lacrosse, war-dances, &c.; but a rain-storm coming on, he was obliged to leave the field before half of them was over.

Before doing so, however, the Boston (U.S.) Fusiliers marched on the ground, filing past the pavilion where the royal party was standing. They presented arms; and their band played " God save the Queen," and afterwards " Yankee Doodle."

From the same pavilion the Prince also witnessed the grand procession of the Temperance Organisation, numbering 500 persons, carrying flags, banners, &c., and headed by a band of music.

At one o'clock, the levee was held at the Court House, when about 2,000 gentlemen were presented; as also a number of Addresses, among others, from the Synod of the Church of England, Natural History Society, McGill College, &c., and one from the inhabitants of Red River Colony, which we give. It was presented by the Bishop of Rupert's Land, (Dr. Anderson).

To His Royal Highness the Prince of Wales.

We, the inhabitants of Red River Settlement, in public meeting assembled, desire to approach Your Royal Highness with feelings of warm attachment to Your Royal Person, and with unfeigned congratulations on your safe arrival in British North America.

Though far distant from the flourishing Provinces honored by the presence of Royalty, and isolated from every other dependency of the kingdom, yet we are not the less sincere in welcoming to the soil of the

Western Empire, a Prince in whom are so happily blended all those high qualities which we respect and revere in His Royal Mother, Our Most Gracious Sovereign the Queen.

Deprived, by reason of our remoteness, of the coveted opportunity of addressing Your Royal Highness in person, we beg, through this humble Address, to convey our sentiments of devoted loyalty to the British Crown, and our high appreciation of the wise and liberal policy pursued by the Imperial Government towards the Colonies; at the same time expressing a fervent hope, that, when called by Divine Providence to the Throne of the Empire, Your Royal Highness may long be spared to reign over a loyal, happy, prosperous, and contented people.

Signed on behalf of the inhabitants of Red River Settlement.

W. MACTAVISH,
Governor of Assineboine, and
Chairman of the Meeting.

Red River Settlement,
June 14th, 1860.

In the evening, H. R. H. attended one of the grandest balls ever given on this continent, at least so it was admitted by all those that attended; and many were there from all parts of the States and Canada. It was given in a large wooden pavilion erected for the occasion. A full description of the interior of the building we take from a Montreal paper, and which appeared before the ball took place:—

The entire circumference of the building is, as we have stated, upwards of nine hundred feet. It consists of one circular apartment of 215 feet diameter, and 82,000 feet of superficial space; and of several others surrounding this, and forming, in a ring between it and the outside wall, the supper-room, the dressing-rooms, and other offices. These last will, of course, be all larger or smaller segments of a circle, and all about twenty-six feet wide. They will be twenty feet high under the eaves, gradually ascending to a height of thirty-six feet at the springing of the dome. The roof of this outer circle of apartments will serve, as we have said, for the floor of an external and open gallery. Thus they will be separated, except by doors, from the main apartment, which will have an outside wall of thirty-six feet high, the roof rising dome-shaped to forty-four feet at the base of the lantern. A gallery surrounds the whole circle, capable of accommodating two thousand persons; and the orchestra, in the centre, will be on a platform of twenty feet diameter, which will be greatly increased by additional staging for the musical festival of a succeeding evening. Eight pillars surround this platform, carrying a circle of gas-burners. The lantern above, twenty feet in diameter and eight feet high, being open, with the exception of its supports, forms, with the heating of the gas below, a most efficient ventilator; fresh air being brought from the numerous doors and other openings at the sides. There will be one other circle of pillars intended to support the roof, besides the pillars supporting the gallery. Mr. Charles Garth has placed on all these lights, to the number of about two hundred.

"Thus far we have to deal with the designs and workmanship of architects and builders; but it is plain that a great part of the effect in such a building must depend upon the colourists. The business of decoration has been judiciously committed to Messrs. McArthur & Spence, and they have amply justified the choice. The front of the gallery, where a portion of the space is reserved for the Prince's box, is panelled. The ground colour predominant throughout is pink, and the arabesque traceries chiefly in white and green. A medallion in a circular fillet of gold occupies the centre of each alternate panel; the central ornaments of the rest being other appropriate designs. The plinth surrounding the room below the gallery will also be finished with drapery having a golden fringe. The dome-shaped roof is divided in its height into two circles, and each of these into compartments; the upper one twelve, and the lower one twenty-four in number. On the upper twelve are painted in bright colours the twelve signs of the Zodiac, in imitation of fresco; the borders of each being made with numerous lines traced in various tints. In twelve of the lower compartments, taken alternately, there is, as a base, a plain geometrical figure with line borders, occupying about one third of the height. Above this a semicircle encloses a brilliantly-coloured representation of the royal arms, with appropriate emblems; and over the arch of the semicircle is a vase, supported on either side by reclining female figures; part of the space left vacant on either side by the narrowness of the design as it rises towards the lantern, being filled with bright-coloured arabesques. The alternate compartments have simpler figures, so as to allow the ground-colour to appear in breadth, and give relief and variety to the rich tone and full designs of those just described.

Rich drapery of scarlet and gold depends from the pillars above the orchestra; and are wreathed with green, and have, at about the middle of their height from the ground, ornamented shields, with pennons on each side. The effect of these shields and pennons is to break the uniformity of outline, and furnish points for the eye to rest on in the wide space between the central pillars and the gallery. On the northern part of the circle, a retiring-room and a compartment separated from the rest of the gallery are prepared for the special use of the Prince and his suite. The retiring-room, occupies a space over the projection for the main entrance, and is about 30 x 50 feet, and together with the compartment is fitted up with crimson and gold drapery. The front of the compartment, which has the appearance of being bowed outwards, is also draped in crimson and gold, and is further decorated by the royal arms, and similar appropriate emblems. The *coup-d'œil* presented by the appearance of this gigantic ball-room, is one in which all the gayest colors vie for brilliancy with the glitter of the golden ornamentation with which they are interspersed,—"A mighty mass, yet not without a plan."

We have only one or two particulars to add to this description. The interior galleries are approached from the floor of the ball-room by a number of stairs, and communicate with the external gallery by doors; and in order to prevent disaster from any possible accident by fire, besides the numerous doors either for the entrance of the company or other purposes, and the means of egress offered by the external gallery, there will be hose laid on within the building sufficient to drown out any conflagration.

We add the following:—

Upon glancing round the room after our entrance, we found that some additions and improvements had been made to it since we last saw it. A line of red drapery immediately below the eaves, made an agreeable contrast to the otherwise rather pale color of the lower part of the ceiling, and added precisely what was required to bring up the tone of the lower circle, to that of the upper one. We observed, too, that the artist who had been employed to decorate the shields and escutcheons on the pillars, and on the front of the gallery, had charged them with the armorial bearings of H. R. H., the Duke of Newcastle, the Governor-General, Lord St. Germains, and several others of the distinguished visitors who have arrived in the suite of His Royal Highness.

The private apartment of H. R. H. had also been fitted up since by our previous visit. The windows had on them blinds in Gothic patterns, and there were mirrors on the other three sides of the room. The furniture was of damask and rosewood, with a crystal gasalier. The ceiling was beautifully ornamented with Cupids on a light ground; and the paper was panelled, the ground being a very light pink, with branches of ribbons in gold, and the bars of purple and gold.

The box appropriated to H. R. H. in the gallery was draped with crimson, relieved by a gold fringe, and opposite to it was a dais with a few chairs for himself and his suite. This was also draped with crimson and gold fringe, and at each side of it there was a piece of statuary.

The ball-room presented the finest appearance of any that the Prince had honoured with his presence. A description from us would be superfluous; so we abstain from attempting a subject which we know our pen is hardly equal to, and which demands our greatest praise.

H. R. H. and suite appeared about ten o'clock, and the Prince immediately took his stand upon the dais. The Duke of Newcastle then presented the Hon. Mrs. Young (wife of the Hon. John Young), and the Prince opened the ball with that lady. He had on his right the Hon. Mr. Cartier, with Mrs. Dumas; and on his left, Major Teesdale and Miss Rogers. Their *vis-à-vis* were the Duke of Newcastle and Mrs. Perrault. On the Prince's right hand were Governor Bruce and Mrs. Denny, Capt. Connolly and Miss Penn; and on his left hand, the Earl of Mulgrave and Miss Delisle, and Capt. De Winton and Miss Tyre.

H. R. H. danced incessantly until half-past four in the morning, with the following ladies :—

Miss Delisle, Miss Servante, Lady Milne, Miss Napier, Mrs. King, Miss E. Smith, Miss Tyre, Mrs. F. Brown, Miss Leach, Miss Fisher of Halifax, Miss Sicotte, Miss De Rocheblave, Mrs. C. Freer, Miss Laura Johnson, Miss Belson, Miss Napier (a second time), Miss King, Mrs. Forsyth, Miss Sophia Stewart, and the Hon. Mrs. J. S. Macdonald.

The following was the order of dances :

1. Quadrille The Queen's Canadian
2. Polka............Minnehaha.
3. Waltz..............Sultana.
4. Lancers............Original.
5. Mazurka..........Billet doux.
6. Galop.............Reception.
7. Quadrille...........Palermo.
8. Waltz.............Trovatore.
9. Polka.............Ariadne.
10. Lancers............English.
11. Galop....The Prince of Wales.
12. Mazurka......Sweet Thought.
13. Quadrille.............Lucia.
14. Waltz.............Satanella.
15. Polka........Sleeping Beauty.
16. Lancers............Original.
17. Galop.............Laughing.
18. Mazurka.............Lurline.
19. Lancers .... Queen.
20. Waltz................ Bertha.
21. Galop..................Charivari.

On Tuesday (28th), the royal party, accompanied by the Governor-General and the Commander of the Forces, went on an excursion to Dickinson's Landing on the Grand Trunk Railway. They occupied on that occasion the splendid new car built expressly for the Prince of Wales, and of which the following is a truthful description :—

The car fitted up by the Grand Trunk Railway Company for His Royal Highness the Prince of Wales, is now in Toronto receiving its finishing touches at the hands of Messrs. Jacques & Hay. A great deal of ingenuity as well as taste has been exercised in its construction. On the outside, it varies in no respect from those used in ordinary by the Company; but once inside, and a great difference is seen. The car itself is divided into five compartments. The first is intended as a sitting-room for the Prince and the noblemen accompanying him, and is fitted up with every possible convenience. In it there are five large arm-chairs and two sofas covered with morocco. The centre is occupied by a small table, on which stands a lamp. A large mirror, a rack for books, and an exceedingly beautiful chronometer, hang from the sides. The ceiling of the car is of the finest bird's-eye maple, divided into pannels by strips of gilded moulding. Contrasting with this are the sides of the carriage of dark walnut, also relieved at regular intervals by ornamental gold-work. Over each panel, running round the entire room, are placed carved and gilt imitations of the Prince of Wales' crest, bearing the motto *Ich Dien*, worn so many years ago on the field of Cressy. The appearance of the room, though exceedingly pleasing, is free of anything like gaudiness or of over-strained display. Entering the next compartment, we find it smaller in width than the preceding one, owing to the fact that allowance had to be made for a passage whereby to communicate with another room at the further end of the car. It is fitted up with many conveniences. Over the roof is placed a large cistern, a pipe from which descends into a filter, communicating with a tap rising from a marble-topped table. The pipe, by being arranged in the same way as the worm of a spit "still," is made to pass through a large quantity of ice, that a supply of cool water may be obtained. Near by this arrangement is a small wine-closet, and a set of drawers, in which are arranged a number of plate and dishes suitable for use under such circumstances, as it may be expected they will be used. Accompanying the china are knives and forks and silver spoons— sufficient altogether for twelve persons. The furniture here is all of black walnut. The next two compartments are state-rooms, with a couple of beds in each. The washing-stand and dressing-table are fitted with marble tops. Mirrors hang from the wall, and various contrivances for holding brushes. Towels and cloths are also supplied. The last compartment in the car, we suppose, is intended for servants. It is supplied with a lounge, and the sides and ceiling are fitted up with much the same description of work as in the first-mentioned room. The doors are each supplied with plain glass panels engraved with the rose, shamrock, and thistle. Very great care has been taken to secure proper ventilation. The invention of Mr. Sheriff Ruttan has been called into requisition, and a contrivance adopted by which the air, after having passed through a cistern of water, where it is cleansed from dust, is admitted into the car through a number of registers. Further to prevent the dust finding admittance, frames of net-work have been provided, fitting in windows, which may thus be opened without inconvenience. The cost of the car, which must be large, we are unable to state.—*Globe*.

On passing the different railway-stations, the people turned out in great numbers and gave him welcome; arches were erected, flags displayed, and everything showed that genuine loyal feeling which he had experienced since his arrival in British America.

At Dickinson's Landing, he took the steamer *Kingston*, and was propelled down the far-famed rapids of the Long Sault, Coteau, Cedars, Cascades, and Lachine, reaching Montreal at seven o'clock, and was immediately driven to his residence.

It is related of His Royal Highness that he was so much fatigued on his return to town, with the exertions of the last few days, that he actually went to sleep over his dinner.

At ten o'clock the royal party attended the Grand Musical Festival at the Crystal Palace which was given in his honour.

The Concert consisted of three parts:—1st. Selections from the Oratorios by the Montreal Choral Society. 2nd. A Grand CANTATA composed in honour of the visit of His Royal Highness by Ed. Sempe, Esq., of St. Hyacinthe, the music by Mr. C. W. Sabatier; 3rd. Selections from the Operas by the celebrated Strackosch's Italian Opera Troupe, composed of Mdlle. Adelina Patti, Mad. Amelia Strackosch, Signor Brignoli, Amodi, Barili, and Susini. The hall was perfectly crowded; there must have been at least 8,000 persons present, and they all presented a most respectable appearance.

The CANTATA was commenced before His Royal Highness and suite arrived at the royal box. On their arrival, however, it was stopped. The entire company rose and cheered, and the Choral Society performed "God save the Queen." The Prince bowed to these compliments. The CANTATA was recommenced, and he remained until the end of it; and then retired, amidst the hearty and enlivening cheers of the assemblage. At his departure his place, by invitation, was taken by Lady Franklin, who was present during the whole of the Festival.

We here give the CANTATA in English, translated by Mrs. Leprohon, the well-known authoress, of Montreal:—

PART I.

From far St. Lawrence' banks to Albion's shore,
A voice hath gone forth and been heard,

And in the royal palace noble hearts
  By love respondent have been stirred.

THE DEPARTURE.

Recitatif.

From Windsor's walls the cannon's boom is heard;
By martial sound the summer air is stirred;
From tower and turret countless chimes arise,
Mingling in silvery carols to the skies.
Steel gleams in sunshine flashing like bright gems,
And shouts awake the echoes of the Thames;
Whilst now behold, in royal pomp arrayed,
Approach a gay and noble cavalcade;
Fiery chargers arching necks of pride;
Flags, banners, standards, floating on each side;
Drum, Trumpet, blending in one martial peal,
That fills each throbbing heart with ardent zeal.
London is all astir; like a stream, the crowd
Follow the Prince with cheers and clamour loud,—
The Prince, who goes to meet, 'neath stranger skies,
Subjects bound to him by Love's closest ties.
The Royal mother now has said Farewell
With tearful eyes to the son she loves so well;
Striving to banish fear of winds and waves,
And storms that slumber in old Ocean's caves.
Ah, calm each anxious fear, illustrious One!
Safe is the bark that bears thy gallant Son :
Too many prayers for him and thee arise
On Albion's shores and 'neath Canadian skies!
Again the cannon's deafening roar is heard :
The vessel's glittering sails are slowly stirred ;
Poised on the wave she spreads the snow-white folds,
As if rejoicing in the priceless freight she holds.
Fair winds and sunshine mark her onward course ;
Neptune restrains the rising tempest's force.
Longing, we wait to gaze on that young noble brow :
Ah, our hopes are crowned and he is with us now.

THE ARRIVAL.

CHORUS :—All hail, old England's Hope and Pride,
Destined to wear one day Earth's fairest diadem,
  Thou who hast left thy home's dear tie
To glad thy people with thy presence new to them.
  Hail! child of hope and victory,

Coming to greet us even on our household hearth,
    Uniting in thyself
Royalty's splendor to that of modest worth.

A Voice :—At thine approach our woods and glens
    Have put on their brightest bloom ;
Our Mountains, erst crowned with hoar-frost,
    A richer green assume ;
The winds of summer on their wings
    Bring a fragrance yet more sweet,
And in humble cot and lordly home
    All hearts with pleasure beat.
From 'mid their leafy summer haunts
    Where airy zephyrs, wild flowers woo,
The birds their silvery notes awake
    As if to bid thee welcome too.

Recitatif.

We hope, great Prince, that thou wilt find
Thy New-World Empire worthy of thy sway,
And thy coming will give us heart
For greater things to strive each day.

A Voice :—Thou hast seen the massive bridge
    That our labour has patient raised ;
Ah! repaid for our toil will we amply be
    If by words from thee 'tis praised.
Lord of our noble river wide,
    Silent it stands in stately pride,
'Mid waters chafing on every side ;
    As firmly based the massive parts,
As thou art throned in thy people's hearts.

PRAYER.

Chorus :—Thou who placest the sceptre in the hands of Kings
    Great Lord whom we praise,
Of our Young Prince, so well, so justly loved,
    Guard Thou the days!
    A mother's hope is he,
Pride and shield of a nation free ;
Father! grant, then, that he may be
Worthy his lofty and his noble state,
And the honours high that on him wait.

Recitatif.

Up even to Heaven's starry domes,
    Its messengers doth bear

Upon their wings to the King of Kings
Our incense and our prayer.

CHORUS OF SOLDIERS.

 War-drums and trumpets,
 Raise your martial voice ;
 Your loud and stirring notes
 Make our hearts rejoice.
 Bind with bright garlands
 Every bridle-rein ;
 Fling wide our banners,
 Free from dishonour's stain.
 Well foes may tremble :
 Our standard floats above;
 We march to do them battle
 For Queen and Prince we love.

PART II.
THE AWAKENING AND RETURN.

Recitatif.

Like a mourner weeping nigh a mausoleum lone,
Canada in darkness lay, obscure, unknown.
Emerging from that torpor deep, at length,
She wakes, and the world admires her young strength.

CHORUS OF YOUNG GIRLS.

 Come let us gather
 Roses and flowers,
 Glit'ring with dew-drops
 From gardens and bowers ;
 Let childhood's small hands
 Fair blossoms cull;
 Branches of eglantine,
 And sweet myrtle, pull ;
 Weave them in garlands :
 Thus well evince,
 On this day of joy,
 Our love for our Prince.

DIALOGUE.

FIRST VOICE.

Rude huts on a bleak wild strand,
Such was once our native land.

SECOND VOICE.

Now harvests of golden grain
Enrich vale, hill-side, and plain.

FIRST VOICE.
'Neath her dreary icy shroud, Nature pulseless lay.
SECOND VOICE.
A robe of emerald verdure she wears to day.
FIRST VOICE.
Once the silence of the tomb reigned all around.
SECOND VOICE.
Now sunny hamlets through our land abound.
BOTH VOICES.
Like Zion, Prince, from out the dust,
Hath risen our city fair ;
With giant steps hath she advanced,
'Neath Albion's fostering care.
Onward her march ; to greater things
Will she aspire and aim each day,
E'er to become more worthy of
Thine and Victoria's sway.
Recitatif.
Proudly be-doing our foes and the tempest's fierce might,
Freely our standard floats out from its height ;
Like an oak in the midst of our forests so wide,
It may bend, but 'twill rise in still statelier pride.

SEXTUOR.

Here, where once forests raised their summits to the skies,
As if by magic power, cities, towns, arise ;
And in lone plains where man's foot the grass ne'er stirred,
The reaper's joyous song, harvest-home, is now heard.
On returning to our Queen,
Some kindly words of us thou'lt say;
Thou'lt tell her how we have prospered 'neath,
And how we bless her wise, just sway.
Recitatif.
Already the trumpet's voice
Sends forth on the air its echoing swell;
It may sadden but not rejoice.
We must part from the Prince we love so well ;
Let us join our voices to say Farewell.

FINAL CHORUS.

Farewell, oh, noble Son of our illustrious Queen.
May thy heart's motto ever be,
Justice, Truth, Fidelity ;
Thy reign prove bright and blessed as *Her's* hath been.
And may our loyal love's deep store
Win thee back to our land once more !
Farewell, great Prince, until we meet again !

At noon on Wednesday, 29th, His Royal Highness reviewed the Volunteer Militia of Montreal, on Logan's Farm, two miles from the city, in presence of an immense concourse of people.

The Volunteers consisted of two troops of cavalry, two companies of light infantry, nine companies of rifles, one company of highlanders, three companies of foot artillery, and three companies of field battery, numbering about 1600 men, all dressed in uniform, well disciplined, and certainly a fine-looking body of men.

His Royal Highness was accompanied by his suite, the Governor General and suite, the Commander of the Forces and suite, and a good many militia officers, all mounted, and forming a very brilliant staff.

A royal salute was fired by the battery as the royal party entered the field, and the whole multitude of people cheered the Prince heartily. The Volunteers were formed in line and presented arms, the band playing "God save the Queen." The Prince and those accompanying him passed down in front, and up in rear, inspecting the whole corps, and then galloped up to the flagstaff from which floated the royal standard. The troops then marched past in quick time, and went through several evolutions representing a sham-fight, with which the royal party was much pleased.

His Royal Highness, on leaving, summoned the commanding officers, Colonel Dyde, Lieutenant Col. Wiley, Lieutenant Col. Thorndike, and Captain Stevenson, whom he personally complimented on the efficiency of their several corps. A *feu de joie* and royal salute were then fired; and, amidst heartier cheers than ever, the Prince left the ground.

The following description of the visit to the late Sir George Simpson's residence at Isle Dorval, which took place the same day, is from the Montreal *Gazette*:—

> On Wednesday the 20th inst., the canoe-excursion given by the Hudson's Bay Company to His Royal Highness the Prince of Wales, came off with complete success, from Sir George Simpson's beautiful country residence,—Isle Dorval,—about three miles above Lachine. The weather, which had been threatening in the morning, cleared up in the afternoon, and was everything that could be desired. After the review, which took place in the morning, was over, the Prince of Wales and suite drove out to Lachine by the upper road, meeting a hearty re-

ception along the whole route; but more especially at the village of Lachine, where the residents had made great exertions to do the Prince due honor. For a considerable distance, pine trees had been planted on each side of the street; a profusion of flags and garlands decorated the houses, and (short as had been the time for preparation) no less than eight or nine triumphal arches spanned the road. The first seen was near the toll-bar, erected by Mr. Duff. Among others, we noticed that at the Hudson's Bay House, the residence of Sir George Simpson; at the Ottawa Hotel; at the Lachine Brewery (Dawes and Sons); and at the residence of Mr. Hopkins (H. B. Co. service).

At a point opposite Isle Dorval (also the property of Sir G. Simpson), the royal party quitted their carriages to embark in boats sent up for the purpose, from the vessels of war lying in our harbour. The scene at this moment was unrivalled in interest, and picturesque effect,—one never to be forgotten by those (comparatively few in number) who witnessed it. His Royal Highness, in warm terms, expressed his surprise and gratification at the demonstration, of which we will endeavour to give some faint idea.

The site was well chosen; the channel, less than a mile in width, flows between fields now ripe for the harvest, sloping to the water's edge, and the dense foliage and verdant lawns of Isle Dorval, fresh with recent showers and brilliant with sunshine. A flotilla of nine large birch-bark canoes was drawn up in a line close to the head of the island. Their appearance was very beautiful; the light and graceful craft were painted and fitted up with great taste, each having flags at the bow and stern; their crew, composed of 100 Iroquois Indians, from Caughnawaga and the Lake of Two Mountains, being costumed *en sauvage*, gay with feathers, scarlet cloth, and paint,—the crews and craft harmonising admirably.

As soon as the barge carrying the Prince pushed off from the mainland, the fleet of canoes darted out from the island to meet him, in a line abreast, and to the inspiriting cadences of a voyageur song. On nearing the royal barge, the line opened in the middle, apparently to let it pass, but, suddenly wheeling round with a rapidity and precision which took every one by surprise, they again formed in line, with the Prince's barge in the middle, and in that form reached the landing-place, when the canoe-song ceased, and a cheer, it did one's heart good to hear, burst from the voyageurs, which His Royal Highness, with a face beaming with pleasure, returned, by saluting his Indian escort.

The Prince of Wales was received on landing by Sir George Simpson; and soon afterwards luncheon was served to a select party, invited to meet His Royal Highness, by Lieut. General Sir Fenwick Williams, who at present occupies the Island as the owner's guest. Being a private entertainment, a complete list of the names of those present has not been furnished us; but we understand that there were about forty at table. Sir F. Williams, as the host, had the Prince on one side of him and Sir George Simpson on the other. Among other guests, were the Duke of Newcastle, Lord Lyons, Marquis of Chandos, Earl Mulgrave, Lord Hinchinbrook, Bishop of Montreal, Bishop of Rupert's Land, General Bruce, Mr. Engleheart, Major Teesdale (Equerry), Col. Taché, Col. Bradford, Col. Rollo, Mr. H. McKenzie (H. B. Co.), Mr. Hopkins (H. B. Co.), Admiral Milne, Captain Vansittart, R. N., Mr. Blackwell, Captain Earl, A. D. C., Captain De Winton, &c., &c. No ladies were invited, nor were any present, except three immediately connected with Sir George Simpson, viz., Mrs. Hopkins, and her sister, Miss Beechey, and Mrs. McKenzie.

Justice having been done to the elegant repast, the party strolled about to admire the beauty of the place, while the band of the Royal Canadian Rifles performed on the lawn, and the birch-bark fleet, in full song, paddled round the island. About half-past four the party embarked in the canoes, and proceeded, in great style and at a rapid pace, towards Lachine; one, bearing the royal standard and carrying the Prince, the Duke of Newcastle, and General Williams, taking the lead, while the remainder, in line abreast, followed close behind it. About the centre of the brigade we observed Sir George Simpson (accompanied by the Earl of Mulgrave and General Bruce, both old fellow-voyageurs of Sir George's), directing the movements in person. Passing down close along the north shore, the flotilla at that point again executed the extraordinary evolution of wheeling round in line, and then crossed the St. Lawrence to Caughnawaga, where crowds of white and red faces lined the bank to see the royal procession pass. After passing along the whole length of the village, a halt was called, and the canoes ordered to head up stream and mount the current in "Indian fyle," till again opposite Lachine, where the line was formed, as before, and the river recrossed to the railroad wharf, where the steamer *Kingston* was lying, to receive the party on board. As soon as the embarkation was completed, the canoes drew off, giving a parting cheer in capital style, which was replied to from the steamer and the crowds on shore. The *Kingston* quickly cast off her moorings, and, running down the Lachine Rapids, landed the Prince and his party in Montreal, about half-past seven, where carriages were in attendance for them on the wharf.

We are enabled to state that the Prince, and all who had the good fortune to be with him, entirely enjoyed the whole affair; which, from its peculiarities and successful management, will probably make a more lasting impression on His Royal Highness than anything else that has been, or will be done, to entertain him in this country.

We consider the Hudson's Bay Company are entitled to the thanks of the Canadian public, for their liberality and spirit in getting up this unique excursion; which, besides gratifying our royal visitor, afforded a most agreeable holiday to several thousand persons, who were enabled to witness the scene from the shores of the noble St. Lawrence.

In the evening, a torch-light procession by the firemen of Montreal took place. They were accompanied by their engines, which were gorgeously lighted up, bidding "welcome" to the Prince. The men, besides their torches, carried rockets and Roman candles, which they continually sent up.

On Thursday, August 30, H. R. H. and suite, the Gov. General, &c., took the royal car for the Eastern Townships, and crossed over the Victoria Bridge. They soon arrived at the town of St. Hyacinthe, which was beautifully ornamented and its streets laid out in a manner deserving the greatest credit; as also does the hearty reception received by H. R. H., when we know that nearly the entire population consists of French Canadians.

Carriages were in waiting; and the royal party were driven through the streets to the R. C. College, where three Addresses were presented from the authorities of the town, the county, and the college. H. R. H., as at the Laval University in Quebec, ascended to the roof and enjoyed the magnificent scenery which he could there behold.

He arrived at Sherbrooke at two o'clock. Here a splendid reception awaited him. Arches, and beautiful ones too, were erected; the streets decorated as no others had been. Flags were flying from every roof, and the whole population far and near turned out to give him a hearty and loyal welcome. Guns fired, bands played, and there was certainly a great commotion.

The following Address was presented to him, under a beautiful pavilion made of green boughs, &c.:—

To His Royal Highness Albert Edward, Prince of Wales.

MAY IT PLEASE YOUR ROYAL HIGHNESS,—

It is with feelings of peculiar satisfaction, that, on behalf of the Corporation and Citizens of the town of Sherbrooke, and on the part of the Eastern Townships, we have the honour of addressing Your Royal Highness, the representative of our Gracious Sovereign Queen Victoria, and of assuring you of our hearty and cordial welcome to the Eastern Townships of Canada. Loyalty to the Crown, and attachment to the person of your illustrious Mother, are as lively and ardent in these

Townships as in any portion of Her Majesty's dominions; and, on your return to England, you can assure Her Majesty of our attachment to the British Crown and to British institutions, and that we feel proud of our connection therewith and of our relation to our Gracious Sovereign, distinguished alike as a Queen and as a woman for those estimable qualities which have won for her the confidence and love of her people. Your Royal Highness can also assure Her Majesty, that, although situated on the borders of the neighbouring republic, and intimately acquainted with the working of its institutions, yet, under our own constitution, connected with and protected by the British Government, we have no desire for any change in the relations existing between us and the Mother Country. We sincerely pray that these may continue for ages to come. In visiting a new country like the Townships, Your Royal Highness will not expect such progress in agriculture and manufactures, or such marks of competence and wealth, as in the older settled portions of the country; still, we hope that what you may see will impress you favourably with the natural beauties and the varied resources of the Townships, and enable you to form an opinion of what they are destined to become through the industry and enterprise of the inhabitants. We sincerely and respectfully thank your Royal Highness for the visit, and would gladly hope that it may afford your Royal Highness as much gratification as it confers honour upon us. Permit us to hope that the Queen, the Prince Consort, and their beloved family, may long be spared to fill and adorn their high positions; and that when it shall please Almighty God in His wisdom to call upon you to assume and exercise the duties and responsibilities devolving upon you as reigning Monarch, your career may, like that of your Royal Mother, be prosperous and happy, benefiting the millions governed, and year by year reflecting additional lustre on your Royal Highness's person.

J. G. ROBERTSON,
Mayor.

His Royal Highness replied as follows:—

GENTLEMEN,—I thank you warmly for your Address welcoming me to this part of Canada, and expressing your loyalty to the Queen. I could not pass on, in my rapid journey through the Canadian provinces, without a visit to the Eastern Townships; and I only regret that the shortness of time in which so much has to be seen does not permit of a longer stay amongst you. Even in this hurried view of your country, I see much to indicate the future destiny which awaits a land to which so great energy and industry are devoted, and whose inhabitants are influenced by such attachment to the institutions in which they have been educated, as is evinced by your Address. Accept my thanks for your kind wishes for my future happiness. In return, I wish you every prosperity.

An Address was also presented from Bishop's College, Lennoxville, near Sherbrooke.

H. R. H. was then conducted to the residence of Hon. Mr. Galt, Minister of Finance, which is situated on the brow of a hill, surrounded by spacious grounds, and which was beautifully decorated with flowers and flags. While on his way, H. R. H. was nearly smothered by the great number of bouquets which came down from the hands of bewitching and captivating maidens.

At Mr. Galt's, a singular levee took place by reason of persons appearing in undress, in which H. R. H. shewed the example by appearing himself in the same costume.

Several hundred gentlemen were presented, and, during the levee, the following incident and noble act of H. R. H. took place, and of which we here give the particulars:—

At the close of this levee the voice of Colonel or Captain Moore was heard;—Colonel, by reason of his militia rank; Captain, because he is a retired naval officer. " Cheer," he loudly cried, " for justice has at last been done to as brave an officer as ever stepped the quarter-deck." He said a few words more, but they were unintelligible, being either choked by emotion or drowned in the cheers which immediately burst forth. Proceeding to the spot to learn if any one were mad or drunk, the writer heard that this was not the cause of the commotion, but that it was from the following circumstance: John Felton, commonly called Old Squire Felton in his own district, was signal midshipman on Nelson's flag-ship the *Victory*, at the battle of Trafalgar. He was also at the battle of Copenhagen, and wears medals for bravery at both those actions. At the blockade of Guadaloupe, West Indies, in 1826, he was the officer of the watch on board the *Curieux*, sloop-of-war, when she struck on a rock and was wrecked. On the court martial, which was of course subsequently held, there were some enemies of young Felton's, and, perhaps to their personal hostility, perhaps to the fact that court-martials were not held in those days with so much care for the ends of justice as now, he owed it that, although the wreck was caused by circumstances beyond his control, he was dismissed the service. His prospects were thus at once destroyed, and he finally emigrated to this country, where for four and thirty years he has lived respected. His Royal Highness having been made aware of the hardships of Mr. Felton's case,—not by him, for he suffered uncomplainingly,—chose this day as the occasion for exercising the prerogative delegated by Her Majesty to him, and, when the old man presented himself at the reception, not only received him with the greatest cordiality, speaking to him kindly words, but intimated that from that moment he was

I

restored to the position he had lost. This it was which caused the ebullition of feeling on the part of his brother-sailor, Captain Moore, and the cheering on the part of that of the crowd. The act was in itself graceful, it was gracefully performed, and it was thoroughly appreciated. Every one looked delighted. Mr. Felton could not conceal his pleasure, though he tried to look unmoved, and Mrs. Felton looked at her husband with more than usual pride as he and she were receiving the congratulation of the people.

After the levee, a luncheon was given by the Hon. Mr. Galt, and to which the royal party did ample justice. The carriages were afterwards brought round, and the Prince took his departure to return to Montreal, amidst a shower of flowers, cheers, salutes, waving of handkerchiefs, &c.; and arrived at Montreal at half-past six, after passing a day which must have been very agreeable. That evening, a grand display of fireworks was given in Montreal; and the next morning, H. R. H. and suite, accompanied by the Governor General, the Commandant, the Ministry, the Members of the Legislature, &c., took his departure by the railway, from the kind and hospitable city of Montreal, amidst a shower of rain. A Guard of Honour, the Artillery of which fired a royal salute, attended, with nearly the entire populace to cheer the Prince and bid him a good speed.

At the bridge of Ste. Anne's, which was decked out with flags and evergreens, the entire party took the splendid new steamer *Prince of Wales*, and had a magnificent sail up the beautiful and far-famed river Ottawa. It was at Ste. Anne's where Moore wrote his celebrated boat-song. The weather had cleared up; the sun shone and the scenery looked most beautiful, everything apparently revelling in the presence of royalty. At every little village and settlement, Two-Mountains, Treadwell, Montebello, Buckingham, Windsor, Plantagenet, &c., flags and decorations were displayed, and the people turned out shouting and hurrahing in honour of the Prince.

At Carillon, H. R. H. and suite again took the cars. Here a Guard of Honour of Militia presented arms, and a royal salute was fired. Arches were erected, and the place generally was profusely decorated. The people also turned out in great numbers, and showed their loyalty by cheering their future king.

At Grenville, the same loyalty was shown; besides, the children sang the National Anthem. Here the royal party took the fine steamer *Phœnix*, which had been entirely renovated and furnished.

When opposite the Gatineau River, they were met by a fleet of river steamers, nicely decorated and crowded with people, who cheered loudly as they passed her. Here also one of the grandest sights ever witnessed appeared in view: 1,200 lumbermen and Indians, attired in red and other colors, in 150 birch-bark canoes, met the steamer and formed into the letter V, and, with the *Phœnix* in the centre, continued so escorting our well-beloved Prince to the future capital of Canada,—Ottawa City.

The Prince, who was in the cabin, on being informed of the cheers of the lumbermen, ascended to the hurricane-deck with the members of his suite and others, and greatly admired this novel and picturesque fleet.

The banks of the river near the city, and the city itself, were perfectly crowded with people. The cheering as the *Phœnix* neared the city, and until she was safely moored at the wharf, was tremendous; nothing could equal it. The people's loyalty as well as gratitude to their Sovereign was clearly shewn.

Ottawa City was beautifully adorned with arches, flags, banners, and every conceivable decoration was used to give a grand and varied appearance to the city.

It was after six before the *Phœnix* came to her moorings, and consequently no time was to be lost. The wharf on which H. R. H. landed was very prettily ornamented and well carpeted; the seats surrounding it were crowded by the most fortunate of the good people of Ottawa, who loudly cheered, as also did all others present, as His Royal Highness landed.

A Guard of Honour of the Light Infantry Militia and Volunteer Artillery of Ottawa saluted him, the former by presenting arms, the latter by a royal salute, which was thundered forth to the cheers of the entire populace; the band meanwhile playing the National Anthem.

He was met by the Mayor (Alex. Workman, Esq.), attired in his robe of office, and the members of the City Council, the Warden and members of the County Council, and the most prominent citizens of Ottawa. The following Address was then presented by the Mayor :—

To His Royal Highness Albert Edward, Prince of Wales, Duke of Cornwall, &c., &c.

MAY IT PLEASE YOUR ROYAL HIGHNESS,—

The Corporation of the City of Ottawa, in Council assembled, most respectfully approach your Royal Highness with the offer of a sincere and loyal welcome to this city, and beg to convey to your Royal Highness sentiments of profound devotion and inalienable attachment to our much-beloved Sovereign.

We consider it a privilege in being allowed to tender to your Royal Highness our hearty congratulations upon your safe arrival in this portion of the extensive empire of which this province forms an integral part, and to assure you of the satisfaction which your visit affords to every class of Her Majesty's liege subjects resident in the Ottawa Valley.

We feel proud in having the opportunity of acknowledging with gratitude the act of your august mother, our most gracious Queen and ruler, in selecting this city as the future capital of Canada ; and your presence upon this occasion is viewed as a further indication of the great condescension and interest manifested by our beloved Sovereign in the welfare of her Canadian subjects in this portion of Her Majesty's dominions.

We hail with the utmost delight the auspicious event of your Royal Highness's visit to Canada ; and sincerely hope, that a personal acquaintance with the resources and varied capabilities of this important part of the British possessions, may be found interesting as well as instructive ; and that the experience acquired during your sojourn in the country may satisfy you that its inhabitants are loyal, contented, and prosperous.

In conclusion, allow us to wish you a pleasant and agreeable tour throughout the Province, with a safe voyage across the Atlantic ; and on your return to your native land, may you enjoy every comfort and happiness this world can bestow.

ALEX. WORKMAN,
Mayor of Ottawa.

To which the Prince made the following reply :—

GENTLEMEN,—I thank you sincerely for this Address, and request you to convey to the citizens whom you represent the expression of my gratitude for the very kind language in which it is couched, and the warm reception with which they have greeted me.

In this city, at your request, I am about to lay the first stone of a building in which, before long, the deliberations of the Parliament of Canada will be held ; and from which will emanate the laws which are

133

to govern the great and free people of these Provinces, extend the civilizing influence of British Institutions, and strengthen the power of the great Empire of which this Colony forms an integral and most important portion.

I do not doubt, that, with its increase of population and influence, this city will prove itself worthy of the country of which it is now the Capital, and will justify the selection which your Sovereign made, at the request of her Canadian subjects.

It has been most gratifying to me to witness the demonstrations which have met me on every occasion during my progress through this magnificent country, and which evince the feelings towards your Queen entertained alike by all races, all creeds, and all parties.

In consequence of rain falling, the Address and reply were rapidly hurried through. The procession organized, and the Prince, escorted by nearly the entire population, started for the Victoria House, which had been leased for his residence. The procession was as follows :—

Sergeant. { Police in Advance Guard. / Chief of Police and Officers. } *Sergeant.*

BAND OF THE ROYAL CANADIAN RIFLES.

The Prince's Standard.
Advance Guard of Cavalry.

Officers of Cavalry.

HIS ROYAL HIGHNESS THE PRINCE OF WALES,
AND SUITE.
Governor General and Suite.
Commander of the Forces and Staff.
Members of the Executive Council.

Officers of Cavalry.

BAND.
City Standard.
MAYOR OF OTTAWA.
Members of the City Council.
City Officials.

Marshals

Members of the Legislative Council.
Members of the Legislative Assembly.
Distinguished Guests.
BAND.
County of Carleton Standard.
Warden of the County of Carleton.
Members of the Co. of Carleton Council.
County of Carleton Officials.

Marshals

{ Marshals ——

BAND.
St. Jean Baptiste Society.
St. Andrew's Society.
St. Patrick's Society.
St. George's Society.
BAND.
Fire Companies in Uniform.
Hook and Ladder Companies in Uniform.

—— Marshals }

{ Marshals ——

Lumbermen in Uniform.
Government Architects.
Government Workmen in Uniform.
Citizens of Ottawa.
Yeomanry of the County of Carleton.
Military to be arranged by the Officer in Command.

—— Marshals }

Meanwhile, the rain came down faster than ever, still the people continued cheering lustily. Precisely at eleven o'clock next day (September 1st), the weather having cleared up in a most propitious manner, H.R.H. and suite left the Victoria House, under a royal salute, to lay the foundation-stone of the new Parliament Buildings of Canada. The place selected for so doing was perfectly crowded with elegantly-dressed ladies and gentlemen, seated upon platforms erected for the occasion, and the chief dignitaries of the Province stood within a railing, which surrounded a space where the stone (which was of Canadian marble) was placed; to adorn which a neat arch and massive crown had been erected by the Board of Works.

Shortly after eleven, the Prince, attended by his suite, the Governor General, Lord Mulgrave, Sir Fenwick Williams of Kars, their several suites, the Ministry, Members of Parliament, and a host of other gentlemen, took their destined places, the Prince standing, and surrounded by his suite, the Governor General, and most of the above gentlemen.

The proceedings were opened by the Rev. Dr. Adamson, Chaplain to the Legislature, reading the following prayer :—

Protect us, O Lord, in all our doings, with Thy most gracious favor, and further us with Thy continual help, that in all our works begun, continued, and ended in Thee, we may glorify Thy Holy Name, and finally by Thy mercy obtain everlasting life, through Jesus Christ our Lord. Amen. Our father which art, &c.

At the conclusion of which, H. R. H. advanced to the stone, which bore this inscription:

THIS CORNER-STONE OF THE BUILDING
intended to receive
THE LEGISLATURE OF CANADA,
was laid by
ALBERT EDWARD, PRINCE OF WALES,
On the first day of September,
MDCCCLX.

On the top of the cube of white marble which composed the stone, was inserted a long six-pointed star of brass, in the centre of which was the following inscription :—

Quod felix faustumque sit Hunc lapidem Ædificii
quod comitiis Provinciæ habendis
inserviret ponere
dignatus est
ALBERTUS EDWARDUS, PRINCEPS WALLIÆ,
Anno Domini MDCCCLX,
die 1° Septembris,
Anno Regni Victoria Reginæ,
XXIV.

On the sexagonic circle around the inscription were these words :— "His Excellency Right Hon. Sir Edmund Walker Head, Bart., Governor General of British America." On each of the points of the star were the names of the architects, builders, &c., as follows :

Hon. J. Rose.................... Com. of Public Works.
Samuel Keefer.................... Deputy Com. P. W.
Fuller & Jones........................... Architects.
John Morris........................ Clerk of Works.
Thomas McGreevy........................ Builder.
Charles Garth........................ Steam fitter.

It was suspended from the centre of the huge ornamental crown by a large pulley, which ran round a gilt block. Under this was a cavity in which was placed a glass bottle containing a collection of coins of the present day, and a parchment-scroll inscribed thus :—

The foundation-stone of the Houses of Parliament in the Province of Canada, was laid on the 1st day of September, in the year of our Lord 1860, in the 24th year of Her Majesty's reign, at the City of Ottawa, by H. R. H. the Prince of Wales. [Here followed the names of all the Members of the Legislative Council, the names of all the Members of the Assembly, the names of the Government of Canada, the names of all the Architects, &c.]

The mortar was then spread by the Clerk of Works, Mr. Merrill, and the Prince gave it the finishing touch with a beautiful silver trowel, presented by Hon. John Rose, on the face of which is the following inscription:—

WITH THIS TROWEL
on the
FIRST DAY OF SEPTEMBER, 1860,
THE CORNER-STONE OF THE BUILDING
intended to receive the
PARLIAMENT OF CANADA,
was laid at the
CITY OF OTTAWA,
BY
ALBERT EDWARD, PRINCE OF WALES.

And on the back is engraved a view of the intended building.

The stone was then finally deposited in its resting-place, H. R. H. giving it three steady knocks with a wooden mallet. The following prayer was then offered up by the Rev. Dr. Adamson:—

This corner-stone we lay in the name of the Father, and of the Son, and of the Holy Ghost; and may God Almighty grant that the building thus begun in His name, may be happily carried on to its completion without injury or accident, and when completed it may be used for the good of the Province, the Glory of our Queen, the happiness of our Prince, and the good government of our people. Amen.

The plummet was applied by Mr. Morris, and the level by S. Keefer, Esq., Deputy Commissioner of Public Works; and these gentlemen having announced to His Excellency the Governor General that the stone was properly laid, His Excellency proclaimed the same in these words, " I proclaim the stone fairly and duly laid in this work." Then three cheers arose for Her Majesty the Queen, such as never perhaps arose in this country before; three for H. R. H. the Prince of Wales; and three for His Excellency the Governor General.

The Architects for the Parliament and Departmental buildings, Messrs. Stent and Laver, and Messrs. Fuller and Jones, and the Clerk of Works, Mr. Morris, were then separately presented to H. R. H., who shortly after took his departure.

Shortly afterwards, a levee was held at the Victoria House, when a number of gentlemen were presented.

In the afternoon, the Government gave a sumptuous *déjeuner* to H. R. H. and suite, and a large number of guests, including the Mayor and Corporation, the Clergy, &c., &c.

At four o'clock, the Prince and suite, attired in their uniforms, entered the apartment, the Ministry also in uniform, and the whole company standing; the R. C. R. Band playing the National Anthem, and which also discoursed sweet music during the time the company were engaged.

After due discussion of the viands, His Excellency the Governor General rose and proposed the health of the " Queen," which was right loyally responded to with a " hip hip hurrah."

Sir N. F. Belleau proposed the "Prince Consort," which was received with cheers.

Sir Henry Smith then proposed " H. R. H. the Prince of Wales," which was received with the greatest enthusiasm.

As it subsided, H. R. H. rose and said, " I propose the Governor General, and both Houses of the Legislature." Cheers again broke forth, long and loud, and the greatest enthusiasm and exultation prevailed.

We must compliment the Ottawaites on the excellent condition of their lungs; for really, on that occasion, they displayed more stentorian powers than all the people in the other cities combined.

H. R. H. and suite, with the Governor-General, &c., took their departure from the room shortly after. They then proceeded to the Chaudière Falls, situated near the city; and viewed the slides over which the timber passes, on a raft which had been previously constructed by Mr. Skead. The Prince and the entire party, including Lord Hinchinbrooke, the Hon. Mr. Eliot, and Lord Mulgrave, embarked and swiftly passed over one of the slides; near the bottom of which, a beautiful new barge, constructed by the Clerk of Works for the Government, met them, and on which they speedily embarked, and were rowed about the river by a party of Ottawa gentlemen. Afterwards the Prince viewed the grand canoe-regatta which there and then took place. There were six races. In each race, only a certain number of paddles and men were allowed, and it was somewhat ludicrous to view it; each one endeavouring to supplant the other, and, in doing so, requiring to be extremely cautious, lest, by a sudden jerk or move, the whole occupants of the canoe should be precipitated into the water.

After a short cruise around the river, the Prince and suite returned to the shore, where carriages were waiting, in which they speedily drove home.

In the evening, a very pretty illumination was given. Of course it was not so extensive or elaborate as that at Montreal or Quebec, yet its very simplicity made one admire it.

A Society calling themselves the "Phisiocarnivalogicalists," which is enough to break any person's jaw-bone in pronouncing it turned out and gave a torchlight procession; and which halted, in front of the Victoria and cheered the Prince, who appeared, and was much interested in the strange "institution."

On Sunday morning, Sept. 2nd, H. R. H., escorted by his suite and the noblemen and gentlemen accompanying him, attended Divine Service at Christ Church, where pews had been provided for them, near the Communion Table.

On entering, he was conducted by the Revds. Messrs. Lauder, Adamson, Stephenson, and Loucks; the entire congregation stood up; and the organ pealed forth the Coronation Anthem (the organist was Mr. Barnby of Montreal.)

The Morning Service was read by the Rev. E. Loucks, of Christ Church; the ante-communion service and Epistle by the Rev. Dr. Adamson; and the Gospel by the Rev. J. S. Lauder, Rector of Christ Church, who also preached.

The Anthem was from the 26th Psalm, "I will wash my hands in innocency: so will I compass thine altar, O Lord."

The following was the—

SERMON.

The text was taken from the 1st Epistle of Peter, ii. chapter, and 9th verse, "Ye are a chosen generation, a royal priesthood, a holy nation, a peculiar people."

The Epistle whence the text is taken, although written for the instruction of the Jews and Gentiles who had embraced Christianity under the Apostle's preaching, was intended more particularly for the Jewish converts: hence the frequent allusions to Jewish customs and historical events which mark the contents of almost every chapter. In the verse I have just read, we cannot fail to recognize a striking allusion to a people who were more than ordinarily circumstanced—who were highly favored amongst the various races of men, and the Apostle used the words which should remind them of what they were under the Law of Moses—to shew them that they were no worse under the new Law of Christ—that they were still a chosen generation, a royal priesthood, a peculiar people, but with this difference, that the chosen was not now confined exclusively to the Jews, as in the days of old, but was extended to all believers in Christ, no matter whether Jews or Gentiles, in every nation under Heaven. We, then, brethren, who are assembled here to-day, are made, by the mercy of God, partakers of the blessed privilege which the text declares. We are now in a position which none but Jews alone once occupied towards God—we are a "chosen generation, a royal priesthood, a holy nation, a peculiar people"— and what blessings are contained in each of those titles! what glorious gifts have been bestowed in consequence!—1st. We are a generation amongst whom God has been pleased to set up His name—a generation who for eighteen hundred centuries have had the Gospel presented to us—a generation enjoying all the privileges which the Jews of old enjoyed, without the heavy burdens of the Law. No types now dim our spiritual vision, nor costly sacrifices have we to make—no tedious journeys to the temple to sacrifice and atone for our sins—no seeing through a glass, darkly, the Redeemer of our race. The Type has long given place to the Antitype—the sacrifice of Christ has made atonement once for all, and the seeing through a glass darkly, has been changed to "face to face." Enjoying as we do all the privileges of the Gospel —having the purest branch of the Holy Catholic Church in which to enrol ourselves as members—a church in which God's word is preached free and unfettered—in which are ceremonies of peculiar solemnity, yet free from superstition—a church blessed with two Holy Sacraments of Christ's ordaining, and, thank God, none of man's—the one, bestowing a Baptism whereby we are made members of Christ, children of God, and inheritors of the Kingdom of Heaven; the other, furnishing a spiritual food and sustenance for the strengthening and refreshing of our souls in this life—hallowed and refreshed by the worship of a "common prayer," in the language of a chaste and time-honoured liturgy, which breathes throughout a spirit of the most fervent piety, and watched over by the pastorship of a three-fold ministry of bishops, priests, and deacons;—having all these privileges amongst us, and enjoying them in the peace and happiness which British liberty affords, may we not well say that we are " a chosen generation, a royal priesthood, a holy nation, a peculiar people," and that God has blessed us in a wonderful manner beyond millions of the people of the earth, who yet sit in darkness and the shadow of death.—But we are also "a royal priesthood." The Jews were styled a "kingdom of priests" by God himself, probably because of their consecration to himself by a peculiar covenant, and their separation from the rest of mankind, as priests are separated from the multitude of men. St. Peter applies the term to all believers, who are priests, not the ministering priests of the church, but priests of a more private character—priests to themselves appointed to offer up a sacrifice of praise and thanksgiving daily for themselves and their households. And our church, in her beautiful Communion Service, recognizes this priestly character of its members, in the words, " and here we offer and present unto Thee, O Lord, ourselves, our souls and bodies to be a reasonable, holy, and lively sacrifice unto Thee." We are called Royal on account of our new privileges, being born again "to be heirs of the Kingdom of Heaven—to reign with Christ hereafter—and to wear an incorruptible crown that fadeth not away." We are therefore "a royal priesthood"—we are a holy nation too. The Jews were called a holy nation, because they were in covenant with God, and because to them were committed the oracles of God—and so are we for the same reason : we are now in covenant with God, and to us is committed the Bible. We are not to suppose that by the term "holy nation" is to be understood a nation in which every individual and thing is holy,—such a state of things did not exist among the Jews; but we are to understand a nation in which holiness is recognized as the chief aim of man —in which religion occupies the chief place—whose people recognize God in all his offices of Creator, Redeemer, and Sanctifier, and the law of His mouth is deemed unto them better than thousands of gold and silver; to whom the Sabbath is a delight, the holy of the Lord honourable—from whose altar the incense of pure and heartfelt prayer ascends to Heaven—a holy nation too, I might say, because that even our civil laws render that justice to every man, which only laws based upon the law of God can bestow, and with which every man is satisfied.

Our last title is—a peculiar people. The word peculiar, as translated in the margin of the Bible, is, "purchased"; and if we take this meaning, what a volume does it not contain? of how much does it not remind us? what remembrances does it not call up?—how that once we were sinners, and not only sinners, but sinners *sold* under sin—the slaves of Satan and of death, but that now we are purchased back again, and with what a price!—purchased by the precious blood of Christ, for which cause you may remember it is said, "Ye are not your own; ye are bought with a price—a purchased people!"—Oh! how does this recall to mind the cross on which the Lord of Glory hung—the spear that pierced his precious side—the blood that flowed from his reeking wounds—the bitter cry, "*Eli, Eli, lama Sabachthani,*" and the last words of this sad scene—"*It is finished!*" A purchased people! Yes; and therefore, perhaps, we may say with some propriety still, "a peculiar people"— peculiar because so much has been done for us—peculiar because God has made us a chosen generation—peculiar because we are a royal priesthood—peculiar because we are a purchased people. There is no verse in the Bible, perhaps, more striking than this, in which our real state as believers in Christ is so forcibly set forth. If the titles therein expressed mean anything, they must show us clearly that we are a people signally favoured by Providence—that we are citizens of no mean city, but fellow-citizens with the saints and of the household of God, and therefore that our responsibilities are great indeed. As persons, then, called by such titles, what manner of people ought believers to be? We should be men formed upon the maxims of Gospel. We should present to the admiration of the world an assemblage of all virtues—fidelity in our discourse, sincerity in our sentiments, uprightness in our conduct, modesty without affectation, humility without baseness. We should feel that we have passions, only to overcome them—pleasures, to sacrifice them to duties, to comply with them. Above all things, we should be men of prayer—accustomed to seek counsel of God in everything that we do, and to ask His forgiveness for everything we do amiss. We should also be men of self-denial, prepared to do and give up much for the sake of Christ, who gave Himself for us, and for our sakes " became poor that we through his poverty might be made rich." We should also show, by a holy conversation, what we are and whose we are. Passed, I know, is the Golden Age of religion, when the name of Jesus Christ and the maxims which he delivered were mixed with all the discourses of Christians. In these times the language of religion is nowhere to be found but in sermons and books of piety. We have scarcely courage enough in company to mention that adorable name of our Saviour. We need not, to be sure, intrude or thrust our religion into every place we come, lest we make it distasteful and ourselves unwelcome ; but we should be careful, in all our intercourse with men, that, by our chaste conversation, we may be recognized as Christians. Let us never forget that this " chosen generation " is made up of individuals, and that we all individually have duties to perform ; and what those duties are, we need be at no loss to discover. We have only to look around us and behold numberless paths of duty clearly marked out. Believe me, we have not been placed in the high position which the text declares, to live a mere earthly life here, to enjoy earth's pleasures and dance along its seducing paths, without a thought for anything but ourselves. God has given us a holy Sabbath—Do we observe it? He has given us a holy Church—Are we faithful members? The poor are hungry—Do we feed them? they are naked—Do we clothe them? they are sick—Do we visit and relieve them? The heathen are perishing for knowledge—Are we sending it out to them? There are few of these conditions that you cannot help to alleviate. Christ meant us to do as He did, and He went about doing good. It is idle to call ourselves Christians, unless we strive to be like Him, who hath left us an example that we should follow His steps. As a "chosen generation," then, depend on it, we have been chosen for some purpose, not only as individuals but as a nation; and the question with us individually and nationally should be, For what were we chosen? I think, to do our work on the earth. The next question with us, then, should be, How is it to be done? Be assured it is not by the power of her spear or her sword that the nation to which we belong, occupies the proud position she does among the nations of the earth. It is England's Bible that is the grand secret of England's greatness. It is that that has made her the most civilized, the most polished, the most refined, and the most Christian nation in the world; it is that that has made her laws so just and her people so happy; and we in this colony of hers, if we are ever to be great, must become so by the same means. The Bible must be our Polar Star to lead us to that kind of civilization which alone exalteth a nation.—Although the waves of the Atlantic roll between us and our Fatherland to-day, let me speak of ourselves as one nation; for that we are, thank God. God, I am persuaded, has chosen us as a nation to spread the Gospel through the earth. He has committed the Holy Scriptures to us, and we are responsible for the manner in which we use that precious gift. We are bound to spread them, not only among ourselves, but to send them to the darkest corners of the earth. We must not withhold their truths, nor sacrifice their holy doctrines to superstition or whims.—If we are chosen to do this work, woe be to us if we neglect our duty. Expediency, I know, is too much the order of the present day; but it must not be carried too far, lest we imitate the fearful expediency recorded of a once-memorable event. "It is expedient that one man die for the people." There must be no halting between two opinions in God's work, neither as individuals, nor as a nation. We must not neglect to send out the glad tidings of a reconciled God and Saviour to every nation we call our own, that they, too, may become a part of this "chosen generation," this "royal priesthood," this "holy nation," this "peculiar people." The salvation of the soul through Christ is too precious a truth to be kept to ourselves, the glorious news of a Saviour's love is too grand a blessing to be kept uncirculated. If we rejoice in Him, let us see that others are partakers of our joy; and if eighteen centuries have passed away since Jesus hung on Calvary's Cross for us, since His blood flowed down its rough hewn wood, let us not grow careless; let us remember, that, though old to us, there are yet millions of human souls for whom that blood was spilt, as well as to whom this great salvation would be new.—Oh! if we are a chosen people, let us try to be a holy nation—a nation that reads the Bible and spreads the knowledge of the truths contained in it, because it believes the Bible —a nation that prays to God and serves its God, because it believes in God and loves its God. It is worth our while, then, brethren, while we have time to do so, to ask ourselves whether we are really the kind of Christians that Christ intended us to be? Oh! what a poor service ours is, after all—what a poor serving of Christ!—what miserable compromises we make!—what sincere striving to be His, and yet afraid to put the world out of temper with us! I fear we are astray, and far astray, in what we do and what we expect. Christ must be our all in all. He wants our whole heart, and we think that, some way or other, though we don't give it to him now, yet he will do something for us in the end, that will gain us an entrance into Heaven. We trust to His good nature, if I might use the term, too much. But it is a sad mistake: we cannot win him even thus.—"Lord, Lord, have I not prophesied in Thy name, and in Thy Name done many wonderful works," will have no effect then either.—Brethren, now is the time to win Christ; now is the time to gain His favour. Remember, I pray you, and I fear too many are apt to forget this fact—remember, that at the last day, Christ is not to be our Saviour, but our Judge! Oh, what a difference! How does this warn us not to be harboring vain imaginations now! "A chosen generation" we are now. Let us take care that we are found in the same position in the great and terrible day of the Lord; for, unless we are, all the more dreadful—because of our being a "chosen generation"— will our sentence be. "They that knew their Lord's will, and prepared not themselves, neither did according to his will, shall be beaten with many stripes. But they that knew it not, and did commit things worthy of stripes, shall be beaten with few stripes. For unto whom much is given, of him shall much be required."

At the conclusion of the service, His Royal Highness and suite left the church in the same order observed on entering, viz. preceded by the church-wardens, the organ playing the National Anthem.

His Royal Highness and suite, attended by the Governor General and other gentlemen, took their departure from the delightful little city of Ottawa on Monday morning at eight o'clock. The steamer *Emerald* had been chartered to carry the royal party as far as the Chats Portage, and on it His Royal Highness and suite immediately went. A Guard of Honour of the Volunteers presented arms, and the artillery, under Major Turner, fired a royal salute. The people cheered to their hearts' content; and to the sweet strains of the National Anthem, the steamer moved away.

The royal party arrived at the Chats after twelve a. m.; and, entering canoes, were quickly rowed up the Ottawa, to Arnprior, which was nicely decorated. They were met by the Sheriff of the Counties of Lanark and Renfrew, as also the Warden and County Council, who presented an Address. Luncheon was partaken of; and at four o'clock they took carriages for Almonte, 20 miles distant, a station of the Ottawa and Prescott Railway. The distance was accomplished in two hours and a half,—through one of the most fertile and best-settled portions of the Province.

On each side of the road were well-laid-out farms, the houses all nicely decorated, and colours flying. Arches were erected and well decorated all along the road; and every farmer and farmer's son turned out, welcoming the Prince with loud cheers.

At Almonte, the royal party took the cars for Brockville; and, amidst the greatest cheering, His Royal Highness standing on the platform, took his departure.

The royal train arrived at Brockville at eight o'clock in the evening; and of course it would then have been quite dark, but for the loyalty of the inhabitants, who lit up their dwellings and stores. The firemen, to the number of 300, turned out with torches. Everything was at once, as it were, turned into day.

His Royal Highness was received, on the arrival of the cars at the station, by the Mayor and Councillors, the Warden and members of the County Council, and the most influential inhabitants of this pretty and well-laid-out town, who conducted him to a pavilion which had been erected near the station, and which was beautifully ornamented with flowers, rosettes, and drapery of many colours. This was lit up with variegated lamps, which gave a very fine appearance. Two Addresses were then presented; one from the Town Council, and the other from the County Council. After replying to both, the Prince, his suite, and the gentlemen attending on him, were immediately conducted to carriages and driven through the illuminated streets, surrounded by the firemen with their lighted torches, &c. Nothing could have been more beautifully sublime; nothing more truly grand than this simple, unostentatious, but truly loyal display.

The royal party was escorted to the Steamer *Kingston*, which was lying at the wharf; and in which the Prince proceeded to Kingston on the following morning (September 3rd), passing through some of the grandest and most beautiful scenery on the continent,* which must have charmed and astonished the Prince and the members of his suite, though much accustomed to some of the best scenery in the United Kingdom.

And now we have to speak of an affair which was most disagreeable, not only to ourselves, but to the whole inhabitants of the Province, and which unfortunately comes specially under our notice as connected with the Prince's visit to Canada. We allude to the Orange disturbances at Kingston and Belleville; occurrences which are universally lamented as having tended to mar the happiness and joy of the Prince's progress.

It is not our province to pass an opinion on the events which have taken place: we shall merely, and as carefully as possible, lay before our candid and discriminating readers, what really did occur, and leave them to form an unbiassed opinion.

During the sojourn of the royal party at Montreal, a report was mooted, which came to the knowledge of the Duke of Newcastle, that the Orangemen of Upper Canada, but more particularly of the cities of Kingston and Toronto, intended to erect arches in those towns displaying partizan objects, and array themselves in full Orange regalia to join in the procession of welcome.

This the Duke was most particularly adverse to (on the grounds stated in the appended letter to the Governor General), and accordingly wrote the following letter to His Excellency:—

MY DEAR SIR EDMUND,—I am informed that it is the intention of the Orangemen of Toronto to erect an arch on the line of route which it is desired by the citizens that the Prince of Wales shall take on Friday next, and to decorate it with the *insignia* of their Association. I am also told that they mean to appear in the procession similarly decorated with party badges.

It is obvious that a display of this nature on such an occasion is likely to lead to religious feud and breach of the peace; and it is my duty to prevent, as far as I am able, the exposure of the Prince to supposed participation in a scene so much to be deprecated, and so alien to the spirit in which he visits Canada.

I trust you may be able to persuade those who are concerned in these preparations, to abandon their intentions; but that there may be no mistake, I hope you will inform them, that, in the event of any such arch being erected, I shall advise the Prince to refuse to pass under it,

---

* The Thousand Islands.

K

and enter the town by another street; and further, if any Orange demonstration, or any other demonstration of a party character, is persisted in, I shall advise the Prince to abandon his visit to the town altogether.

I have heard, but with less certainty, that a similar demonstration is contemplated at Kingston. I need not say that my remarks apply equally to that or any other town.

I am, &c.,

NEWCASTLE.

To the Right Hon. Sir E. W. Head.

Accordingly, the Governor General wrote the following letter to the Chief Magistrates of Toronto and Kingston (Adam Wilson, Mayor of Toronto, and O. S. Strange, Mayor of Kingston) :—

OTTAWA, August 31, 1860.

SIR,—I have the honor to enclose a copy of a letter addressed to me by the Secretary of State for the Colonies, now in attendance on His Royal Highness the Prince of Wales.

In explanation of this letter, I desire to call your attention to the fact, that, according to an advertisement which has appeared in a Toronto paper, it is the intention of the Orange body in that city to display in the procession which is to take place on the reception of His Royal Highness, and in the streets through which he is to pass, certain emblems and decorations belonging specially to their own Society.

I may state in the most explicit terms, that any such display, or any attempt to connect with His Royal Highness's reception, the public and open recognition of the Orangemen or any party association, would be viewed with extreme dissatisfaction.

You will bear in mind, Sir, that His Royal Highness visits this Colony on the special invitation of the whole people, as conveyed by both branches of the Legislature, without distinction of creed or party ; and it would be inconsistent with the spirit and object of such an invitation, and such a visit, to thrust on him the exhibition of banners or other badges of distinction which are known to be offensive to any portion of Her Majesty's subjects.

I feel satisfied that His Grace's reasons for expressing these views will, on consideration, be deemed satisfactory; and I have to request that you, as Chief Magistrate of the City of Toronto, will take care that no such cause of complaint may exist, either in the procession itself, or in the decoration of the streets through which His Royal Highness will pass.

I have further to request that you will, by letter addressed to me at Kingston, inform me explicitly whether any doubts exists as to a compliance with the wishes expressed by the Duke of Newcastle in this matter ; as the course likely to be pursued at Toronto may materially affect the route to be taken by His Royal Highness in his future progress through the Province.

I have the honor to be, &c.

EDMUND HEAD.

The Roman Catholic inhabitants of these cities, who became indignant that the Orangemen should build arches and endeavour to demonstrate their allegiance, immediately called meetings and appointed deputations to proceed to Ottawa, to have an interview with the Duke of Newcastle, and to protest against such demonstrations; which they accordingly did, and were completely successful, the Duke promising that the Prince would not land where any Orange demonstrations should take place.

The Orangemen on their part fancying that it was through the Catholics' influence that their arches and intended procession had been denounced by the Duke of Newcastle, then remained firmer to their absurd purpose than ever: they came to a decision, that, come what would, they would stand their ground and carry the day.

Kingston had made good preparations, and every one expected that the Orangemen would ultimately "cave in," to have the pleasure of the Prince's presence; but no, they would not! they remained firm to their decision. In this lamentable state of affairs, the *Kingston*, with the Prince and suite on board, appeared off the town, escorted by a small fleet of boats, &c. A royal salute was fired by the Volunteers, and every expression of joy was manifested by the people at the Prince's presence.

An enquiry was made by the Duke of Newcastle if the Orangemen still persisted in their conduct; and, to the regret of all, the answer returned was that they did. A message was then sent to say that sixteen hours would be given for the city to give a final decision, a decision by the City Council; and if at the end of that time they did not consent to give up their partizan demonstration, the *Kingston* (with the Prince on board) would proceed on her way to Belleville, the next place of call.

During this time, a special meeting of the Council was held, to determine whether the Council should proceed to present the Address on board the *Kingston*, or on the wharf,—or not present it at all, if His Royal Highness should not land.

After a long debate, the following resolution was carried:—

That we, the loyal Roman Catholics, in conjunction with the liberal loyal Protestants of this city, do hereby cordially unite in requesting as a special favor that His Royal Highness will land at the place appointed, and then proceed to the City Hall, in order to give Her Majesty's dutiful subjects an opportunity of being presented to her royal son.

The Orangemen, in full regalia, were assembled in vast numbers to greet the Prince, the Rifles were on the wharf to salute him, and the whole population was out to welcome him; but His Royal Highness was obliged to refuse landing after his request was treated in such a manner, and the *Kingston* proceeded on her way at 3 p. m., 5th Sept.; not, however, before Addresses were presented on board, from the Magistrates of the United Counties of Frontenac, Lennox, and Addington, and the Moderator of the Church of Scotland. To the former, and to the Sheriff of the United Counties, His Royal Highness expressed his extreme regret at the circumstance which had transpired to debar his landing, but doubted not the loyalty of the parties.

With the greatest regret the loyal inhabitants of Kingston viewed the steamer's departure; and the city, that should have been all gaiety, was turned, in a few minutes' time, into woe and discontent.

This unfortunate event drew forth the following correspondence. The first letter is from the Duke of Newcastle, written on board the *Kingston*, prior to her departure for Belleville.

OFF KINGSTON, 5th Sept., 1860.

SIR,—It is with the utmost regret that I now find myself compelled to take the extreme course contemplated as possible in my letter to Sir E. Head, of the 30th August, which was immediately communicated to you by His Excellency, and to advise the Prince of Wales to proceed on his way without landing in the city of Kingston. When we arrived yesterday, we found an arch covered with Orange decorations, and an organized body of many hundreds, wearing all the insignia of their Order, with numerous flags; a band and every accompaniment which characterized such processions. I could hardly bring myself to believe, that, after seeing you and the other gentlemen who accompanied you on board the steamboat, and fully explaining to you the motives which actuated my advice to the Prince, the objections I took to those party displays on such an occasion, and the necessary consequences which must ensue if the Orangemen would be so misguided in their own conduct and act so offensively to the whole of their fellow-citizens, Protestant and Roman Catholics, as to persevere in their intention of preventing the Prince from accepting the hospitality of your city. I have been disappointed. The Prince consented to wait twenty-two hours to give the Orangemen time to reconsider their resolve. They have adhered to it; and it is my duty therefore to advise the Prince to pursue his journey. What is the sacrifice I asked the Orangemen to make? Merely to abstain from displaying, in the presence of a young Prince of 19 years of age, —the heir to a sceptre which rules over millions of every form of Christianity,—symbols of religious and political organization which are notoriously offensive to the members of another creed, and which, in one portion of the Empire, have repeatedly produced not only discord and heart-burning, but riot and bloodshed. I never doubted the loyalty of the individuals composing the Orange body. I based my appeal to them on the ground of that loyalty and of their good feeling. I did not ask them to sacrifice a principle, but to furl a flag and to abstain from an article of dress. I wished the Prince to see them, but not to give countenance to a Society which has been disapproved of in the Mother Country by the Sovereign and Legislature of Great Britain. I am told that they represent this act of mine as a slight to the Protestant religion. Until they can prove that the great mass of Englishmen are also not Protestant, it is quite unnecessary for me to repudiate so unfounded and absurd a charge. I am well aware that such party processions are not illegal in this country, as they are in England. This is a conclusive answer, if I asked you as Mayor to exercise your authority; but it is no answer to my remonstrance. I made it not as Secretary for the Colonies called upon to force a law; but as Minister of the Queen, attending the Prince of Wales by command of Her Majesty, in an official visit to this Colony, at the invitation of its Legislature; and I ask in what position would the Prince be placed by sanction, if he were now to pass through such a scene as was prepared for him (which happens not to be forbidden by the Colonial Legislature), and next year visit the North of Ireland, where he could not be a party to such an exhibition without violating the laws of his country? His Royal Highness will continue the route which has been prepared for him; but in any place where similar demonstrations are adhered to, a similar course to that pursued at Kingston will be taken. I cannot conclude this letter without an expression of regret that the Corporation did not accept the offer which I made them, through you, to present their Address on board the steamer; an offer readily accepted by the Moderator and Synod of the Presbyterian Church in connection with the Church of Scotland. It is impossible to believe that the members of the Corporation were influenced by sympathy with the conduct of the Orangemen, but I fear such a construction is too likely to be put upon their decision.

I am, Sir,
Your very obedient servant,
NEWCASTLE.

To the Worshipful Mayor of Kingston.

The Mayor made the following reply :—

THE CITY HALL,
Kingston, 11th Sept., 1860.

MAY IT PLEASE YOUR GRACE,—I have the honor to acknowledge the receipt of Your Grace's letter dated 5th instant, and have laid the same before the Council of the City of Kingston.

In reply, I am instructed by the Council to thank Your Grace for the exposition of your motives in the advice given by your Grace to H. R. H. the Prince of Wales, in pursuance of which the citizens of Kingston have been debarred from the pleasure of seeing him, presenting the Address of welcome to their city which they had prepared, and assuring His Royal Highness that the loyalty and devotion to the British Crown exhibited by the inhabitants of this district during times of internal disaffection and foreign aggression have not decreased, whilst the feelings of love and admiration entertained for Her Most Gracious Majesty by the people of England are fully shared by their fellow-subjects here.

The Council have carefully weighed the arguments used by your Grace to sustain the decision communicated on the 30th ult. to Sir Edmund Head, to the effect that His Royal Highness would be advised to abandon his visit to this city in case any Orange demonstration were persisted in, it being your duty to prevent the exposure of the Prince to supposed participation in a scene likely to lead to religious feud and breach of the peace ; and they respectfully call your Grace's attention to the fact, that the present state of the law affecting the Orange Society in Upper Canada is not the result of chance or neglect of the Legislature, as your Grace appears to suppose, but the designed intention of Parliament after several years' experience of a law of repression ; and that the Orange Society, so far from being contrary to law, was publicly recognized by His Excellency the present Governor General on the 12th of July, 1857, when they presented an Address and received an official reply ; that neither the Council nor any other constituted authority in Canada had the power to put your Grace's wishes in force, in opposition to the settled policy of the country, by endeavoring to prevent that body from wearing such dress or displaying such banners as they saw fit ; that the fear of religious feud and breach of the peace must have arisen from wrong information regarding the state of Upper Canada, and ought to have been set to rest by the official guarantee of the Mayor for the peace of the city ; that the general procession in which your Grace objected to the appearance of the Orangemen in regalia was, as you were informed at Brockville, entirely abrogated, and their subsequent appearance was therefore without any semblance of sanction from the civic authorities ; and the act of His Royal Highness entering the city would not, therefore, in the slightest degree have identified him with any particular party, political or religious. Nor could he be held to participate more in the Orange demonstration by the display before him of flags of the Order than he was compromised by viewing the purple robes and insignia of the Roman Catholic Bishops and others who attended him at Quebec—a demonstration in which His Royal Highness could not have participated in England. And the Council consider that your Grace's protest was sufficient to prevent any one from supposing that the Prince was giving his sauction to a display which you had clearly stated you desired would not take place. Had your Grace, on landing on this cohtinent, made known His Royal Highness's desire that no party-emblems should be used on the occasion of his visit, and that it was your intention to advise him to pass by any place where this was disregarded, the Council are convinced that the late complication would not have occurred, as it is believed the Orange Society would never have thought of acting counter to His Royal Highness's wish; but your Grace's own experience must satisfy you of the extreme difficulty of, at the last moment, reasoning with men who, looking upon their colors as the badge of their religion, had imbibed the idea, however erroneous it may have been, that your Grace's command (for, considering the penalty, it amounted to such) was intended as a slight to the Protestant community ; the restrictions now imposed being in such striking contrast to the attention and respect shown to the Roman Catholics in Lower Canada.

Had the Prince visited Kingston upon the invitation of the Orange Society, it would have been within your Grace's province to have affixed any condition you thought proper to the acceptance of the invitation. But this was not the case. The invitation was given in the name of the citizens, and unconditionally accepted; and the Council cannot but feel that the expectations of the people, after being raised by that formal acceptance, and by the Prince's promise to attend a ball to be given in his honor, have been arbitarily disappointed without good reason, moral, religious, or political, but simply to meet the unreasonable demands of a small section of the citizens.

Neither the anthorities nor the inhabitants were responsible for the acts of the Orangemen who visited Kingston on the 4th and 5th inst. ; and from the fact of so few of the large assemblage being residents of the city, the members of the Council could exercise little, if any, influence over them. And yet, because these parties choose to assert their rights as British subjects, and appear to greet their Prince in a peculiar costume, not contrary to law, your Grace has caused a disappointment of the most poignant kind to thousands of Her Majesty's most devoted subjects assembled here, after months of eager expectation, to testify their loyalty to the Throne, and to give His Royal Highness a warm and affectionate welcome.

The Council cannot admit of any analogy between His Royal Highness landing in a town in Canada where Orange emblems were exhibited, and being a party to a similar scene in the North of Ireland; and in proof need only refer to your Grace's letter, which states that, whilst in this country such a party display is legal, in Ireland it is the reverse. His Royal Highness could not, therefore, by any possibility, be made a party to an exhibition which, being illegal, could not occur. Nor can they see any similarity between the position of the Moderator of the Presbyterian Church, residing in Lower Canada, and with whom a special appointment to receive an Address (the reading of which by some accident had not been permitted in Montreal), and that of the citizens of Kingston, whose invitation, after being accepted, was now slighted, and their dearest hopes doomed to disappointment, because parties over whom they had no control thought proper to wear Orange ribbons and unfurl a flag bearing the likeness of a former King of England.

There appears, however, to be a great similarity between the course adopted by the Council of the Counties of Frontenac, Lennox, and Addington, and that of the City Council; and this is natural, as in both cases the Addresses welcoming his Royal Highness to Kingston would have been inappropriate, and might as well have been presented at St. James' as on the bosom of Lake Ontario.

The Council, without justifying the want of courtesy exhibited by the Orangemen, firmly believe that they were actuated by an earnest desire to do the Prince honor; and that the disappointment is all the keener to them because their efforts have been misunderstood, and the display of the emblems which they conceive to be typical of their loyalty to the Throne and their attachment to the Protestant faith, made a reproach to them.

In conclusion, the Council desire to express their deep regret at the recent occurrences; and refer to the strenuous efforts made by them, during the whole period of the late difficulty, to induce the Orangemen to waive their rights and lay aside their regalia, so as to remove the difficulty which your Grace's decision has raised to His Royal Highness landing, as the best proof that they were not actuated by sympathy for the Orangemen in declining to present the Address on board the steamer, but by a due sense of the important trust committed to them by their fellow-citizens, and a determination that they would not, by any act of theirs, assume the responsibility or appear to sanction the soundness of the advice tendered by your Grace to His Royal Highness—advice which the Council believe would not have been given had your Grace consulted the Government of the country, who, from their intimate knowledge of the state of feelings and circumstances, as well as the laws of the Province, would have probably been able to satisfy your Grace of the injustice and impolicy of the course which has been adopted.

I have the honor to be your Grace's
Most humble and obedient servant,
O. S. STRANGE, *Mayor.*

To His Grace the Duke of Newcastle, &c., &c.

The Duke was in London, C.W., when he received this, and wrote the following in reply :—

LONDON, C.W., 13th September, 1860.

SIR,—I have the honour to acknowledge your letter of the 11th inst., which reached me this afternoon.

It would be easy to refute the arguments and contradict the statements advanced by you on behalf of the Council of the City of Kingston, but I have neither time nor inclination for the task. I have only therefore to express my hope that it is your intention to publish your letter without delay.

If you do not, I shall feel it my duty to do so, in order that it may receive an answer from the good sense of the Canadian people.

I am, Sir, your very obedient servant,

NEWCASTLE.

The Worshipful the Mayor of Kingston.

The following was the resolution of the City Council upon this last letter :—

Resolved,—That in consequence of the letter from the Duke of Newcastle, now read, calling in question, as it does by implication, the truth of the statements contained in the letter addressed to His Grace by the Mayor, under date of 11th inst., the Council are compelled, in justice to themselves, to reiterate the facts and arguments therein set forth ; the former being known to be true, and the latter believed to be unassailable.

Carried by a majority of 13.

The *Kingston* arrived at Belleville at nine o'clock that evening. The bells of the churches rang out gaily, and the greatest joy was manifested by the inhabitants. Great care had been bestowed on the ornamentation of the town, and on the intended reception. The arrangements perfected were extremely good.

Nine arches had been erected. The ladies of the town, with commendable zeal, had been, for a long time, working to give the place a fine appearance. The town was filled with farmers from miles around, together with their whole families; with strangers, and others. Everything in fact promised to come off well; but, by some very unaccountable means, everything went off in the opposite direction.

The Orangemen who reside in, and near here, in great numbers, had erected two arches, but no party emblems were displayed on them. The Orangemen themselves consented not to walk ; but next morning (6th) outside influence began to work. Flags of a partizan nature were hung from them, and the Orangemen mustered in full numbers; in full regalia, with their bands of music, paraded the street, determined to receive the Prince. When this state of things became known to H. R. H., no alternative was left him but to remain on board, and proceed to Cobourg, which he accordingly did at half-past nine o'clock. It was perfectly touching to witness the sorrowful countenances of the good portion of the people of the town of Belleville; all their exertions, all their toil, destroyed in an hour, by the mere caprice of strangers. But at the town of Cobourg he received a welcome which he will not easily forget.

No partizan displays were warranted or tolerated there; everybody worked with a will and love that will ever be commendable.

The *Kingston* appeared off the town near nine o'clock at night. the beach was crowded to give the Prince a regular demonstrative welcome; and when, therefore, the steamer came up to the wharf, ay, and long before, the enthusiasm displayed was intense.

The whole city was brilliantly illuminated, and presented one of the finest effects ever witnessed. Rockets were set off, a royal salute fired, and a Guard of Honour of the Volunteer Rifles presented arms as His Royal Highness landed. His carriage was drawn by a newly-organized Society composed of the gentlemen of Cobourg, called "Native Canadians," with silver maple-leaves on their breasts, who carried lighted torches, and were escorted by the National Societies, the Volunteer Cavalry and Rifles, and by the people generally, who cheered and hurrahed until they were hoarse. The Prince and his suite were taken through the lighted streets to the Town Hall, a fine new building, which was gorgeously illuminated. Here H. R. H. received the several Addresses from the Mayor, Victoria College, the Magistrates, Brighton Council, &c., &c., and gave his replies; and immediately after, entered the building, and opened a ball at eleven o'clock, dancing until broad daylight. The following are the names of the fortunate ladies he danced with, fifteen in all :—

Miss Beaty (daughter of the Mayor), Miss Ewart, Mrs. Reid, Miss Fortune (Sheriff's daughter), Miss Pringle, Hon. Mrs. Sidney Smith, Miss Dainty, Miss Powell (Niagara), Miss Burnham, Miss Bennet, Mrs. Cubitt, Miss Hall, Miss M. Boswell, Miss Gaver, Miss Barron.

After the ball, H. R. H. and suite, with the Governor General and the other gentlemen, retired to the mansion of the Hon. Sidney Smith (Postmaster General); and, after a slight repose, left Cobourg on the morning of the 7th, by railway for Peterboro, amidst the most hearty demonstrations of loyalty and joy.

The train arrived at Rice Lake in due time. And here the royal party took the steamer *Otonabee*, named after the river of that name. The lake is called Rice on account of the great quantities of wild rice that grow in it.

After crossing the lake in saftey, the royal party again took the cars.

The scenery in and around this lake, abounds with singular beauty : the many small islands that dot its surface give it a very enchanting aspect.

On one side of the lake, the Mississaga tribe of Indians (one of the first that held Upper Canada) had erected an arch, which for them was not so bad, as some fastidious mortals would make us believe that it was perfectly wretched; but it was not so. They fired a royal salute; and had a brass band, which, we confess, could not come " God save the Queen ";—at any rate, they made an attempt.

The train stopped at this place, and the whole tribe advanced to welcome the son of their " Great Mother."

An Address was presented by the Chief,—who, by the by, is 100 years of age. A number of Indian curiosities were presented to His Royal Highness, who took his departure under another royal salute and National Anthem.

At Peterboro, the same enthusiasm was shewn as at Cobourg. Thousands upon thousands were present to give His Royal Highness a right loyal welcome.

The place was nicely decorated. Fine arches had been erected, and highly adorned. Under all these the royal party were escorted in carriages to the Court House; where the Corporation Address, &c., were presented, and replied to. A short interval elapsed, when His Royal Highness took his departure, under showers of bouquets and the deafening cheers of the populace.

We note not a very agreeable incident which here took place: a man, with an enormous amount of *brass*, stretched out his brawny arm to shake hands with His Royal Highness, who graciously complied. Many others followed his example; and at last the Prince had to turn to the other side.

At Port Hope, the next landing-place, quite as much enthusiasm was manifested. The people of this usually quiet little city were as enthusiastically excited as the inhabitants of the other cities. They had worked, and worked well, to have a fitting display; and the consequence was that several fine arches spanned the principal streets; the houses being as handsomely adorned as at the cities heretofore visited.

A well-organized procession escorted His Royal Highness, his suite, &c., through the principal street to the Town Hall; where the Mayor (James Scott, Esq.) presented the Corporation Address, amidst the greatest cheering from the immense concourse of people assembled. The Prince, after replying, entered the Town Hall, and, with his suite, partook of luncheon. After the Mayor had proposed the toast of the Queen and Royal Family, His Royal Highness left for Whitby; where the train arrived somewhat late in the afternoon.

The people here exhibited as many marks of loyalty and attachment to the Crown as at any of the places where the Prince had been. Their cheers were most hearty and uninterrupted, and their demonstrations were also very fine; a continuous salute being kept up while His Royal Highness was in the town, and until the *Kingston*, on which he embarked for Toronto, was long out of sight.

An Address was presented and replied to, and the whole population escorted His Royal Highness to the boat.

But perhaps one of the finest receptions the Prince ever received, was from the true and loyal inhabitants of the city of Toronto, the capital of Upper Canada.

Here, where the greatest number of Orangemen reside, and where the greatest gathering from all parts of the country was about to take place; on being told that such a a display was against the Prince's wish, they very good-naturedly laid down the insignia of their order, and appeared in the procession and manifested their joy as private citizens; and by this act, they shewed their good sense, by complying with the wish of their future king.

But they had erected an arch on King Street, the principal thoroughfare of Toronto and the finest in Canada, and through which the procession escorting the Prince was to pass. This arch was intended to be decorated with all the Orange paraphernalia; but, on becoming aware of what had taken place at Kingston and Belleville, they wisely consented to abstain from making the arch a party one, but they allowed a statue of King William III. to be on its summit, as also pictures of the Queen and the Prince Consort; a Bible and a Crown, with several mottoes, but totally of an unpartizan character. The Mayor (A. Wilson, Esq., M. P. P.) had been written to by the Duke of Newcastle to ascertain if the arch was to be decorated with party colours; and that functionary, putting the state on a footing with the people, took some Roman Catholic gentlemen before it and asked them if *they* had any objections to the statue. Of course, it being the representation of a king of England, *they* could not have any objections; so Mr. Mayor telegraphed His Grace that there would be no partizan display on the arch or in the city, and the *Kingston* steamed up Lake Ontario for the "Queen City of the West."

Never had people made greater exertions than the people of Toronto in honour of the Prince's visit, to give their fair and fine city a better appearance than it possesses, and in this they were completely successful. Magnificent arches arose as if by magic; every house was well decorated, and displayed either flags or something better, according as circumstances permitted; and everything presented as fine, and perhaps finer, appearance than did any other place yet visited by the Prince.

On the esplanade, a magnificent large amphitheatre with seats had been built, capable of accommodating thousands of persons, and which was filled to its utmost capacity with well-dressed ladies and gentlemen. Near this, a fine dais had been erected, well carpeted, and very nicely decorated with flags, banners, &c. On this dais was an Address from the city to be presented, by the Mayor and Corporation. For many hours before the appointed time, thousands congregated here; but it was nearly dusk before the *Kingston* was sighted coming up the Lake, escorted by the magnificent lake-steamers *Peerless, New York, Cataract,* and *Zimmerman,* and the small steamer *Fire Fly*; and on her being perceived, three guns were fired by the York Field Battery, as a signal to make all ready.

The cheering on the *Kingston* nearing the wharf, and while the Prince landed, knew no bounds. The assembled thousands congregated everywhere, raising their voices in honour of the son of our beloved Queen. The people in the amphitheatre rose *en masse;* and such waving of handkerchiefs, clapping of hands, and presenting bouquets to H. R. H., was seldom, if ever, seen before or since.

One thing is certain, joy was more open and intense at Toronto than at any other city, town, or village visited.

His Royal Highness was received by the Members of the Cabinet and the Mayor and Corporation, the Bishops and Clergy, the Judges, the Members of the University, and the boys of U. C. College, the chief Militia and Regular officers of Toronto, the St. George's, St. Andrew's, and St. Patrick's Societies, in full regalia, the British Canadians, the Temperance Organization, and Bands of Hope, the Coloured Society, and several other guilds.

H. R. H. was then conducted to the dais, the Guard of Honour of the Toronto Militia presenting arms, the bands playing the National Anthem, and a royal salute being fired by the Field Battery; and here, surrounded by his suite and the other gentlemen, the following Address was presented by the Mayor:—

MAY IT PLEASE YOUR ROYAL HIGHNESS,—

We, the Mayor, Aldermen, and Councilmen, on behalf of the citizens of Toronto, respectfully offer to your Royal Highness a most cordial welcome on your arrival in the capital of Upper Canada, and gratefully express our high appreciation of the distinguished honor which you have conferred upon us by your visit.

The annals of our youthful city present but little more than the record of improvement steadily advancing in almost unbroken tranquillity; and the brief interruptions of its peaceful progress are now worthy of notice, as evincing an early attachment to British connection, so strong as to stand the severe test of fire and sword, and so illustrating the happy influences of commercial and social intercourse in uniting the combatants of bygone feuds as good neighbours and valued friends.

The generations which saw the settler's log-house succeeding to the red-man's wigwam on the site of Little York, has not yet wholly passed away, and yet we venture to hope that your Royal Highness will look with satisfaction on the evidences which our city presents—in our streets, our railways, our private buildings, and our public institutions

—of the successful results of industry and enterprise, fostered by constitutional liberty; and that you will regard our provision for the relief of misery, for the diffusion of education, for the administration of justice, and for the worship of God, as manifestations of that spirit which has been mainly instrumental, under Providence, in placing our mother country in the glorious position which she occupies amongst the nations of the earth.

We desire again most respectfully to offer our grateful thanks for the honor which your Royal Highness has been pleased to confer upon us; and gladly avail ourselves of the opportunity to renew the assurance of our devoted loyalty to the Queen, under whose benignant rule we enjoy the estimable blessings of civil and religious liberty, and to express our undoubting confidence that our rights as freemen and our interests as subjects will continue to be faithfully maintained by Her Majesty's hereditary successor, whom we now rejoice to honor as our future Sovereign.

The Mayor then handed the Address to His Royal Highness, who replied as follows :—

GENTLEMEN,—I receive this Address with the most lively satisfaction; and I request you to convey to the citizens, whom you represent, the expression of my gratitude for the more than hearty welcome which I have just experienced.

You will not doubt the readiness with which I undertook the duty entrusted to me by the Queen of visiting, for her, the British North American dominions; and now that I have arrived at this distant point of my journey, I can say with truth, that the expectations which I had formed of the pleasure and instruction to be derived from it, have been more than realized. My only regret is, that the Queen has been unable, herself, to receive the manifestations of the generous loyalty with which you have met her representative—a loyalty tempered and yet strengthened by the intelligent independence of the Canadian character.

You allude to the marvellous progress which a generation has witnessed on this spot. I have already been struck throughout my rapid journey by the promise of greatness, and the results of energy and industry which are everywhere perceptible, and I feel the pride of an Englishman in the masculine qualities of my countrymen—in the sanguine and hardy enterprise—in the fertility of conception and boldness of execution which have enabled a youthful country to outstrip many of the ancient nations of the world.

The school children, to the number of 5,000, under the superintendence of Mr. Carter (the Cathedral Organist), sang "God Save the Queen," the multitude uncovering.

The following verses were added for the occasion :—

>Victoria's son and heir!
>No title canst thou bear
> More proud, more dear.
>Thou, o'er the mighty sea,
>Hast come, our guest to be :
>Warmly we welcome thee ;
> Thrice welcome here!
>
>God bless our matron Queen!
>Her sons of manly mien,
> And daughters fair.
>May Heaven's perpetual grace
>Rest on her rising race ;
>May they her footsteps trace,
> Her virtues share!
>
>Hail! Britain's hope and ours!
>Though here no regal towers
> Receive thy train,
>Strong arms shall thee surround,
>And loyal hearts shall bound,
>And every voice resound
> Our joyful strain.

The royal party were then conducted to carriages, and, escorted by the procession, drove through the streets to Government House, or what was formerly the residence of the Governor General. The whole line of the procession was one perfect ovation; the Torontonians nobly sustaining their good name.

The procession was as follows :—

MARSHAL OF FIRST DIVISION.
F. ROBINSON, ESQ.

York Volunteer Cavalry.
The Loyal United Colored Society.
The Canadian Order of Odd Fellows.
The Fire Brigade.
The Native Canadians.
St. George's Society.
St. Patrick's Society.
St. Andrew's Society.

161

MARSHAL OF SECOND DIVISION.
P. COSSAGE, ESQ.

The Toronto Grammar School.
The Officers and Members of Boards of School Trustees.
The Normal and Model Grammar Schools.
The Officers of Educational Department and Council of Public Instruction.
Upper Canada College.
The University of Trinity College.
The University of Toronto, and University College, with other Affiliated Colleges and Institutions.
The President and Members of the Board of Trade.
The Chairman of the Medical Board and Members of the Profession.
The Treasurer of the Law Society and Members of the Profession.
Officers of the Army, Navy, and Militia, on Foot.

MARSHAL OF THIRD DIVISION.
H. J. BOULTON, JR., ESQ.

The Yorkville Municipal Council.
The Chief Constable.
The Magistrates of the United Counties.
The Treasurer, Clerk of the Peace, and the County Officers.
The County Council.
The High Sheriff, Warden, and County Crown Attorney.
The Judges of United Counties.

MARSHAL OF FOURTH DIVISION.
ROBT. BEARD, ESQ.

Members of Reception Committee.
The Junior Officers of Corporation.
The Chief of Police and High Bailiff.
The City Clerk and Chamberlain.
The Aldermen and Councillors.
The Recorder and Police Magistrate.
THE MAYOR.
The Members of the House of Assembly.
The Members of Legislative Council.
The Members of Executive Council.
His Excellency the Commander-in-Chief and Staff.
Their Excellencies the Lieut. Governors and their Suites.
His Excellency the Governor General and Suite.

L

THE PRINCE.

His Grace the Duke of Newcastle, the Earl St. Germains.
Major Gen. the Hon. Robert Bruce and the other Members of His Royal Highness's Suite.
Mounted Officers of the Army and Militia.
York Volunteer Cavalry.
Police.
CHIEF MARSHAL.
R. L. DENISON, ESQ.

In the evening, a grand illumination of the town took place, which, although not quite up to Montreal, was pretty good; but the joy occasioned by the visit was somewhat dimmed by the unforeseen difficulties that arose out of that unfortunate Orange arch, and which were ultimately overcome.

The Duke of Newcastle perceiving the statue of William III. on the arch, and taking it for a party design, naturally thought that he had been wilfully deceived by the authorities of the place, and naturally looked to His Worship the Mayor for an explanation.

Next day (8th), the following correspondence took place. Happily the difficulties were overcome, and the Corporation presented on a subsequent occasion :—

The Duke of Newcastle to the Mayor.

GOVERNMENT HOUSE,
Toronto, Sept. 8, 1860.

SIR,—I deeply regret that you have not thought fit to send any explanation of the occurrence of which I made complaint to you last evening. I would not willingly revert to any cause of offence, after the most magnificent and warm-hearted reception which the Prince of Wales met in the city yesterday, but there are matters which cannot be overlooked without the loss of honor and position.

You distinctly informed me that the transparency of William III. was removed, and one of the Prince of Wales substituted. I relied upon your word, and the consequence was that the Prince was thereby led into doing what I had distinctly informed you he would not do.

As the levee is announced to be held at this house, no alteration will be made; but I hope you will see the propriety of not attending it so long as your part in this matter is unexplained and no reparation offered.

. I am sir, your very obedient servant,
NEWCASTLE.

To the Worshipful the Mayor of Toronto.

P. S.—I re-open my letter to say that yours has been this moment (11 o'clock) received. I trust that the result of the meeting may be satisfactory, but I am sure that you will feel that the reparation must precede any further communication.

The letter alluded to in the above Postscript.

MAYOR'S OFFICE,
Toronto, Sept. 8, 1860.

MY LORD DUKE,—In consequence of the very painful interview your Grace did me the honor of holding with me last evening respecting the portrait of King William III. which has been placed over the arch erected by the Orangemen of this city, and which was to have been dispensed with, and one of his Royal Highness the Prince of Wales adopted for it; and respecting also the communication specifying the proposed change which I had the honor of addressing to his Excellency the Governor General a few days since, and which was permitted to remain uncontradicted, either by the latter communication to his Excellency or by any personal statement, I have convened the Council for this morning at 9½, when I trust to be enabled to make an explanation and an apology to your Grace and to His Excellency which I hope may be accepted as satisfactory. I should have had this meeting last night, but I could find neither clerk nor messengers, and I was told I should have had greater difficulty in finding the members.

I have the honor to be, my Lord Duke, your Grace's most obedient and humble servant.

ADAM WILSON, *Mayor.*

The Mayor's reply to the Duke's Letter.

MAYOR'S OFFICE,
Toronto, Sept. 8, 1860.

MY LORD DUKE,—Adverting to the interview which Your Grace did me the honor of holding with me last evening, on the subject of the transparency of King William III. on the Orangemen's arch in this city, and the letter which I had the honor of addressing to his Excellency the Governor General, stating that such a decoration was not to have been placed there, I am now desirous of acknowledging to Your Grace that I ought most undoubtedly to have stated the change which was subsequently proposed to be made, and which was afterward in fact made; and although the Roman Catholics were quite willing to acquiesce, and did acquiesce in the alteration, it was, nevertheless, only due to your Grace and to His Excellency that such a deviation from the understood arrangement should have been promptly transmitted. And looking back to what I have done from the present view of matters, it may appear that it was presumptuous on my part to judge whether your Grace or

His Excellency would or would not have esteemed this deviation as of that consequence which it has now assumed.

There has been much difficulty in arranging satisfactorily the late threatening and serious state of affairs here, and I trust I have not been wanting in my efforts to bring about this pleasing result. It is painful to me, therefore, to feel, that I have, even unintentionally, failed in discharging my duty in this particular. But it is infinitely more painful to me to think that your Grace should think that I have omitted to communicate this information from any unworthy motive, or for the purpose of compromising His Royal Highness the Prince of Wales, your Grace, or His Excellency the Governor General, or even for the sake of complaisance towards any portion of my fellow-citizens. I can safely appeal to any one who knows me, and who, I am sure, will satisfy your Grace, that I would not, unless I were to depart from the whole tenor of my life, act in the manner to which your Grace alluded to last evening; but I admit again, that much does appear in what has occurred to have induced your Grace to form the strong opinion which your Grace gave expression to on the occasion in question. I have now only to implore your Grace that whatever omission or offence I may be chargeable with, it may not be visited in any manner upon this loyal city, for as toward your Grace and his Excellency I am alone to blame.

I have the honor to be, my Lord Duke, your Grace's most obedient, humble servant,

ADAM WILSON, *Mayor*.

To his Grace the Duke of Newcastle, Secretary for the Colonies, &c.

The Duke's letter accepting the Apology.

GOVERNMENT HOUSE,
Toronto, 8th Sept. 1860.

SIR,—I am so sincerely anxious that all the painful events of the last few days should be at once and forever buried in oblivion, and nothing remembered but the heart-stirring scenes which last night proclaimed to the world the unanimous and enthusiastic loyalty of the city of Toronto, that it is a relief to feel that I can, without any sacrifice of duty to the Prince of Wales, accept the apology which is offered by your last letter just received. In this spirit I will not continue a discussion which must have been so painful to you, and has certainly been no less to me. But I must point out to you that it was your letter which really gave an obnoxious character to the transparency of William III. Nobody can object to a representation, in itself, of one of the most illustrious of our Kings; but when you informed me that the transparency was to be removed by the Orangemen as an acknowledged party symbol, it at once assumed the objectionable feature of the display which I advised the Prince not to countenance, and its restoration made it impossible for the Prince to pass under the arch without violating the terms of my letter to the Governor General. I can only hope from this moment that all differences may as completely vanish from the minds of others as they will from that of, Sir, your very obedient servant,

NEWCASTLE.

To the Worshipful the Mayor of Toronto.

On Saturday (8th) His Royal Highness held a levee at Government House, when about 1,000 gentlemen were presented; but the Mayor and Corporation were excepted.

Addresses were also presented from the Upper Canada Bible Society, by its President, Hon. G. W. Allan; from the Synod of the Church of England, by His Lordship the Bishop; from the Trinity College University, by the Chancellor, &c.; from the Synod of the Presbyterian Church, by the Ministers and Elders; from the St. George's Society, by S. B. Harman, Esq.; from the Temperance Organization, by Hon. R. Spence; from the County Council, by D. Ressor, Esq.; from Knox's College, by Dr. Willis. All these were replied to by His Royal Highness.

The weather being very disagreeable, His Royal Highness, accompanied by the Governor General, only visited the Racket Court, and played a game with His Excellency. An immense crowd was gathered outside, who, when His Royal Highness left, cheered him lustily.

In the afternoon, His Royal Highness and suite attended the evening reception given by the Benchers of the Law Society of Upper Canada, at Osgoode Hall (The Court of Law).

On His Royal Highness stepping from his carriage, he was met at the entrance of the Hall by Hon. J. Hillyard Cameron, Treasurer of the Law Society; who welcomed him, and escorted him to the Centre Hall; the band of the Royal Canadian Rifles and a band from Buffalo (U. S.), playing " God save the Queen."

Here on a dais, His Royal Highness received the following Address from the Law Society, which was presented by Mr. Cameron, surrounded by members of the Bar of Upper Canada:—

MAY IT PLEASE YOUR ROYAL HIGHNESS,—

We, Her Majesty's faithful and loyal subjects the Law Society of Upper Canada, beg leave to offer to Your Royal Highness our warmest congratulations upon your safe arrival in the capital of Upper Canada, and our most earnest gratitude for the kindness you have manifested in permitting us to welcome you at Osgoode Hall.

This Hall, now dignified by the presence of Your Royal Highness, contains within its precincts the new Superior Courts of Law and Equity, which have been lately opened in Her Majesty's name; and it is with pride and gratitude that we acknowledge the condescension of Her Most Gracious Majesty's goodness in affording to Your Royal Highness the opportunity of inaugurating the event in the name and on behalf of Her Majesty.

In this new country, our Society, with but little more than half a century of existence, cannot exhibit to Your Royal Highness those many memorials of eminent servants of the Crown, who have passed away, which adorn the Halls of the Inns of Court at home; but we offer (in their stead) to Your Royal Highness, in the dignity and purity of our Bench, in the just and impartial administration of the laws, and the respect of the people for constituted authority, a living testimony of the exertions which have been made among us for promoting sound legal education, and aiding in giving stability to the system of Jurisprudence which we have adopted from the Mother Country.

We humbly entreat Your Royal Highness to convey to your Royal Mother, our most August Sovereign, our expressions of attachment and devotion for her person and government; and we pray that the Lord may grant to Your Royal Highness a long and happy life, and that in years to come the remembrance of your visit, in your early manhood, to these Provinces, may be as pleasant to your memory, as the recollection of it will be enduring in the minds of the Canadian people.

His Royal Highness replied as follows:—

GENTLEMEN,—I have accepted your invitation to this Hall with very great pleasure, and must thank you warmly for the Address just presented to me.

The purity of the Bench and the independence of the Bar are the proud characteristics of the legal profession in England; and I rejoice to think that this Province equally with the mother country enjoys these great securities for liberty and order.

I hope that this Hall may in future generations continue to have enrolled in its list of members, men as illustrious as those whose names are loved and venerated in the United Provinces.

The Prince was then escorted to the Society's magnificent Library; and here, on being requested, and amidst great cheering, became an honorary Member of the Society, as did also the Duke of Newcastle and Earl St. Germains.

The Hall was crowded with fashionably-dressed ladies and gentlemen, together with most of the Officers of the City in uniform. These did not fail, and especially the ladies, to show their high appreciation of the honor conferred on Toronto by the visit of His Royal Highness.

Dancing now commenced; the Prince opening the reception by dancing with the Hon. Mrs. J. H. Cameron, and afterwards with the following ladies: Miss Boulton, Miss MacNab (daughter of Sir Allan), Miss Widder, Miss Robinson, Miss McCaul, Miss Draper, and Miss Powell (of Niagara).

After partaking of supper at half-past eleven o'clock, the Prince danced until twelve. It then being Sunday morning, the party broke up, and the Prince and suite retired, the band playing the National Anthem.

On Sunday morning, His Royal Highness and suite, accompanied by the Governor General, his aides, and the Commander of the Forces, attended Divine Service at St. James's Cathedral.

He was met at the entrance by the church-wardens, Bishop and Clergy, who escorted him to the Governor General's pew; the organ pealing forth the Coronation Anthem.

The service was as follows:—

Revd. Mr. Grasett, Rector, read the Prayers; Revd. Mr. Geddes of Hamilton, the Lessons; The Ven. Archdeacon Bethune, Revd. Mr. Baldwin, and Rev. Mr. Boddy, assisted at the Communion Service.

His Lordship Bishop Strachan delivered the following—

SERMON.

Psalm LXXII. 1st verse, " Give the king thy judgments, O God, and thy righteousnes to the king's son."

In this prophetical prayer, the aged Monarch of Israel, about to resign the kingdom into the hands of his son Solomon, makes to God for him the request of a wise and affectionate father. He asks such a portion of wisdom and integrity from above as might enable the young Prince to govern aright the people of God, and to exhibit to the world a fair resemblance of that king of Israel, who was in the fullness of time to sit upon the throne of his father David—to reign in righteousness, and to have all judgment committed unto him. This tender and affectionate prayer was afterwards more fully shadowed forth at Gibeon, where the Lord appeared to Solomon in a dream, and said "Ask what I shall give thee;" and Solomon said, " O Lord my God, thou hast made thy servant King instead of David my father, and I am but a little child. I know not how to go out or come in. Give therefore thy servant an understanding heart to judge thy people, that I may discern between good and bad, for who is able to judge this thy so great people!" and it pleased the Lord that Solomon had asked this thing. Such was the wise and manly answer made by a youth about twenty years of age. Now reflecting on what almost all youths in his circumstances, with strong passions, a love of magnificence, and in possession of the proudest throne in Asia, would ask, we cannot but strongly admire Solomon's modesty and wisdom, and that diffidence in himself which turned him in confidence to God. Thus guided by heavenly principles, which can alone triumph in conflicts which monarchs have to undergo as well as others, he took upon himself the royal power as God's vice-gerent upon earth, and as his appointed instrument of blessedness to his people. He was the predecessor of one far greater than himself, and prefigured him who was to gather all the earth under his dominion. He was, as it were, riding in a glorious procession which his orderly conduct would bring happily towards its end; and although great, he was only the harbinger in that mighty procession, and wore the livery of that heavenly Sovereign who, as in triumph, closed up the rear. The principles which Solomon had chosen are like the soul of man, which cannot be affected by the elements of this world, but are able to defy their most violent assaults, and are like the wind which throws down palaces, but is itself unassailable; while, on the other hand, worldly principles, like the body of man, yield before the assaults of kindred elements, and break up, and waste away by being exposed to stronger and more corrupt principles of the same world. Solomon proved himself by his choice to be filled with that spirit which became him, who had been anointed by God—Prophet and Priest. And the inward grace bestowed in that outward unction had been put to such good use that it carried more grace, and the wisdom shown in this petition obtained the gift of more wisdom. God gave him a wise and understanding heart, so that there was none like him, before him, neither after him should any arise like unto him—God also proved in him the rule which his blessed son, Jesus Christ, afterwards laid down when he commands us to seek first the kingdom of heaven and its righteousness, and then all earthly blessings shall be added to it. Because Solomon had asked this heavenly gift only, and mentioned none that were earthly, God gave him the earthly also,— "I have also given thee that which thou hast not asked, both riches and honor, so that there shall not be any among the kings like unto thee all thy days. And if thou wilt walk in my ways, keep my statutes and my commandments, as thy father did walk, then I will lengthen thy days." From the Tabernacle, at Gibeon, Solomon returned to Jerusalem to offer sacrifice before the Ark of the Covenant of the Lord. Thus he consecrated the first days of his reign, and commenced his course under the most happy auspices. He made God the beginning, happy if he had made him also the end, of all his doings. It is not, however, my desire, on the present auspicious occasion, to touch upon the last and melancholy years of King Solomon's life, but rather to connect the few observations I shall offer at this time with the youthful and more early portion of his reign—while his heart was yet pure and the Lord preserved him. I would observe, in the first place, that there is not, perhaps, in the history of mankind a more beautiful picture than that which is here represented. A young man in the bloom of life, when everything was gay and alluring around him—in the moment of ascending to a brilliant throne, where pleasure and ambition were before him—betaking himself thus humbly to God, and imploring of him that wisdom which might enable him to resist the temptations with which his situation surrounded him, and to fulfil the duties to which he was called. Had it been in the latter periods of his reign, when, satiated with pleasure and disappointed in ambition, when fatigued with the cares and pageantry of a throne, he looked abroad for better comforts;—had it been at such a time, when Solomon directed his soul to heaven, much of the merit of his piety would have been lost. It would then have appeared only as the last refuge of a discontented mind, which interest, not disposition, had led to devotion; and which only sought for repose in piety, because it had been disappointed in everything else. But at such a season to be guided by such sentiments, in such an hour to betake himself to God, bespeaks a mind so humble and yet pure, a disposition so ardently and yet so rightly inclined, a soul so well fitted for every kind of excellence, that no language of praise seems too strong. It is not, however, from the peculiar situation of Solomon, that the beauty of this memorable instance of devotion arises. Its charm chiefly consists in its suitableness to the season of youth, in its correspondence to the character and dispositions which distinguish that important age, which we eagerly desire to see in the young. Piety or the fear of God in youth has in it something singularly graceful and becoming—something which ever disposes us to think well of the mind in which it is found, and which, better than all other attainments of life, appears to promise honor and happiness in future days. It is suited to the opening of human life, to that interesting season when nature in all its beauty first opens on the view. It is suited still more to the tenderness of young affections—to that warm and generous temper, which meets everywhere the objects of gratitude and love. But, most of all, it is suited to the innocence of the youthful mind —to that sacred and sinless purity, which can lift up its unpolluted hands to heaven; which guilt hath not yet torn from confidence and hope in God, and which can look beyond this world to that society of kindred spirits, " of whom is the kingdom of heaven." The progress of life may indeed bring other acquisitions; it may strengthen religion by experience, and add knowledge to faith. But the piety which springs only from the heart—the devotion which nature and not reasoning inspires—the pure homage which flows unbidden from the tongue, and which asks no other motive for its payment than the pleasures which it bestows, these are the possessions of youth and of youth alone. I would, in the second place, remark, that the feelings of piety are not only natural and becoming in youth, but they are still more valuable as tending to the formation of future character. They spring up in the first and purest state of the human mind. When the soul comes fresh from the hands of its Creator, and no habits of life have contracted the reach of its powers, they come in that happy season when life is new and hope unbroken, where nature seems everywhere to reign, to rejoice around, and where the love of God rises unbidden on the soul. They come not to terrify or to alarm, but to present every high and pleasing prospect in which the heart can indulge. They come to withdraw the veil which covers the splendors of the Eternal mind, and to open that futurity which awakens all their desires to behold and attain, and in the sublime occupations of which they feel already, as by some secret inspiration, the home and destiny of their souls. At such a period religion is full of joy. It is not an occasional, but a permanent subject of elevating their meditations—a subject which can fill their solitary hours with rapture, and which involuntarily occurs to them in every season when their hearts are disposed to feel, and to which they willingly return from all the disappointments or follies of life, and resume again their unfinished joys. If there be a moment of human life in which the foundation of a virtuous character can be laid, it is at this period. If there can be a discipline which can call forth every noble faculty of the soul, it is such early exercises of piety. They not only suggest but establish a tone and character of thought which is allied to every virtuous purpose; they present those views of man and of the ends of his being, which awaken the best powers of the soul; and they afford prospects of the providence of God, which can best give support and confidence to virtue. But again, there is no man perhaps, who, in some fortunate moments of thought, has not felt his soul raised above its usual state by religious considerations. There are hours in every man's life when religion seems to approach him in all her loveliness, when its truths break upon his soul with a force which cannot be resisted, and when in the contemplation of them he feels his bosom swell with emotions of unusual delight. In such moments every man feels that the dignity and purity of his whole being is increased. The illusions and temptations of the world appear beneath his regard, his heart opens to nobler and purer affections, and his bosom regains for a while its native innocence. In the greater part of mankind, however, these moments are transient; life calls them back again to their usual concerns, and they sometimes relapse into all the folly and weakness of ordinary mortals. Now it is the tendency of early piety to fix this character of thought, and endeavour to render that temper of mind permanent, which in many is only temporary and transient. By the great object to which it directs the minds of the young, by its precedence to every other system of opinions which might oppose its influences by its power to arrest and return their attention, it tends gradually to establish in the soul a correspondent dignity in every other exercise. While yet the world is unknown and the calm morning of life is undisturbed, it awakens desires of a nobler kind than the usual purposes of life can gratify, and forms in secret those habits of elevated thought which are of all others the most valuable acquisitions of youthful years, and fit it for future attainments in truth and virtue beyond the reach of ordinary men. Once more: another fruit of early piety is that it presents those views of man and of the end of his being which will call forth the best powers of our nature. We readily accommodate our acquisitions to the opinions we entertain of the scene in which they are to be employed, and take expectations which are formed in respect to us. It is hence that the different situations of human life produce so great diversities of character and improvement. The poor man whose life is to pass in obscurity and on whose humble fortunes the regard and observations of the world are never likely to fall, is seldom solicitous to distinguish himself by any other acquisition than those which are suited to the humility of his station, and which the exigencies of his station demand of him. The great and the opulent, on the contrary, who are born to be the objects of observation and attention feel themselves called upon to suit their ambition to the opinions of mankind; and, if they have the common spirit of men, usually accommodate themselves to these expectations. It is in this manner that early piety has an influence in forming the future character. It represents man as formed in the image of God, "as but a little lower than the angels," and as crowned with glory and honor. It represents life, not as the short and fleeting space of temporary being, but as the preparation only for immortal existence; as a theatre on which he is called on to act in the sight of his Saviour and his God, and of which the rewards exceed even the powers of his imagination to conceive. It represents all this in the season when no lower passions have taken the dominion of his heart, and when his powers are all susceptible of being moulded by the ends which are placed before him. In such views of man, all the best qualities of his nature arise involuntary in the soul—the benevolence which loves to diffuse happiness and to be a fellow-worker with God in the designs of his providence—the fortitude which no obstacles can retard and no dangers appal in the road to immortality—the constancy which, reposing in the promises of Heaven, presses forward in the path of strenuous and persevering virtue. Such views have also the tendency to fortify the mind against all those narrow and unjust conceptions of life, which are the source of the greatest part of the follies and weaknesses of mankind. They level all those vain distinctions among men, which in one class of society are productive of oppression and pride, and in the other of baseness and servility. They silence that feeble and grievously complaining spirit which is so often mistaken for sensibility and superior feeling, and which, from whatever cause it springs, gradually poisons the source of human happiness and undermines the foundation of every real virtue. They dispel those dark and ungenerous views of man, and of his capacity for happiness and virtue, which are in general only the excuses for indolence or selfishness, and which, wherever they have prevailed, have so often withheld the arm that was made to bless, and silenced the voice that was destined to enlighten them. "Whatsoever things are just, whatsoever things are pure, whatsoever things are lovely and of good report," these are the objects at which the spirit of early piety forms the mind to aim wherever the production of happiness or virtue is to be acquired, or by the performance of duty praise is to be won. It is true that we sometimes find the pious and the wise, to whom religion ought to have taught better things, complaining under the unequal distribution, and nourishing in their hearts those secret murmurs against providence, which unnerve every virtuous purpose of the soul, and cover religion itself in gloom and melancholy. It is the piety of youthful days which can afford the best preservative against those dark and unjust conceptions. Before the experience of life has made any impression on the minds—before they descend to the wilderness through which they are to travel, it shows them from afar "the promised land." It carries their views to the whole course of their being, and, while no narrow objects have yet absorbed their desires, shows them its termination in another scene, in which the balance of good and evil will be adjusted by the unerring hand of God. Under such views of nature, the system of Divine Providence appears in all its majesty and beauty. Beginning here in the feeble state of man, it spreads itself into forms of ascending being, in which the heart expands while it contemplates them, and closes, at last, in scenes which are obscured only from the excess of their splendour. With such conceptions of their nature, life meets the young in its real colours—not as the idle abode of effeminate pleasure, but as the school in which their souls are formed to great attainments; not as the soft shade in which every manly and honorable quality is to dissolve, but as the field in which glory and honor and immortality are to be won. Whatever may be the aspect which it may assume, whatever the scenes in which they are called to act or to suffer, the promises of God still brighten in their view, and their souls, deriving strength from trial, and confidence from experience, settle at last in that humble but holy spirit of resignation, which, when rightly understood, comprehends the sum and substance of religion; which, reposing itself in undoubting faith on the wisdom of God, accepts, not only with content, but with cheerfulness, every dispensation of his providence; which seeks no other end but to fulfil its parts in his government; and which, knowing its own weakness and God's perfection, yields up all its desires into his hand, and asks only to know his laws and to do his will. Such are some of the natural effects of youthful piety upon the formation of human character, and to which more might be added; and especially the certainty which it affords of the favor of God, and of the continued assistance of his Holy Spirit, as appears in our Heavenly Father's dealings with the young throughout the whole of Revelation. Rejoice, then, O young man, in thy youth—rejoice in those days, which are never to return, when religion comes to you in all her charms, and when the God of Heaven reveals himself to thy soul, like the mild radiance of the morning sun, when he rises amidst the blessings of a grateful world. I would offer my young hearers, of both sexes, a parting word of lovingkindness, for God is the Creator and Father of us all. If, then, piety hath already taught you her secret pleasures—if when revelation unveils her mercies, and the Son of God comes forth to give peace and hope to fallen man—if at such a time your eyes follow with astonishment the glories of his path, and pour at last over his cross those pious tears which it is a delight to shed; if your souls accompany him in his triumph over the grave, and enter on the wings of faith into that heaven " where he sat down on the right hand of the Majesty on high, and beheld the society of angels and of the spirits of just men made perfect," and listen to the everlasting song which is sung before the throne; if such be frequently the meditation in which your youthful hours are passed, renounce not, for all that life can offer you, these solitary joys. The world that is before thee—the world which thine imagination paints in such brightness—has no pleasures to bestow which can compare with these; and all that its boasted wisdom can produce has nothing so acceptable in the sight of Heaven as the pure offering of youthful souls.

The following selections of music were performed under the leadership of Mr. Carter, the organist, during the service:—

Venite—Chant—Gregorian.
Glorias—Chant—Goss, from Beethoven.
Te Deum.
Jubilate.
Anthem, " Bow down Thine ear, O Lord."
Introit—Sanctus—Spohr.
Responses—John Carter.
Gloria—(before and after Gospel)—Tallis.
Before Sermon—" But the Lord is mindful of His own "—Mendelsohn.

While the collection was being taken up, " Handel's Sampson," and " We worship God, and God alone," from " Judas Maccabeus," were performed; and when H. R. H. was leaving the sacred edifice the National Anthem was played.

Outside an immense concourse of people was gathered, who cheered loudly as His Royal Highness stepped into his carriage and drove away.

On Monday (10th), H. R. H. and suite, accompanied by the Governor General, Sir Fenwick Williams, and their suites; Hon. Messrs. Galt, Vankoughnet, Sherwood, W. B. Robinson (President, Canada Co.), J. H. Cameron, Angus Morrison, M.P.P., Major Denison, Captains Dick and Storm, General Robinson and Hon. Mr. Denny (the two latter gentlemen from Pittsburg, Pa.), embarked upon the Northern Railway for an excursion to Collingwood, Georgian Bay.

His Royal Highness was received at the station by the Hon. J. C. Morrison, President of the Company, and Messrs. Cumberland, T. Galt, Grant, Fleming, and Beaty, of the Company, and by them conducted to the car, which was a beautiful open one, constructed expressly for the occasion, and which, together with others, left Toronto a little after nine A.M., a large concourse of people cheering heartily. The train was drawn by the *J. C. Morrison* engine, and was preceded by a pilot one named the *Cumberland*.

The Northern Railway runs through a fine and well-settled portion of the Province, and some places along the route are very picturesque and exceedingly pretty. Thus His Royal Highness had an ample opportunity, not only of witnessing how rapidly some parts of Canada West had been developed, but of seeing some very good scenery.

Crowds of people were gathered at every station along the route, who cheered right heartily. Every place was adorned with flags, banners, and arches, in honour of the auspicious occasion.

At Newmarket, Aurora, Bradford, and Barrie, Addresses were presented by the municipalities, &c., and replies given by the Prince. At the latter place a very good display was made, the town being well set off. The Rifle Volunteers and Firemen turned out, the band of the former playing the National Anthem;—indeed this air had been struck up at nearly every station on the route!

After passing Angus, Sunnidale, and Nottawasaga, the train arrived at Collingwood, at about one o'clock, where a fine reception awaited H. R. H. The Rifle Companies were out and saluted; the children sang the National Anthem; Addresses were presented; and H. R. H. was escorted to the *Rescue* steamer, at the wharf, by a delighted and enthusiastic people, who cheered as they, no doubt, never cheered before. The *Rescue* cruised about the Bay for a short time, during which H. R. H. and suite, and those accompanying him, had time to enjoy the pretty scenery that adorns the coast, and to take luncheon. On returning to Collingwood, the royal party again took the train, and arrived at Toronto at half-past six p.m.

Here H. R. H. thanked Mr. Cumberland for the kind attention he had received, and alluded to the good management of the road.

During the day, the Grand Scottish Gathering of the Canadian Highland Society was held at Toronto, in honour of the Prince's visit, where prizes were given to the successful competitors at the manly games of Scotia.

On Tuesday (11th), although raining in torrents, H. R. H., his suite, &c., &c., attended the Regatta, under the auspices of the R. C. Yacht Club, Toronto Bay. At the amphitheatre he received and replied to an Address from the Royal Canadian Yacht Club, presented by Commodore Durie and the Officers, who were attired in their handsome uniforms. Here, the children again sang the National Anthem, and a Guard of Honour was drawn up.

H. R. H. witnessed the start of the fine yachts of Upper Canada, which were evidently well manned, but he was compelled to depart to fulfil other engagements. Before leaving, at the request of the Club he became their Patron. The next features in this important day's proceedings, were the opening of the Queen's, formerly University Park; the laying of a pedestal for a Statue of the Queen; and a review of the Volunteer Corps of Toronto.

On H. R. H. arriving at the Park, he was met by the committee appointed from the Reception Committee, viz. Rev. Dr. McCaul, President of University College; Messrs. Cumberland, Brunot, A. Morrison, and Pattison; who, with a portion of the Cabinet, &c., escorted H. R. H. to a handsome canopy, where the following Address was presented him by Rev. Dr. McCaul :—

MAY IT PLEASE YOUR ROYAL HIGHNESS,—

As Chairman of the Committee on Programme and Arrangement, I am deputed, on behalf of the Citizens of Toronto, to request that Your

Royal Highness will be graciously pleased to lay the foundation-stone of the pedestal of a Statue of the Queen. Our object in erecting the Statue is, that there may be a permanent manifestation of our grateful sense of the manifold blessings which we enjoy under Her Majesty's benignant rule. I am deputed further to request that Your Royal Highness will be graciously pleased to inaugurate that portion of the University Park, which has been set apart for the use of the Citizens; and I feel assured that I speak the sentiments of every member of the community, when I give utterance to the confident hope, that this and succeeding generations, whilst availing themselves of the opportunities which this place of public resort presents for healthful recreation, will ever associate their enjoyment of these advantages, with the reign of a Sovereign, to whose throne and person the citizens of Toronto are devotedly attached, and with the visit of a Prince, whose presence amongst us is welcomed with enthusiastic joy.

To this the Prince was graciously pleased to give his assent.

Then Mr. Angus Morrison, M.P.P., handed His Royal Highness a crystal bottle, containing several gold and silver coins of the present reign, together with copies of the Toronto papers; the whole of which the Prince deposited in a cavity of the stone for the purpose.

Alderman Carr then presented a brass plate, with this inscription engraved on its face:—

Hunc Primum Lapidem
Basis cui
Statuam Victoriæ Reginæ
Cives Torontonenses
Imposituri sunt
Posuit
Albertus Edoardus
Princeps Walliæ
VI Id. Septembr. MDCCCLX
Victoria
Annum vicies et quartum
Regnante
Edmundo Walker Head, Baronetto
Vice Regia Rerum Summam
Per Provinc. Britann. in America Septentr.
Administrante
Eodemque die
Princeps Celsissimus
Agrum e Praedio Academico
In salutem oblectationemque civium sepositum
Dedicavit.

Previous to which, a handsome silver trowel was presented to His Royal Highness by the Mayor. It bore this inscription :—

Presented to
His Royal Highness the Prince of Wales,
by the Citizens of Toronto,
On laying the Foundation-Stone
for a Statue of the Queen,
at the Inauguration
of the Queen's Park,
Sept. 11th, 1860.

The stone was then, with the usual ceremony, lowered upon the cavity, and Rev. Dr. McCaul declared the Park inaugurated and opened to the public, by the name of the Queen's Park. This was received by the half-drowned people with shouts of enthusiasm. Three cheers were then given for the Prince, in which every one joined enthusiastically. The ceremony then terminated.

The review of the Toronto Volunteer Corps then took place, notwithstanding the drizzling rain that continued to fall.

The Companies on the ground were No. 1 Rifles, Captain McDonald; No. 3 Rifles, Captain Smith; Highland Rifles, Captain Fulton; the whole of the Yorkville Cavalry, Captain G. T. Denison; and the Companies of the Field Battery, Captain R. L. Denison: the whole under Lieutenant-Colonel Denison, Commandant of the Active Force.

The royal party, with the Governor General, Sir W. F. Williams, &c., stood on the Grand Stand as the corps went through their several evolutions, which were not many, seeing that the weather was so unpropitious; but what little they did go through was done with a soldier-like precision that reflected great credit on the officers who commanded.

First of all, the entire corps presented arms; the bands playing the National Anthem, and every civilian uncovering. They then marched past in quick time to the tune "British Grenadiers," and, with a few other quick movements, the affair ended.

Colonel Denison then, at the request of the Prince, presented himself at the Grand Stand. His Royal Highness personally expressed his satisfaction to him, at the efficient appearance and standing of the Toronto Force.

The Prince and suite then paid the University of Toronto a

visit. The University is situated a short distance from where the stone was laid, consequently the royal party had not far to go.

The Entrance Hall of this noble structure, conspicuous from its Norman roof of sombre hue, its tessellated pavements, and mullioned windows, was, in its stern grandeur, very successfully ornamented by the simple addition on the wall of the Prince's plume, and, on a scroll beneath, the graceful classic salutation, " Salve Princeps."

At the entrance, His Royal Highness was met by the Chancellor (Hon. Mr. Justice Burns), the Vice Chancellor (J. Langton, Esq., Auditor General), the President of University College (Rev. Dr. McCaul), and the President of the University Association (Hon. James Patton).

These gentlemen conducted H. R. H. and suite to the Convocation Hall, which was crowded with fashionably-dressed ladies and gentlemen; in fact, only the *elite* of the town was admitted. Through a lane made of Graduates and Students, H. R. H. and suite passed to a raised dais at the end of the room, on which was a throne surmounted by the royal arms in gold. Opposite to them were these pretty words, which he could not help seeing:—
" *Imperii spem Spes Provinciæ salutat.*"

The following Address was then presented to H. R. H. by the Chancellor:—

MAY IT PLEASE YOUR ROYAL HIGHNESS,—

We, the Chancellor, Vice-Chancellor, Senate, and Graduates of the University of Toronto, and the President, Council, and Members of University College, desire to welcome Your Royal Highness with loyal and dutiful respect on your visit to the Capital of Upper Canada; and gladly avail ourselves of this auspicious occasion to renew the assurance of our devoted loyalty to the Queen, and to express our grateful appreciation of the manifold blessings which we enjoy under Her Majesty's benign sway.

Fresh from the advantages of England's most ancient University, Your Royal Highness now honors with your presence the Academic Hall of this young Province. The pleasures and profit united in the purest of Collegiate studies have already been enjoyed by you; and we doubt not that our efforts to extend the same educational privileges among our Canadian youth will command your sympathy, framed as our system is upon the model of the Institutions of our mother country, while adapted in its details to the special want of this portion of the Empire.

To this great work, which involves the intellectual advancement of

Canada, our best energies have been directed. By its means the first advantages of liberal culture, and Academic honors and rewards, are placed within the reach of all who are prepared to avail themselves of their untrammelled facilities; and, under the Divine blessing, our exertions have already been crowned with such success as encourages us to anticipate a noble future for our Provincial University and College.

The high gratification which we feel on welcoming, in the heir of the British Crown, the destined successor of our royal founder, is especially enchanced to us by the consideration, that, alike by study and travel, Your Royal Highness is being trained for the duties of the exalted position you are born to occupy. In these halls, devoted to the training of the youth on whom the future hopes of Canada rest, we welcome you as the hope of a great Empire. We rejoice to recognize in our Prince the promise of qualities which will render him worthy to inherit the Crown of our beloved Queen, whose virtues are associated with the glories of the Victorian era, and whose sceptre is the guarantee of equal liberties enjoyed in this, as in every Province of her world-wide dominions.

To which His Royal Highness made the following reply :—

GENTLEMEN,—I rejoice to receive the assurances of your loyalty to the Queen, and your appreciation of the blessings enjoyed under her sway by every portion of her Empire.

I am at this moment a member of a more ancient University, but I am not on that account the less inclined to respect and honor those whose efforts are directed to the spread of knowledge and learning in a young country.

I sympathize heartily with the efforts which you are making on behalf of science and literature.

I believe that much depends on your exertions; and I earnestly hope that the best evidences of the successful exertions of the University of Toronto may hereafter be found in the progress and prosperity of Canada.

A resolution was then moved by the Vice Chancellor, seconded by the President of the College, to the effect " that the Prince having expressed his willingness to become a student of the college, he moved that he be admitted as one of the second year," which was of course carried with enthusiastic cheers.

The Registrar (Mr. Moss) then presented a book, which His Royal Highness signed.

The Principal and Masters of Upper Canada College then presented an Address; and the Prince, after receiving it, was conducted through the building, and must have experienced great pleasure at witnessing the progress which has been made by one of our many public institutions.

On the same day, H. R. H. also inaugurated the Botanical Gardens of the Toronto Horticultural Society by planting a Canadian maple. He received an Address from the Society; which also presented him with the handsome silver spade used in planting the tree.

He next visited the Educational Department of Upper Canada, under the Rev. Dr. Ryerson, where 450 school teachers sang the National Anthem, and a new song entitled " Hurrah for Canada." Here Judge Harrison presented an Address from the Educational Department, to which H. R. H. was pleased to reply.

Knox's College was next visited; and, after remaining a short time, H. R. H. departed for Government House, after a very hard day's work.

The ball given to the Prince and suite at the Crystal Palace in the evening, and which he attended, was all that could be desired, and will long be remembered in the " Queen City" as the best ever gotten up. His Royal Highness danced until after four in the morning with the following ladies :—

1, quadrille, Mrs. Wilson, Lady Mayoress; 2, polka, Miss De Blaquière; 3, galop, Miss Blackwell; 4, quadrille, Mrs. M. C. Cameron; 5, valse, Miss Killally; 6, galop, Miss E. Ridout; 7, lancers, Miss Powell; 8, galop, Miss MacNab; 9, valse, Miss Helen Gzowski; 10, quadrille, Mrs. J. B. Robinson; 11, polka, missed; 12, Miss Wallace; 13, lancers, Miss Young, (daughter of the Chief Justice of Nova Scotia); 14, valse, Miss Moffatt; 15, polka redowa, Miss McCaul; 16, quadrille, Miss Harris; 17, galop, Miss Shanly; 18, valse, Miss Denison; 19, lancers, Miss Spragge; 20, valse, Miss S. Jarvis, and 21, galop, Miss Murney.

On Wednesday (Sept. 12th), the royal party, accompanied by the Governor General, the Commander of the Forces, together with their suites, and a portion of the Cabinet, &c., took his departure from Toronto for London, C. W., by the Grand Trunk Railway state-car, amidst an enthusiastic farewell from the whole populace of the Queen City.

The route was through a very splendid portion of Canada

West; indeed it is about the best cultivated and settled of any portion of the Upper Province.

As on the previous trips on our Canadian railways, great displays were made all along the line; every village and town vieing with each other to do the Heir Apparent honour; each place turning out its whole population to shew their loyalty, by loud and continuous cheering, and by dressing out their places in holiday attire. At every station, two or more neat arches were to be seen; flags and evergreens abounded in great abundance. Salutes were fired at some places from cannon of heavy calibre, and at others from fire-arms. All joined together, to shew their great joy and hapiness at the visit of His Royal Highness.

At Guelph, an Address was presented, and the Volunteer Corps turned out and fired a royal salute. National Societies and others assembled, the National Anthem was sung by the school-children, and the greatest joy was manifested.

At the German settlement of Peterburg, an Address in their native tongue was presented, and a reply given by H. R. H., verbally, in that language.

At Stratford, an Address was also presented, and replied to. The Volunteer Rifles turned out as Guard of Honour; the Fire Brigade also made a fine display. Every manifestation of joy was shown.

The royal train arrived at London shortly after four a. m., where a most heartfelt welcome awaited the royal visitor. A royal salute was fired by the Volunteer Artillery; and the Volunteer Rifles, Highlanders, and Cavalry served as a Guard of Honour and escort. The whole town was out, dressed in its best, in honour of the occasion; the city was very nicely decorated; arches, flags and streamers lined the thoroughfares, and the greatest joy was manifested by the people.

The Mayor, City Council, City Members, and the Reception Committee received H. R. H. at the Station; and carriages being provided, H. R. H. and those accompanying him, were driven to a handsome pavilion, where the following Address was presented by the Mayor (James Moffat, Esq.), and replied to:—

To His Royal Highness Albert Edward, Prince of Wales, &c., &c.
MAY IT PLEASE YOUR ROYAL HIGHNESS,—

We, the Mayor, Aldermen, and Committee of the City of London, in Upper Canada, do, in the name of the inhabitants, most cordially welcome Your Royal Highness. We rejoice that our city should be thus highly honoured by the presence of the son of our beloved Queen, and the Heir Apparent of the powerful and glorious empire over which Her Majesty has for so many years, so wisely and auspiciously, reigned. It has given us unmingled satisfaction to be made acquainted with the enthusiastic reception accorded to Your Royal Highness during your progress westward, from the day of your first landing in these Provinces; but less than such a welcome we never imagined you would receive, for the North American Colonies are peopled by those who will yield to none in their devoted attachment to the British Crown, and in affection for the reigning Sovereign. The fact that at most it is only forty years since, in the locality where you now stand, none but the red Indian dozed under the shade of the primeval forest, will sufficiently explain to Your Royal Highness why we can conduct you to no magnificent buildings, to no sacred historic monuments, such as those which are familiar to your eye; but we are persuaded you can well appreciate the results of an industry which, in our circumstances, are necessarily more marked by the useful than the ornamental. We trust that Your Royal Highness may return home in safety, gratified with your visit to these colonies, and retaining pleasing recollections of their inhabitants. Do us the distinguished favour to convey to Her Majesty assurance of our most devoted loyalty to Her Crown and Person. We pray the Almighty to guide and bless you through life.

JAMES MOFFAT,
Mayor.

His Royal Highness replied as follows:—

GENTLEMEN,—I accept with great satisfaction the Address in which you proclaim your deep attachment to the person and government of the Queen, and offer me so kind a greeting in your loyal city. You do no more than justice to the other parts of this splendid Province, when you speak of the enthusiastic reception which has been everywhere accorded to me as the son of your Queen. I know the attachment to the British Crown of the people of the North American Colonies; but all the expectations I had formed of their devotion have been more than realized by the demonstrations I have witnessed. The country through which I have passed this day, presents the spectacle of a population prosperous and happy. Its progress excites alike admiration and astonishment, and the industry evinced on every side has nearly supplanted the trackless forest of past generations, by smiling fields and pastures reminding you of those which so many of you have quitted in your youth. That this prosperity may continue and this industry meet with its fair reward, will ever be the constant prayer of your Sovereign, of myself, and of the people who share with you the blessings of free institutions, and are bound to you by identity of interest and affection.

Then the carriages were again called into requisition, and the grand procession of Volunteers, National Societies, Members of Parliament, Lawyers, Clergymen, and Firemen, of whom there was a great gathering, many having come from adjoining towns and villages.

All along the route of the procession the greatest demonstrations of respect, esteem, and love for the Prince took place.

The National Anthem was sung by 2,000 children, under the directorship of Mr Longman, and in this manner H. R. H. was escorted to the Tecumseth House, leased for the occasion by the Government. At this place the cheering was tremendous; and, shortly afterwards, the Prince appeared on the balcony in front, to the people's delighted gaze. His appearance was hailed by thousands of cheers, hurrahs, and cries, all expressive of their great delight. Subsequently, cheers were also given for the Governor General and the Canadian Ministry.

In the evening, there was a very fair illumination, and a splendid firemen's torchlight procession, which did honor to the originators. Indeed, for a city of its size, London is entitled to the highest praise for one of the best demonstrations and displays. On the following day (Thursday, Sept. 13th) the royal party took the Grand Trunk state-car for an excursion to Sarnia, a distance of sixty-two miles.

Starting at nine, His Royal Highness arrived at Sarnia at eleven, a. m., where he received as great a demonstration (though of course on a smaller scale) as at any previous place. There were the usual decorations, cheering, and joy.

On a large platform, surmounted by a handsome canopy, His Royal Highness received the Addresses of the Town and County Councils, and replied to them; including one from the Indians, there being a representative from most of the tribes of the Upper Province, tatooed and dressed in their native gear.

The head man of the Indians, a tall, powerful fellow, delivered the following speech in the Indian language, which was interpreted for the Prince:—

GREAT BROTHER,—The sky is beautiful. It was the wish of the Great Spirit that we should meet in this place. My heart is glad that the Queen sent her eldest son to see her Indian subjects. I am happy to see you here this day. I hope the sky will continue to look fine, to give happiness both to the whites and the Indians. Great Brother, when you were a little child, your parents told you that there were such people as Indians in Canada; and now, since you have come to Canada yourself, you see them. I am one of the Ojibbeway Chiefs, and represent the tribe here assembled to welcome their Great Brother. You see the Indians who are around : they have heard that at some future day you will put on the British Crown and sit on the British Throne. It is their earnest desire that you will always remember them.

The Prince replied verbally, that he was grateful for the Address, that he hoped the sky would always be beautiful, and that he should never forget his red brethren.

His Royal Highness then presented each with large silver medals, having ribbons attached, in commemoration of the event.

His Royal Highness then entered a carriage, as also did the members of his suite, and was speedily driven to the Grand Trunk Railway Station, where a luncheon was provided.

After the Queen and Prince Consort's healths had been drunk, Mr. Blackwell, Vice-President of the Grand Trunk Railway Company, proposed the toast of His Royal Highness the Prince of Wales, which was drunk with unbounded enthusiasm. The Prince then proposed the health of Mr. Blackwell, which was received with great cheers.

On leaving the station, the royal party went on board the Steamer *Michigan* to take a short trip on the Lake, and a brief view of the scenery. After which, the royal car was again taken; and in an hour and a half, the royal party arrived back at London.

A levee was held shortly afterwards, when quite a number of gentlemen were presented.

In the evening, a grand ball was given by the city, in rear of the Tecumseth House. About six hundred ladies and gentlemen were present. This affair was got up with a great degree of spirit and energy, as the arrangements testified. His Royal Highness danced with great "gusto" until three o'clock in the morning.

The following ladies had the honour of dancing with His Royal Highness on that occasion :—No. 1, quadrille, Miss Moffat (daughter of the Mayor). No. 2, polka, Mrs. Watson. No. 3, waltz, Miss Becher. No. 4, lancers, Mrs. Howell. No. 5, waltz, Miss Prince. No. 6, galop, Miss Askin. No. 7, quadrille, Mrs. Judge Small. No. 8, waltz, Miss

Hamilton. No. 9, lancers, Mrs. W. L. Lawrason. No. 10, ——. No. 11, galop, Miss J. Meredith. No. 12, quadrille, Miss Bell. No. 13, waltz, Miss Gzowski. No. 14, galop, Mrs. Rivers. No. 15, lancers, Miss Gzowski, No. 16, galop, Miss Hope. No. 17, quadrille, Miss Dalton. No. 18, waltz, Miss Paul. No. 19, lancers, Mrs. Taylor. No. 20, waltz, Mrs. James Daniell. No. 21, Sir Roger de Coverly, Miss Brough.

The Prince had seen all that was to be seen in and about London, and had gratified its inhabitants by his presence for a considerable time, so, on the morning of the 14th at ten o'clock, with a renewal of the kind manifestations of loyalty and love from the people, and the general royal salute, and "turn out," of Volunteers, Firemen, Trade Societies, and the people generally, His Royal Highness took his departure from the "Forest City," *en route* for Niagara Falls, accompanied of course by his suite, the Governor General, the Commander of the Forces, the Members of the Ministry, &c.

The royal party occupied on this occasion a new car, built expressly for the use of the Prince by the Great Western Railway Company, and of which the following is a good description:—

Yesterday we enjoyed the privilege of a peep at the truly magnificent car just completed for the use of His Royal Highness by the Great Western Railway Company. The grand saloon is a perfect gem of a room, painted in pure white, with delicately gilded mouldings and cornices, and presents an appearance at once rich and chaste. The window-curtains are of a royal blue silk, and so fixed, that, by touching a spring, they are instantly drawn up. Above each window is a panel covered with fluted crimson silk, over which hangs a blue silk curtain, looped in the centre, and bound with heavy gold bullion-fringe. The furniture is composed altogether of curled maple of the finest description, and the cushions are covered with blue silk damask. The furniture of the room consists of four sofas, two large arm-chairs, and four small ones. The arm-chair intended for His Royal Highness is most elaborately carved. On the back is the Prince of Wales' feathers and coronet, surrounded by the rose, shamrock, and thistle, while a wreath of maple-leaves is gracefully entwined amongst them. The Duke of Newcastle's chair is similar to the Prince's, but less elaborately carved. In the carving of the sofas, the beavers are quite prominent. On each side of the door leading to the ante-room is a large mirror, with a marble stand beneath, upon which vases of flowers will be placed. Over the doors the Prince's crest is beautifully painted. The floor is covered with

Brussels carpet, and the car will be lighted by three lamps in three cent. In the centre is a table, in the top of which, in a small diamond-shaped space, has been inlaid fourteen specimens of our finest Canadian woods, and very beautiful they are. Between the grand saloon and the ante-room, is the dressing-room, &c. Nothing has been spared to make everything complete. The ante-room is painted similarly to the grand saloon; but here the similarity ceases. The furniture is of black walnut, with crimson plush cushions. In this room there are two lamps. The exterior of the car is very handsome. On each side there is a large oval panel, in the centre of which is painted the royal arms, with the Prince's crest at the top. This is really a magnificent work of art, and reflects the greatest credit on the painter. Over each door and at each corner the Prince's crest appears worked in with other decorative painting. The platforms are much wider than those in the common car, and have silver-plated hand-rails. The trucks are painted a very dark crimson, and ornamented with gilding; all the iron work is bronzed; while the wheels—of which there are twelve—have all the spaces between the spokes filled up with wood, in order that they may be attended by little or no noise. The ventilation is said to be as nearly perfect as it is possible to make it. The ventilators are constructed on a new principle, under Mr. Sharpe's personal supervision. Persons who have seen the Grand Trunk car, and that built by the B. & L. H. Railway, say that neither of them can approach this either for beauty of design or workmanship.—*Spectator*.

At Woodstock, a pretty little town on the route, a very nice display was made. On landing, the Prince was escorted to the Mayor's residence, where was congregated an eager throng, consisting in a great part of the *elite* of the place, who cheered as heartily as the populace on his arrival.

Here Addresses were presented by the Mayor (Mr. Cottle), and the Warden (Mr. Harrington), on behalf of the Town and County Councils, and others from the Council of Ingersoll, and the Baptist College. A levee was also held, at which a great number of gentlemen were presented. The children sang the National Anthem, and the people cheered lustily for the Queen, the Prince Consort, the Prince of Wales, and the Governor General; after which a *déjeuner* was partaken of, and the royal party again took the cars.

On arrival at Paris, the Volunteers turned out, under Capt. Patton, and acted as a Guard of Honour. An Address was presented by the Mayor (Mr. Whitlaw), and replied to; and here a change of cars took place, H. R. H. being transferred from the

Great Western, to the Buffalo and Lake Huron Railway; which had also built a splendid state-car for the occasion.

Brantford was the next stopping-place, and be it said the people did not fail to shew their loyal enthusiasm.

The Address on behalf of the inhabitants was presented to H. R. H. by the Mayor (Mr. Clements), and replied to. The royal party were then conducted to carriages, and driven to the Kerby House, through well-adorned streets, and a loyal and devoted people, who cheered immensely. Here, luncheon was partaken of; and shortly afterwards the party returned to the cars.

Dunnville and Port Colborne were passed. The former place turning out its Volunteers, under Capt. Amsden.

At Fort Erie, the Prince and those accompanying him had a view of the great Lake; and took the steamer *Clifton* for Chippewa, where they did not arrive until the shades of night had advanced. The good people of this place had a large bonfire, so that a light was thrown upon the subject.

Here the Magistrates, Sheriff, and Members of the County received the Prince, and conducted him, together with the noblemen and gentlemen accompanying him, to carriages in waiting. The firemen, and many ladies also, lighted up their torches and escorted him to the Pavilion Hotel, where an Address was presented from the County, and replied to.

H.R.H. and suite were then conducted to the late residence of Mr. Zimmerman, which had been leased and furnished expressly for the royal party; and there let us hope that H. R. H. enjoyed a good night's rest, after a very hard day's work.

In the evening, the Falls were gorgeously illuminated by lines of fires along the cliffs; Bengal lights, &c., which appeared magnificently in the extreme, being more like crystals of different colours, than water,—more like paradise than earth. H. R. H. and suite, with several of the privileged, went out to view them from several points.

On Saturday (15th), the Prince and suite witnessed Blondin, the celebrated *acrobate*, crossing on a rope over the awful chasm of Niagara; firstly carrying a man upon his back, and safely depositing him upon the opposite side; and secondly, walking on stilts, and performing several *evolutions* on the rope. It is said that His Royal Highness presented Blondin with a gift of $400. During that day the royal party "did up" everything interesting in and around the Falls; going under them, before them, behind them; and sailed near the spray, in the little steamer *Maid of the Mist.*

On Sunday (16th), the Prince and suite attended Divine Service at Chippewa Church.

On Monday (17th), H. R. H. paid the American side a visit, crossing in an open ferry-boat. The small crowd there greeted him with a hearty cheer, which speaks well for Brother Jonathan's hospitality. Here, a Yankee took his portrait, uniting hospitality with "trade."

His Royal Highness visited the Terrapin Tower; and a party of men sent an immense log over the Falls for his edification.

A visit was paid to the Suspension Bridge, where an Address was presented to His Royal Highness from the Directors, by the Hon. W. H. Merritt. To this His Royal Highness replied; and, with his suite, &c., took the royal car and crossed to the centre, whence the visitor has a capital view of the Falls. After a few minutes' time, the bridge was entirely crossed.

After returning, he drove on horseback into the country, and saw a portion of the Welland Canal, as also the fine farms that adorn this part of the country.

On Tuesday (18th), His Royal Highness and suite left Clifton, in carriages, for Queenstown, under a royal Volunteer salute and a grand display.

Queenstown is a beautiful spot. The Heights can be seen for a great distance; and at a greater distance still, can be seen the monument to the immortal, brave, and glorious Brock, erected, as a slight acknowledgment for his glorious deeds, by a grateful and affectionate country. Here it was that the Prince found about 160 survivors of the sad but glorious campaign of 1812, assembled to present him with an Address, and to acknowledge the services of their late immortal leader.

The Address was presented by the Hon. Sir J. B. Robinson, Bart., Chief Justice of Upper Canada, one of the survivors, and replied to by His Royal Highness.

189

The following is the Address presented :—

MAY IT PLEASE YOUR ROYAL HIGHNESS,—

Some of the few survivors of the Militia Volunteers who assisted in defending Canada against the invading enemy during the last American war, have assembled from different parts of the Province, in the hope that they may be graciously permitted to offer to Your Royal Highness the expression of their loyal welcome, upon your arrival in this portion of Her Majesty's dominions. In the long period that has elapsed, very many have gone to their rest, who, having served in higher ranks than ourselves, took a more conspicuous part in that glorious contest. They would have delighted in the opportunity which we now enjoy of beholding in their country a descendant of the just and pious sovereign in whose cause they and their fellow-soldiers fought, and whom they were from infancy taught to revere for his many public and private virtues

We feel deeply grateful to Her Majesty, whose condescension to the wishes of her Canadian subjects has conferred upon us the honor of a visit from your Royal Highness; and we rejoice in the thought that what your Royal Highness has seen, and will see, of this prosperous and happy province, will enable you to judge how valuable a possession was saved to the British Crown by the successful resistancem ade in the trying contest in which it was our fortune to bear a part; and Your Royal Highness will then be able to judge how large a debt the Empire owed to the lamented hero Brock, whose gallant and generous heart shrank not, in the darkest hour of the conflict, from the most discouraging odds, and whose example inspired the few with the ability and spirit to do the work of many.

We pray that God may bless your Royal Highness with many years of health and happiness, and may lead you by His providence to walk in the paths of our revered and beloved Queen, to whom the world looks up as an illustrious example of all the virtues that can dignify the highest rank, support worthily the responsibilities of the most anxious station, and promote the peace, security, and happiness of private life.

His Royal Highness replied as follows.:—

GENTLEMEN,—I accept with mixed feelings of pride and pain the Address which you have presented on this spot ; pride in the gallant deeds of my countrymen, but pain from the reflection that so many of the noble band you once belonged to, have passed away from the scenes of the bravery of their youth, and of the peaceful avocations of their riper years.

I have willingly consented to lay the first stone of this monument. Every nation may, without offence to its neighbours, commemorate its heroes, their deeds of arms, and their noble deaths. This is no taunting boast of victory, no revival of long-passed animosities, but a noble tribute to a soldier's fame; the more honorable, because we readily acknowledge the bravery and chivalry of that people by whose hands he fell.

I trust that Canada will never want such Volunteers as those who fought in the last war, nor her Volunteers be without such a leader; but no less and most fervently I pray that your sons and your grandsons may never be called upon to add other laurels to those which you have so gallantly won.

Accept from me, in the Queen's name, my thanks for your expressions of devoted loyalty.

The Prince and suite then ascended to the top of the monument, whence they had a magnificent view of the fine surrounding country. After descending, His Royal Highness proceeded to lay the top-stone of an obelisk to mark the spot where the late departed General had died a soldier's death. It bears this inscription:—

Near this spot
Major General
SIR ISAAC BROCK, K. C. B.,
Provisional Lieutenant
Governor of Upper Canada,
Fell on the 13th of October, 1812,
While advancing to repel
The invading enemy.

Upon the other side were the simple words:—

This stone
Was placed by His Royal Highness
Albert Edward, Prince of Wales,
On the 18th September, 1860.

A handsome silver trowel was used by the Prince on the occasion, and afterwards presented to him by the committee of the monument. An immense crowd of people and militia from all parts of the country were present, who did not fail to shew their loyalty by making the welkin ring.

Shortly afterwards, the royal party proceeded on board the steamer *Zimmerman* for the town of Niagara, accompanied by the magistrates and others, and by some Niagara Militia as a Guard of Honour.

Niagara was reached in due time. It was well ornamented for the occasion; fine arches spanning the streets, and flags flying from the house-tops.

Two Addresses were presented ; one by the Mayor (Mr. Clench), and the other from the magistrates, by Judge Lauder.

After some presents, in the shape of fruit, had been presented by some ladies of Niagara, the boat took its departure; but had to return, when a short distance from the shore, for the Prince's steward (Mr. Sanderson), who had been left behind.

Port Dalhousie was soon reached. Here another Address was presented; and H. R. H. and suite took the royal car, and shortly afterwards arrived at St. Catherines, where a fine display was made by the Volunteers, Firemen, and the citizens generally. Here another Address was presented, by the Mayor (Mr. Currie), and an exchange of cars took place. Grimsby having been reached, an Address was presented from the Loyal Canadian Society, by Col. Clarke. And now for Hamilton, the end of the route, which was reached at five o'clock p. m.

A description of the reception here would be but a repetition of the receptions at the other loyal cities of the Province. We need only add, that the " ambitious little city " fully sustained her good name ; the decorations being superb, and the loyalty of the people as intense as could be.

The Mayor (Mr. McKinstrey) presented the following Address on behalf of the city :—

MAY IT PLEASE YOUR ROYAL HIGHNESS,—

We, the Mayor, Corporation, and citizens of Hamilton, desire to tender you a hearty welcome to this part of Her Majesty's dominions, and to assure you of the deep and affectionate interest we feel in all that concerns your prosperity and happiness.

Your Royal Highness has already witnessed many gratifying proofs of the devotion and attachment of the people of this country to the person and government of our beloved Queen ; and we beg to assure you, that these sentiments, in which we heartily concur, are inspired equally by our admiration of Her many public and private virtues, and by the love of justice, the impartial administration of the laws, and those liberal and enlightened principles of government which have signalised her administration, and enabled her to reign in the affections of her people.

The inhabitants of these Provinces have ever been conspicuous for their unwavering loyalty to the British Crown,—a loyalty which, in the earlier periods of their history, was tried by perils and sacrifices from which their fellow-subjects nearer the Throne have happily been exempt, and they have ever participated with a just pride in the glories and achievements of the great Empire to which they belong.

But if anything could tend still to deepen and perpetuate this feeling, it would be this gracious mark of Her Majesty's royal regard in sending amongst us one in whom she feels so deep an interest, and who, we trust, is destined to inherit equally her vast possessions and her eminent virtues; and we beg you to assure her how highly this proof of her confidence and esteem is appreciated.

Your Royal Highness has visited as yet but a portion of these extensive territories reaching from the Atlantic to the Pacific Ocean; but we trust you may have seen sufficient to impress you favorably with their magnitude and importance, as a valuable portion of your own future heritage; and we esteem it a further mark of your Royal Highness's obliging consideration that your visit should be made on this interesting occasion, when the annual exhibition (to which you will receive a cordial welcome) will enable you to judge of the richness and variety of the productions of this part of Canada, and the energy and enterprise of its inhabitants. Comprehending some four million square miles of territory, with an unrivalled system of natural and artificial communication, and teeming with patriotic and enterprising people, devotedly attached to British institutions and proud of their connection with the mother country, it is not too much to predict that at no distant day the British American Provinces will be the most powerful support to that Throne, which, as the bulwark of civil and religious liberty, has for ages stood the wonder and admiration of the world.

We trust that a bright and glorious career awaits you. To the Government of an Empire embracing over two hundred millions of subjects, with its arduous duties and its heavy responsibilities, you are destined, if it be God's purpose, to succeed; and our anxious prayer is, that " He by whom Kings reign and Princes decree justice," may give you a wise and understanding heart; that He may make you rich in wisdom, and thus prepare you for your great work; and that His protecting care, which has been over you thus far through life, may guard and guide you through a long and useful career.

His Royal Highness replied as follows :—

GENTLEMEN,—This is the last of the very numerous Addresses which have flowed in upon me from Municipal authorities as well as other bodies, throughout the Queen's dominions in North America, which I have traversed from East to West; and I can say with truth, that it is not the least fervent in its declarations of attachment to the Queen; nor the least earnest in its aspirations for the success and happiness of my future life; and in its prayers that my career may be one of usefulness to others and of honor to myself.

You cannot doubt the readiness with which I undertook the duty which was intrusted to me by the Queen, of visiting in her name, and in her behalf, these possessions of her crown. That task is now nearly completed; and it only remains for me to report to your Sovereign, universal enthusiasm, unanimous loyalty, all-pervading patriotism, general contentment, and, I trust, no less general prosperity and happiness.

I can never forget the scenes I have witnessed during the short time which I have enjoyed the privilege of associating myself with the Canadian people, which must ever be a bright epoch in my life. I shall bear away with me a grateful remembrance of kindness and affection, which as yet I have been unable to do anything to merit; and it shall be the constant effort of my future years to prove myself not unworthy of the love and confidence of a generous people.

H. R. H. and suite were then conducted to carriages, the procession formed in, and, escorted by Capt. Bull's troop of Cavalry, soon reached the former fine residence of Mr. Juson, which had been engaged for the royal party,—not however before a large number of school-children had sung the National Anthem, " Rule Britannia," and a new piece called " Hurrah for the Prince of Wales!"

The procession was as follows :—

Assistant Marshal.
Police.
Band.
Guard of Honour.
Abolition Society.
Temperance Societies.
Band.
Fire Brigade.
German Society.
Canadian Order of Odd-Fellows.
Band.
St. Andrew's Society.
St. Patrick's Society.
St. George's Society.
Highland Society.
Band.
Sedentary Militia.
Officers of Militia.
The Magistrates of the County.
The Registrar, the Treasurer, the Clerk of
the Peace, and other County Officers.
The County Council.
The Warden.

N

<pre>
                 The County Judge.
                 The High Sheriff.
           Members of the Reception Committee.
              Officers of the Corporation.
           The High Bailiff and the Chief of Police.
              The City Clerk and Chamberlain.
              The Aldermen and Councillors.
            The Recorder and Police Magistrate.
                     The Mayor.
Cavalry.   Members of the House of Assembly.   Cavalry.
            Members of the Legislative Council.
            HIS ROYAL HIGHNESS AND SUITE.
           The Commander of the Forces and Suite,
                       mounted.
            Mounted Officers of the Army and Militia.
                Field Battery of Artillery.
                       Police.
                Chief Marshal—Major Gray.
</pre>

In the evening, the rejoicings gave vent to a general illumination, and a grand display of fire-works. There was also a splendid concert by the Philharmonic Society of Hamilton which the Prince and suite honoured with their presence.

On Wednesday (Sept. 19th), His Royal Highness and suite visited the Central School of Hamilton; where the Prince received an Address from the Rev. Dr. Ryerson, Superintendent of Education for Upper Canada, on behalf of the institution. His Royal Highness then passed through the building, examining the school-children, who were dressed very nicely, and who greeted him by singing the new song of "Welcome," and the National Anthem.

Thence the Prince and party drove to the Royal Hotel, where a levee was held and Addresses presented.

After the levee, a visit was paid to the Exhibition in the new Crystal Palace. His Royal Highness was received by a royal salute from the Volunteer Battery, a Guard of Honour of the Volunteer Rifles and Highlanders, and by an excited and enthusiastic multitude (representatives from nearly every city, town, and village in Upper Canada), whose cheering was immense. As this was intended merely as a private visit, nothing of importance transpired. His Royal Highness and suite merely went through the building, examining and admiring its contents, and afterwards viewed the cattle and agricultural implements outside, and, before taking a final leave, drove round the grounds; an immense concourse of people cheering him on all sides. A luncheon was then partaken of at the Royal Hotel. In the afternoon His Royal Highness inaugurated the splendid Water Works, situated on the Burlington Beach, a short distance from the city; previous to which, he received and replied to an Address from its Commissioners, presented by Mr. Adam Brown, Chief Commissioner.

In the evening, he attended the grand ball given in his honour at the temporary building, in rear of the Royal Hotel. This was certainly a very grand affair; being well conducted by the committee, and well attended by the *elite* of the place. His Royal Highness joined in every dance, and retired at three o'clock next morning.

As we have given a list of the ladies who were honoured with the Prince's hand at the previous balls, it would be unfair to omit the names of those who danced with him at Hamilton. They are as follows :—

No. 1, quadrille, Mrs. David McNab. No. 2, polka, Miss Mills (daughter of the Hon. Mr. Mills). No. 3, galop, Miss MacNab (daughter of Sir Allan MacNab). No. 4, lancers, Miss Blanche Widder. No. 5, waltz, Miss Smith. No. 6, galop, Miss Thomas (daughter of the Sheriff). No. 7, lancers, Miss Lawrason (of London). No. 8, galop, Mrs. Strickland. No. 9, waltz, Miss Murray. No. 10, Mrs. Brydges. No. 11, quadrille, Miss Powell (of Niagara). No. 12, lancers, Miss E. Murray. No. 13, waltz, Miss Powell. No. 14, galop, Miss Proudfoot (of Toronto). No. 15, quadrille, Miss Benson (of St. Catharines). No. 16, galop, Miss Gedd. No. 17, lancers, Miss Reynolds.

On Thursday (20th), His Royal Highness and suite proceeded to the Crystal Palace, escorted by the Hamilton Cavalry, when the last Canadian Address was presented him by the Agricultural Society of Upper Canada, which was as follows :—

To His Royal Highness Albert Edward, Prince of Wales, &c., &c.

MAY IT PLEASE YOUR ROYAL HIGHNESS,—We, the agriculturists, artizans, and manufacturers of Upper Canada, beg to approach your Royal Highness with our expressions of devoted loyalty to Her Gracious

Majesty's crown and person, and to offer to Your Highness a most cordial welcome to this Exhibition of the products of our soil and of our labor. This is the fifteenth exhibition of the Agricultural Association of Upper Canada ; and we think it demonstrates to those who have witnessed the successive exhibitions from year to year, that they have been successful in stimulating the industrial classes in the improvement of all those productions upon which the prosperity of this portion of Her Majesty's dominions mainly depends.

Blessed with a fertile soil and healthful climate, and forming a portion of that extensive empire over which Her Majesty's benign rule extends, and in which it is exercised in the maintenance of the religious and civil rights of all classes of Her subjects, we hail with delight the auspicions event of Your Royal Highness's visit to this Colony, and rejoice that we have this opportunity of exhibiting to your Royal Highness—as we take what we call an honest pride in exhibiting to our future sovereign—such proofs of the industry, skill, and intelligence of the inhabitants of this country.

We gladly embrace this opportunity of expressing our ardent desire to maintain the connection of this Province with the great and glorious empire of which we rejoice in forming an integral part, and from which we have in great part derived our agriculture as well as our existence; and whilst availing ourselves of the example and improvements of the older portions of the empire, and of the many natural advantages we possess in our soil, climate, and navigable waters, we trust that our efforts may result in affording convincing proof that this province is really a valuable jewel in the crown of our beloved sovereign.

We hopefully pray that the intercourse of Your Royal Highness with the inhabitants of Canada, and the opportunity you have had of witnessing the efforts we are making to advance the material interests of our country, may, during your future life, leave a pleasing impression in your memory.

That your Royal Highness may be placed in possession of statistics and their facts connected with the rise and progress of this Association, we beg that your Royal Highness will condescend to accept these volumes, containing a record of the transactions of this Association from its establishment.

The Prince replied as follows :—

GENTLEMEN,—I return you my warm acknowledgements for this Address which you have just presented upon the occasion of opening the fifteenth exhibition of the Agricultural Society for Upper Canada ; and I take this opportunity of thanking the agriculturists, artizans, and farmers, who are now assembled from distant parts in this City of Hamilton, for the more than kind and enthusiastic reception which they gave me yesterday and repeated to-day.

Blessed with a soil of very remarkable fertility, and a hardy race of industrious and enterprising men, this district must rapidly assume a most important position in the markets of the world ; and I rejoice to learn that the improvements in agriculture which skilled labor and science have of late years developed in the mother country, are fast increasing the facilities of your soil, enabling you to compete successfully with the energetic people whose stock and products are now ranged in friendly rivalry with your own within this vast enclosure.

The Almighty has this year granted you that greatest boon to a people,—an abundant harvest. I trust it will make glad many a home of those I see around me, and bring increased wealth and prosperity to this magnificent Province.

My duties as representative of the Queen, deputed by Her to visit British North America, cease this day ; but in a private capacity I am about to visit, before I return home, that remarkable land which claims with us a common ancestry, and in whose extraordinary progress every Englishman feels a common interest. Before I quit British soil, let me once more address through you the inhabitants of United Canada, and bid them an affectionate farewell.

May God pour down his choicest blessings upon this great and loyal people.

A shower of rain descending, the royal party entered the Palace, and once more inspected a part of the products of Upper Canada. The Prince, being slightly indisposed, retired with his suite; but the Duke of Newcastle shortly afterwards returned to inspect the cattle, with which he was much pleased.

Shortly after two in the afternoon, His Royal Highness took his departure from Hamilton, in the royal car of the Great Western Railway.

The Volunteers and National Societies turned out, and the Field Battery boomed forth a royal salute.

The evening was far advanced when the royal train arrived at Windsor, which is situated nearly at the extreme south-western point of the Province, where a royal salute was fired by the London Field Battery. An Address was presented by the Mayor on behalf of the Council of Windsor; and, after a brief reply, His Royal Highness and suite stepped on board the steamer *Windsor* awaiting him, and, amidst the most enthusiastic, hearty, and soul-stirring cheers of the Canadians, left British America for the United States.

Reception in the United States of America.

On board the steamer were the Governor of Michigan, the Mayor of Detroit (Mr. Buhl), and a large party of the most influential citizens of Detroit.

The whole harbour was lit up by the ships and steamers in port; the majority of which had variegated lamps from stem to stern.

It was not very long before His Royal Highness landed at Detroit, which is situated directly opposite Windsor.

On the Prince stepping on the American soil, the Mayor welcomed him to the United States as Lord Renfrew; the immense concourse of spectators cheering lustily. His Royal Highness and suite put up at the Russel House, where apartments had been provided for them; and here His Excellency the Governor General and suite, a portion of the Canadian Ministry, and the Officers of the Civil Service engaged during the tour, took leave of him, and returned to Canada.

On Friday (Sept 21st), His Royal Highness, after driving round Detroit with the Mayor, took the special train provided for him on the Michigan Central Railroad for Chicago; at which city he arrived at 7.30 in the evening.

A great crowd of persons had congregated at the railway station; but, with the exception of an attempt at cheering, no enthusiasm was displayed, which went to prove that his "incog" was somewhat respected.

The Prince had taken apartments at the Richmond House, whither he and his suite procceded, accompanied by the Mayor (Mr. Wentworth). On Saturday, 22nd, His Royal Highness, after visiting several of the public buildings of the city, accompanied by his suite, took his departure from Chicago, by the same car that had brought him thither. His Royal Highness's destination was Dwight Station, on the Prairies, where he intended to have a few days' shooting; game being very plentiful on the Prairies.

His Royal Highness and suite were located at the residences of Messrs. Spencer and Morgan.

On Sunday, the royal party attended Divine Service in the old

Presbyterian Church of Dwight, where the Rev. Dr. Young delivered an excellent sermon.

The Prince and suite remained at Dwight until the 26th, and regretted that they could not prolong their stay. His Royal Highness was greatly delighted with the sport in which he so actively engaged.

At Alton the cars were exchanged for the steamer; and as the royal party embarked, a salute was fired, and the people cheered in a most demonstrative manner.

St. Louis was reached at six o'clock; where the Mayor (Mr. Filley) met His Royal Highness and welcomed him to the city, escorting him to Barnum's Hotel, where apartments had been taken for him and his suite.

On Thursday (27th), His Royal Highness and suite visited the State Fair, and inaugurated the Western Academy of Arts. In the evening he was serenaded by the entire Fire Brigade. He took his leave of St. Louis for Cincinnati, in a special train, on the following morning (28th); where he arrived next day at one o'clock, and was received by the Mayor (Mr. Bishop), who escorted him to the Barnet House.

During the day His Royal Highness visited Mount Auburn, Clifton; and in the evening attended a grand ball given in his honour, at Pike's Opera House, where he danced until half-past eleven, and then retired.

On Sunday (30th Sept.), he attended Divine Service at St. John's Church where Bishop McIlvain preached the sermon.

At ten o'clock on the morning of Monday, 1st October, His Royal Highness and suite left Cincinnati for Pittsburg; where he arrived the same day.

On Thursday (2nd October), after receiving a short Address from the Judges, the royal party took their leave of Pittsburg, and were escorted to the cars by a grand procession of the Civic Authorities, City Guards, &c., and, amidst enthusiastic cheers, took their departure for Harrisburg. At this place he was received by the Mayor (Mr. Ticknor), and City Council, who conducted them to the principal hotel.

On Wednesday (3rd October), after visiting the Governor of the State (Mr. Parker), in the Capitol, the royal party took their departure; the men cheering heartily, and the ladies waving their 'kerchiefs in a most inspiring manner.

At Baltimore, where they arrived at one o'clock, they were received by the Mayor and City Council, and nearly the entire populace, who cheered the Prince frantically. His Royal Highness passed through the town to the Washington depôt, where he and his suite immediately took the cars for the Capital of the United States, which was reached at four o'clock.

Here he was received by General Cass, who, upon being introduced to him by Lord Lyons, welcomed His Royal Highness, in the name of the President, to Washington.

The President's carriages were in waiting. His Royal Highness and suite entered them, accompanied by General Cass; the people cheering heartily on the route to the White House.

The Chief Magistrate of the United States, President James Buchanan, was here introduced by General Cass; who also welcomed His Royal Highness in the name of the people.

In the evening, a grand dinner party was given to the Prince by the President.

On Thursday (Oct. 4th), the President held a levee at the White House in his honour, when a good number of gentlemen were presented. The President shook each gentleman warmly by the hand as presented; he Prince, who was on his right, slightly inclining his head.

Afterwards the royal party visited the Capitol of Washington, and many of the public buildings and institutions; the Prince, and in fact the whole royal party, paying much attention to everything of interest.

In the evening, another grand dinner party was given; at which a number of the diplomatic corps, in full uniform, attended.

A grand display of fireworks also took place in the evening; the Prince viewing them from the balcony of the White House.

On Friday (Oct. 5th), the royal party, accompanied by the President, Cabinet, and Diplomatic Corps, embarked on board the steam revenue-cutter *Harriet Lane*, and proceeded up the Potomac, to Mount Vernon, the memorable home of Washington; where the Prince viewed the great General's former residence, and the curiosities contained therein; not failing to visit the tomb where his ashes lie. Upon being requested, the Prince planted a small horse-chesnut tree, in commemoration of his visit. On returning to the cutter, luncheon was served up; and immediately after, dancing commenced, the Prince dancing first with Miss Lane (the President's niece).

On returning to Washington, a salute was fired from the Arsenal; and the whole party proceeded to the residence of Lord Lyons, where the royal party partook of dinner. His Royal Highness and suite afterwards, accompanied by the President, returned to the White House.

On Saturday morning (Oct. 6th), the royal party took leave of the President and his niece, Miss Lane, who had so nobly done the honours of the hospitable White House, and, embarking on board the *Harriet Lane*, accompanied by the Cabinet, sailed down the Potomac, with parting salutes from the Arsenal and Navy Yard.

At Acquia Creek, His Royal Highness took the cars for Richmond; which he reached at about seven o'clock, and was received by the Mayor, together with a committee of citizens, and amidst every demonstration of joy on the part of the inhabitants, who escorted him to the Exchange Hotel.

On Sunday (Oct. 7th), he attended Divine Service at St. John's Church, and visited the Governor of the State (Mr. Litcher).

On Monday morning (Oct. 8th), he left Richmond for Baltimore; where he arrived at 8 p. m., and received a grand welcome from the civic dignitaries, and the military corps of that place.

On Tuesday, he drove out with the Mayor, with whom he visited some of the public buildings; and departed for Philadelphia at noon, where he arrived at half-past four, and was received by the city authorities, and conducted to the Continental Hotel, where apartments had been taken for him and suite.

On Wednesday, he visited the most interesting portions of the city; and in the evening attended Strakosch's Opera House, where selections from the operas of *Martha* and *Traviata* were performed. On entering the building, the National Anthem was performed, the whole audience rising and uncovering.

On Thursday (Oct 11th), His Royal Highness and suite left for New York. At Amboy, the steam-cutter *Harriet Lane* was moored, with a party of gentlemen on board from New York; among whom were Mr. Archibald, British Consul at that place, and General Winifield Scott, U.S.A. The Reception Committee was also on board, to bid him welcome.

His Royal Highness was received by General Scott and the principal gentlemen of the committee, and was afterwards introduced to the whole party on board. The *Harriet Lane* shortly afterwards steamed up and left for her destination. A collation was partaken of on board, and the royal party ascended to the deck. On passing the several forts on the river, salutes were fired, and other marks of strong attachment shown to the royal visitors.

At two o'clock, the cutter made New York, and the batteries poured forth their deafening thunders, accompanied by the cheers of the whole populace of that great, industrial, and commercial city. Castle Garden had been chosen as the landing-place; and there the cutter was, in a few minutes, safely moored, the people cheering most heartily. His Royal Highness was received by the Mayor (Fernando Wood, Esq.), the Councillors of New York, and the chief personages of the place.

The Mayor welcomed him in these words :—

YOUR ROYAL HIGHNESS,—

As Chief Magistrate of this city, I welcome you here, and believe that I represent the entire population without exception.

The Prince replied :—

It affords me great pleasure to accept your hospitalities, which I have no doubt will be worthy the great city of New York..

His Royal Highness then entered an apartment and attired himself in his colonel's uniform; and in a few minutes reappeared, mounted a splendid horse which awaited him, and, accompanied by his suite, the Mayor, and the party of gentlemen who formed an escort, proceeded to the Battery, where he reviewed a portion of the troops, the whole concourse of people there collected cheering frantically.

A procession was then organized, and His Royal Highness and suite, entering their carriages, were driven through the principal streets. The troops on Broadway made a fine display, and thousands gave tokens of joy and welcome, every house and thoroughfare being crowded with spectators. It was dark and late in the evening before the Fifth Avenue Hotel was reached, yet great crowds were collected around the building, who cheered him again and again.

In the evening the Caledonian Club serenaded him.

On Friday (Oct. 2), the royal party visited the University of New York, the Astor Library, and the Cooper Institute.

At the former institution, the Prince received an Address from Chancellor Ferris, and listened to Professor Morse speaking on the "Electric Telegraph."

In the evening he attended the grand ball given in his honour by the citizens of New York, at the Academy of Music, which was a magnificent and gorgeous affair, and, but for the accident in the falling of the floor, would have been a complete success and a great credit to our American neighbours in that locality.

His Royal Highness opened the ball with the lady of Governor Morgan, of New York, dancing secondly with Mrs. Goold Hoyt, and afterwards with the following ladies: Miss H. Russell, Miss Jay, Mrs. Edward Cooper, Mrs. Belmont, Mrs. H. B. Field, Miss Van Buren, Mrs. Kernochan, and Miss Butler.

He retired from the room at five a. m.

On Saturday the royal party visited several public and private places of interest, and among them the celebrated Barnum's Museum.

In the evening, the Prince viewed, from the balcony in front of the hotel, the grand torch-light procession of the Firemen in his honour; which was a most magnificent spectacle, the whole Fire Brigade turning out in uniform, with their engines, which were gaily decorated and lit up with transparencies. The procession extended several miles, and was one of the finest sights ever witnessed.

On Sunday, the Prince and suite attended Divine Service at Trinity Church, where the following clergymen took part in the services: Bishops Potter, Odenheimer, and Talbot; Rev. Messrs. Paine, Ogilby, Creighton, and Vinton. The latter gentleman preached the sermon.

On Monday morning (Oct. 15), the royal party left New York for West Point, embarking on board the *Harriet Lane*. Salutes were fired, and the great mass of people congregated cheered as "republicans seldom or ever cheered before;" showing their sincerity, and good wishes for England's Heir. The cutter arrived at her destination at a quarter to three in the afternoon, when a national salute of thirty-three guns was fired from the battery.

The Prince was received by Colonel Delafield, who, we understand, is the Commandant of the place, and a staff of American officers. A company of Dragoons formed the royal escort to the Commandant's quarters, where the staff of officers was presented to His Royal Highness, who shook hands with each.

Shortly afterwards, a review of the Cadets of the Academy took place; the Prince and suite, in plain walking-costume, accompanying the staff, in front and in rear of the reviewed. The royal party next day (16th), after examining several of the most interesting parts around this locality, embarked on board the steamer *Daniel Drew* for Albany (having been invited thither by Governor Morgan).

About twenty miles below Albany, the *Drew* met the steamer *Young America* with the Mayor and Corporation of that city on board, having come to welcome His Royal Highness, and escort him to their city; at which they arrived at half-past four, receiving a very enthusiastic reception from the Albanians, who crowded the wharves and cheered long and loud. We should also note that the city throughout was nicely decorated.

Two regiments of Volunteer Militia acted as Guard of Honour, presenting arms as the Prince passed to the carriage provided for him. His Royal Highness was escorted to the Capitol, where he was received by Governor Morgan, and welcomed to Albany.

The Governor then escorted His Royal Highness and suite to the several public buildings; and afterwards to the Congress Hall Hotel, where apartments had been engaged for their accommodation.

In the evening, the royal party dined at the Governor's residence; where a brilliant company had assembled by invitation, the Heads of Departments, Mayor, City Staff, &c. attending, and which did not break up until a quarter after ten.

On the following morning (17th), the Prince and suite took the cars for Boston; where they arrived at four o'clock p.m., receiving a very fine reception from the civil and military authorities, and the people of that place.

The royal party was escorted into the city to the Revere House by Governor Banks,—several detachments of dragoons and infantry forming a grand procession,—amidst the greatest cheering from the inhabitants, who crowded and jammed the streets.

The following day (18th) was a general holiday in Boston, by proclamation; consequently the many places of business in the city were all closed, and everything presented a quiet and Sunday-like appearance.

In the morning, at 11 o'clock, the Royal party proceeded to the State House, where the Governor formally welcomed the Prince to Boston, addressing him as follows:—

It is with great pleasure that I welcome your Royal Highness to the Commonwealth of Massachusetts, and extend to you the most cordial greetings of its people. They have regarded with profound gratification your visit to this continent, so auspicious in its opening, so fortunate in its progress, and now, I regret to say, so near its termination. Be assured, Sir, you will bear with you the united wishes of the people of Massachusetts for your safe return to your friends and to your country; to which we are attached by so many ties of language, law, and liberty. In their name, I bid you welcome. I welcome, also, with unfeigned pleasure, the distinguished and honorable gentlemen of your suite. Permit me to present to you my associates in the Executive Department of the Government,—His Honor the Lieutenant-Governor, the Gentlemen of the Executive Council, and the Secretary of State."

The several gentlemen referred to were recognized by the Prince, who shook hands cordially with the Aids, whom he had met before.

The Representatives' Hall was filled to overflowing by ladies. The Governor led the Prince through the hall, while the ladies rose *en masse*, greeting him with smiling faces and waving handkerchiefs. The Senate Chamber was occupied by some forty members of the Valuation Committee, who were also permitted to gaze on the face of His Royal Highness.

The Prince and suite then witnessed a review of several regiments of Volunteer Militia and troops of Cavalry, with which they were much pleased.

After the review, the Prince partook of a slight collation, at the State House, with the Hon. Edward Everett and other distinguished guests.

In the afternoon, the royal party attended the Music Hall, where the school-children had been collected to give the Prince a welcome, by singing, amongst other select pieces of music, a grand national ode, written by the celebrated Dr. Oliver Wendell Holmes.

The following is the ode:—

AIR:—GOD SAVE THE QUEEN.

God bless our Fathers' Land;
Keep her in heart and hand,
  One with our own.
From all her foes defend,
Be her brave people's friend,
On all her realms descend,
  Protect her throne!

Father, in loving care
Guard thou her kingdom's heir,
  Guide all his ways.
Thine arm his shelter be
From harm by land and sea;
Bid storm and dangers flee,
  Prolong his days!

Lord, let war's tempests cease,
Fold the whole earth in peace
  Under thy wings!
Make all thy nations one,
All hearts beneath the sun,
Till thou shalt reign alone,
  Great King of Kings!

How touchingly must this have fell on the Prince's ears, sung by over a thousand little voices, and joyfully reiterated by the immense assemblage present, who cheered vociferously and clapped their hands, all joining in one fervent prayer for his welfare.

In the evening, he attended the ball given in his honour at the Boston Theatre, and the last prior to his departure for England.

This was quite as grand, and far more successful, than the one given him at New York.

The Prince opened the ball by dancing a quadrille with Mrs. Lincoln (the Lady Mayoress), and afterwards danced with the following ladies:—Mrs. Governor Banks, Mrs. Wise (daughter of Hon. Edward Everett), Miss Fanny Crowninshield, Miss Susan Emery, Miss Bigelow, Mrs. Col. Chickering, Mrs. Harrison Ritchie, Miss Lombard, Miss Fanny Peabody, and Miss Kitty Fay. The Prince retired at a late hour.

On Friday (19th October), the royal party visited Cambridge, near Boston, where the Prince received a hearty welcome from the inhabitants. He also paid a flying visit to Mount Auburn Cemetery, and Harvard College, both in Cambridge; receiving at the latter place a very spirited reception from the Faculty and Students, and partook of a slight collation after visiting the several departments of that celebrated institution.

On the following morning, His Royal Highness and suite took the cars, and, amidst every demonstration of esteem and affection from the distinguished personages that had helped to entertain them, and the whole people of Boston, took their departure from that interesting city for Portland, where the royal squadron was in waiting to convey them to England.

Portland was reached at half-past one, when a salute of 33 guns was fired. The Prince received a fitting and enthusiastic reception here; not from the worthy Portlanders alone, but from a crowd of Canadians and other visitors, who had arrived in the cars from all parts to have a last look at His Royal Highness, to bid him an adieu, and to wish him good speed and a prosperous voyage. The royal party was received by Mayor Howard and the members of the City Council, a number of distinguished gentlemen from various parts of the Union, and a large body of State Militia. A procession was organized, and the Prince and suite, having been conducted to carriages, were escorted through the principal streets of Portland to the Victoria Pier, amidst the deafening cheers of the many thousands who had congregated to witness his departure. It was not long before the royal party had embarked on board the barge which awaited to convey them from the shores of America, perhaps for ever. Friends' hands were shaken sadly, but warmly; expressions of mutual kindness spoken, the people looking on in sadness as the royal barge pushed off. Then the cannons roared, people cheered, bells rang, and every expression of loyalty was given in that American town, with such warmth, with such feeling, that one imagined himself on British ground.

The royal squadron weighed anchor at half-past four, and, with a fair wind and flowing tide, steamed out on the broad Atlantic, amidst the heart-stirring cheers of the multitude. Although no doubt not heard on board the royal vessels, yet it was a glorious satisfaction to the people to raise their voices in honour of the son of the model Sovereign, and the future monarch of the first throne on the face of the globe.

Our task has now drawn to a conclusion, and it has been a most agreeable one. We have, to the best of our ability, drawn a slight sketch of the Prince of Wales' glorious and commemorative tour through a portion of the vast continent of North America; and our honest and candid readers will acknowledge, that, regarding the accuracy of our narration, we are entitled to claim their sympathies, even though the treatment of the subject has not been elaborate.

We have not devoted so much attention to the receptions and festivities in the Lower Provinces or the United States, simply for the reason that the *object* of this royal tour was Canada; still the loyal devotion of the one, and the courteous kindness of the other, are subjects of which every true Briton may justly feel proud. To see a great Republic like the United States, one of the only two free nations on the earth, and which at one time fiercely waged war against Great Britain, entertain and nearly idolize a scion of that same power, is something not easily to be forgotten, and binds the ties that already greatly endear us to our Republican friends, and makes us feel that we are closely allied together. It makes the British people respect what they have not until now perfectly understood,—the true American character. Oh, may nothing ever sever a friendship such as this, bound together by one so illustrious!

Long as we had wished and patiently waited for the Prince's visit, it came at last. We will not here recapitulate Her Majesty's generous reasons for acceding to our petition: they are so well-known, so highly appreciated, and so often referred to in this little volume, that it would be idle to repeat them. The Queen sent, not a junior member of the royal family, but the Heir Apparent himself. He came, and he has gone. He has received an ovation, which, for costly magnificence, generous display, and the grand exhibition of enthusiastic and loyal feelings, can, if even equalled, never be surpassed, and, what is certain, can never be forgotten by him or ourselves. No, not in his proudest days, perhaps, when he will be all-glorious on the throne or the battle-field (as destiny may direct), will he ever forget the cordial, the loyal reception which he received from all shades of parties and countrymen on his visit to America.

And this visit to Canada, at least, will be productive of much good; irrespective of the political party who wished to force false grievances on the royal ear, and the religious differences in Upper Canada.

Sorry should we be to turn the enthusiastic reception which the Heir Apparent received from the Canadians, into base capital; but the interest evinced in the growing advancement of the country by the royal party is sure to propagate deep surmise as to our "future state." We may be assured, that, although the great question of the day—i. e. the Federation of the Colonies —is not at once determined, our good position at the Court of St. James will not suffer; and when that great policy of a great head can be safely attempted, we may hope for no insurmountable barriers to its being properly carried into execution.

In another view of the matter, we are of opinion that we have gained a great success over the other dependencies of the Crown. To be visited by a Prince of the Royal Family is certainly a great honour; but when that Prince is the Heir Apparent to the Throne, —the one that some day (though, let us wish, for our beloved Queen's sake, a far distant one) may mount the Throne of England to rule and to be obeyed,—then is the success enhanced tenfold. He has seen the country and its people; he is acquainted with its vast resources and growing prosperity; he knows our wishes, and what this vast tract of country requires,—wishes and requirements far too many to be enumerated, but not too many to receive attention.

Let us, then, patiently await the great harbinger of all events,— time; and in so doing, remember that we have now the most powerful of friends in Europe, who are ready and willing to advance the interests of our country and our homes.

O

Recapitulation of Places visited by His Royal Highness Albert Edward, Prince of Wales.

Leave.	Arrive at	Miles.
July 10, Plymouth, England.	July 23, St. Johns, N.F.......	—
" 26, St. Johns, N. F.	" 30, Halifax, N.B.........	900
Aug. 2, Halifax.	Aug. 2, St. John, N.B........	120
" 7, St. John, N.B.	" 9, Charlottetown, P.E.I..	250
" 11, Charlottetown.	" 12, Gaspé..............	200
" 13, Gaspé.	" 15, Quebec, Canada East.	650
" 20, Quebec.	" 20, Chaudière Falls, and back..............	30
" 23, Quebec.	" 24, Montreal, C.E........	170
" 29, Montreal.	" Caughnawaga and back..............	180
" 30, Montreal.	" Sherbrooke and back..	50
" 31, Montreal.	Sept. 1, Ottawa..............	180
Sept. 3, Ottawa.	" 4, Kingston............	100
" 6, Kingston.	" 6, Cobourg............	90
" 7, Cobourg.	" 7, Toronto.............	70
" 10, Toronto.	" 10, Collingwood........	95
" 13, Collingwood.	" 13, London............	25
" 15, London.	" 16, Chippewa..........	126
" 17, Chippewa.	" 17, Queenston..........	10
" 18, Queenston.	" 18, Hamilton...........	25
" 20, Hamilton.	" 20, Detroit, Michigan.....	150
" 21, Detroit.	" 21, Chicago, Illinois.....	284
" 22, Chicago.	" 22, Dwight............;	70
" 25, Dwight.	" 25, Stewart's Grove and back..............	30
" 27, Dwight.	" 27, St. Louis, Missouri....	212
" 29, St. Louis.	" 29, Cincinnati, Ohio......	340
Oct'r 2, Cincinnati.	Oct'r 2, Harrisburg, Pa.......	615
" 3, Harrisburg.	" 3, Washington, via Baltimore..............	123
" 5, Washington.	" 5, Mount Vernon and back	34
" 6, Washington.	" 6, Richmond, Va........	130
" 8, Richmond.	" 8, Baltimore, Md........	150
" 9, Baltimore.	" 9, Philadelphia.........	98
" 11, Philadelphia.	" 11, New York...........	90
" 15, New York.	" 15, West Point.........	51
" 16, West Point.	" 16, Albany.............	99
" 17, Albany.	" 17, Boston, Mass.........	200
" 20, Boston.	" 20, Portland, Me........	187
" 20, Portland for England.		
Total distance travelled................·......6,134		

N. Y. Herald.

APPENDIX.

ADDRESSES
PRESENTED DURING THE ROYAL TOUR.

WINDSOR, NOVA SCOTIA.

To the Most High, Puissant, and Illustrious Prince Albert Edward, Prince of the United Kingdom of Great Britain and Ireland, Prince of Wales, Duke of Saxony, Prince of Coburg and Gotha, Great Steward of Scotland, Duke of Cornwall and Rothsay, Earl of Chester, Carrick, and Dublin, Baron of Renfrew, and Lord of the Isles, K. G. :—

MAY IT PLEASE YOUR ROYAL HIGHNESS,—

We, the loyal inhabitants of the township of Windsor, of the county of Hants, in the Province of Nova Scotia, beg leave to approach your Royal Highness to offer the humble expression of a heartfelt welcome, and to thank Your Royal Highness for the unprecedented honour of this opportunity, condescendingly offered us, of avowing our devoted loyalty and unwavering attachment to the throne and person of our Most Gracious Queen, and to her illustrious house and family; our exalted admiration and respect for the eminent talents and virtues of her Royal Consort, and our fervent aspirations and hopes for a long career of happiness and glory for Your Royal Highness. Representing on this happy occasion the loyal feelings of the oldest university town in Her Majesty's widely-extended colonial possessions, we view it as our highest privilege and singular honour to be permitted to greet Your Royal Highness in the immediate neighbourhood of an institution founded by his Majesty King George the Third, the august and illustrious ancestor of Your Royal Highness. Believing that the University of Windsor has continued during successive years to answer the wise and benevolent purposes of its founder, and knowing that in King's College, under the Royal Charter then granted, have been educated in religion, in literature and science a great number of the clergy, many of the most distinguished members of the bench and bar in this and the neighbouring colonies, many military men, whose heroic achievements have been widely celebrated, and several others, including members of the different religious denominations, equally conspicuous in the various walks of life, all of whom have ever manifested the firmest allegiance to the British Throne and Government. But we are aware that your Royal Highness has only a few moments to bestow for the brief but ever-memorable occasion. We are extremely grateful, and we hope that Your Royal Highness's visit to Nova Scotia may be agreeable to Your Royal Highness, as it is most welcome and most gratifying to us; and that on your happy return to Windsor Castle and to the renowned University in which Your Royal Highness is enrolled, Your Royal Highness may convey to her Gracious Majesty, our beloved Queen, the assurance of the sentiments of inviolable loyalty to the throne and of affectionate veneration for the Constitution, which pervade all ranks and classes of her Majesty's subjects in this portion of Her dominions; and not least, of the youth of our University, educated in a town whose fortress was honoured by the presence and still bears the name of her Majesty's illustrious father.

REPLY.

GENTLEMEN,—The Address which you have presented to me demands my acknowledgments. It is a pleasure to me to visit, even though it be but in passing, this seat of learning in British North America; to find that the sons of these Provinces are successfully pursuing, within the precincts of your town, the studies which I have myself abandoned only for a time, that I might come to these lands. I thank you for your kind recollection of my grandfather, and for your loyal sentiments.

HANTSPORT, N. S.

To His Royal Highness Albert Edward, Prince of Wales, &c., &c.

MAY IT PLEASE YOUR ROYAL HIGHNESS,—

We, the inhabitants of Hantsport, would humbly represent that, in favouring our quiet village with your presence, Your Royal Highness confers on us an honour greater than our words can express, or any demonstration of ours can testify. Yet, though our language and our means may fail, that honour is not the less appreciated, nor less that deep and lasting sense of obligation our hearts must ever acknowledge through the gracious permission of your August Mother. We joyfully accord to Your Royal Highness, as the representative of our Queen, the reception we would accord to Her Majesty. We do not exhibit to Your Royal Highness anything to interest, beyond such bounties as nature has bestowed upon us. We boast of no imposing edifices, no grand triumphal arch, no meritorious work of art, nor can we proudly point to scenes of classic or historic fame; but, better far than these, we welcome our Prince with the earnest affections of a devoted, manly race; we greet the first-born son of our beloved Queen with feelings of deepest respect, and proudly hail the future monarch of that glorious, globe-encircling empire of which we are a part. We would represent our interest to be maritime, and chiefly in other trade with the brother land, thus adding the strong tie of commerce to the pre-existing ones of blood, of language, and religion. Our pride is in the British institutions, laws, and flag; to uphold which, in time of need, we will ever aid with enthusiastic Volunteers. Should this village ever become the city of the beautiful basin beyond, of touching historic interest, and in which Your Royal Highness is about to sail, the rise of that city will date from the royal selection of this port for your embarkation to-day; in commemoration of which it has been designated by the people, and we humbly trust will also meet the approbation of your Royal Highness, as Princeton. Long live Your Royal Highness. Long may you grace the mighty throne of Britain; and when in after years, if your august name shall be inseparably associated with deeds as great and onerous as ever hallowed the memory of earth's noblest, may we hope, presumptuous though it may seem, that, when relaxing from the toils of state, the mind of the king shall revert, may it ever be with joy and pride, to his youthful days, the hour spent in Hantsport may not have been forgotten.

REPLY.

GENTLEMEN,—I thank you warmly for your hearty and kind welcome. With agricultural capabilities on one side, and maritime advantages on the other, your town bids fair to rise in consequence and wealth, and I very sincerely wish you every prosperity.

PICTOU, N. S.

To His Royal Highness Albert Edward, Prince of Wales, &c., &c.

MAY IT PLEASE YOUR ROYAL HIGHNESS,—

The inhabitants of the county of Pictou beg leave to express their sincere gratitude for the distinguished honor conferred upon them by the visit of Your Royal Highness, and they now greet you with a warm and cordial welcome. They hail the visit of Your Royal Highness to Her Majesty's North American Colonies as a pledge and assurance of the deep and lively interest which our most gracious Queen takes in the prosperity of her extended dominions, and they rejoice in this opportunity of being enabled so directly to manifest their devoted attachment and loyalty to the crown and sovereignty of Great Britain. Enjoying the great happiness of being British subjects, and the recipients of the blessings which that glorious privilege confers, their hearts are knit in indissoluble bonds of loyalty to the British throne. The wisdom and justice which have distinguished the reign of our most gracious Sovereign, and the virtues which adorn Her Majesty's court and life, have secured from her subjects in Nova Scotia feelings of the most devoted attachment to Her Majesty's royal person and family. Within a century past the primeval forests covered the soil where, in the progress of Your Royal Highness this day, many happy homes and productive fields have presented themselves to the eye. Those have been acquired under the fostering care of the parent state, and from the influence of the virtues and industry which have always characterized the inhabitants of the British islands, whence this county was originally settled. The inhabitants of the county of Pictou offer their sincere prayers that Your Royal Highness may have a prosperous and pleasant journey through the dominions of Her Majesty in North America ; and that Your Royal Highness may return safe and gratified to that country which, even in this distant land, is designated by the endearing name of home.

REPLY.

In your town I close a visit to the Province of Nova Scotia, which has given me unmixed pleasure, and has brought forth proof of devotion to the Queen and to your mother country, which must ever remain engraved on my memory. I thank you warmly for an Address which, so short can be my stay in this place, is at once a welcome and a farewell. My journey this day through your beautiful country has impressed me with an additional sense of the great destiny which awaits these lands. I heartily wish success and happiness to the settlers whom I have passed, and a speedy and productive development of the vast mineral wealth which lies beneath and around you.

CANADA.

GASPÉ.

MAY IT PLEASE YOUR ROYAL HIGHNESS,—

We, the Clergy, Merchants, and other inhabitants of Gaspé, beg leave most respectfully to welcome Your Royal Highness on your first arrival on the shores of Canada, and to express the pleasure we feel at this distinguished mark of condescension.

This visit proves to us, that, though isolated and few in number, we are not forgotten, amid the many gay, wealthy, and populous cities where the presence of Your Royal Highness is joyfully expected ; it gladdens our hearts and imparts new life to the principles of loyalty, which, we are proud to say, exists in all our breasts.

'Tis true we cannot receive Your Royal Highness with the sound of music; we cannot exhibit to your view the waving plume of the conqueror, or the glittering sword of the warrior: all we have to offer you is the tribute of warm hearts, and a beautiful specimen of the work of the God of nature; our scenery is unrivalled in loveliness in the Province, and our harbour, although it may be equalled, cannot be surpassed, in point of safety, facility of approach, and extent of accommodation. It would ill-become this small and comparatively poor community to speak boastfully; yet we may venture to express the hope that Your Royal Highness will not regret calling at our port, but rather that, when in the order of God's providence Your Royal Highness shall be called upon to wear Britain's crown, you will sometimes think of Gaspé and its inhabitants.

It may not be uninteresting to Your Royal Highness to know that many of the inhabitants of this place are descended from English families, who, rather than renounce their allegiance to the British crown, emigrated here during the American Revolution; others are descended from the French who first colonized this country; but, although we thus differ in our native origin, we are happy to say that we have hitherto lived in peace, and in friendship, respecting each other's particular views and creeds, and acting on the golden rule, " Do unto others as you would have others do unto you."

It now only remains for us to express our most ardent hope, that, in Your Royal Highness's farther progress through the Province, the sights that will burst upon your view, whether in our thriving and beautiful cities, or in our agricultural districts, Your Royal Highness shall be convinced that the Province of Canada is indeed a bright jewel in Britain's Crown; and that the spirit of loyalty, everywhere manifested, is an earnest of our permanent attachment to, and dependence upon, Great Britain, the star of nations, and the land of liberty and peace.

Wishing Your Royal Highness a pleasant journey through the Province, and a safe return home, we are Your Royal Highness's most respectful and obedient servants.

His Royal Highness replied in brief, complimenting the Gaspé people very highly on the appearance of the harbour, as to the beauty of the scenery surrounding it, and the industry displayed in all directions.

The Mayor of Gaspé then presented His Royal Highness with the following Petition:—

MAY IT PLEASE YOUR ROYAL HIGHNESS,—

We, the Mayor and Councillors of Gaspé Bay South, and York, beg leave most respectfully to request, that, in consideration of this Port being the first that has been honoured by the presence of royalty in this Province, they may be permitted hereafter to call it Port Albert, to perpetuate the remembrance of Your Royal Highness's visit.

We are Your Royal Highness's humble and obedient servants.

CHICOUTIMI.

To His Royal Highness Albert Edward, Prince of Wales, &c., &c.

MAY IT PLEASE YOUR ROYAL HIGHNESS,—

To allow me, in the name of the municipality and inhabitants of the county of Chicoutimi, to wish and offer you a hearty welcome on your arrival amongst us.

Still occupied in penetrating into the primeval forest, our population can only associate in heart and soul with the brilliant manifestations which the presence of Your Royal Highness will create all over Canada; but we shall always be proud and happy, if Your Royal Highness departs from amongst us with the feeling and conviction that in no other part of her Majesty's dominions are to be found subjects more devotedly attached to their Queen, or more determined, as much as it lies in their power, to add to the glory of the reign of your illustrious mother.

While our compatriots of the older portions of the Province are advancing in the arts and sciences, as well as in commerce and industry, and doing their utmost to make it a great star of the British Empire, we are advancing into and clearing away the forest, and as it were, conquering a new province to add to the Crown, which at some future period Your Royal Highness may be called on to wear.

We humbly pray Your Royal Highness to lay these expressions of our attachment and loyalty at the foot of the Throne, and to make them known to our most gracious Sovereign.

JOHN KANE,
Reeve of the County of Chicoutimi.

Grand Bay, 15th August, 1860.

REPLY.

H. M. S. "HERO," 15th August, 1860.

SIR,—I have the honour, by desire of His Royal Highness the Prince of Wales, to acknowledge the receipt of the Address which you have this day presented to him from the Municipality of the County of Chicoutimi.

His Royal Highness is much gratified by the expressions of loyalty to the Queen, and of kindness towards himself, which that Address contains, and he is much disappointed that the state of the weather this morning prevented him from proceeding sufficiently far up the waters of the magnificent Saguenay to enable him to receive and answer it in person.

I have the honour to be,
Sir,
Your very obedient servant,
NEWCASTLE.

David Price, Esq., M.P.P.

QUEBEC.

CHURCH OF ENGLAND SYNOD.

MAY IT PLEASE YOUR ROYAL HIGHNESS,—

We, the Bishop, Clergy, and Laity of the United Church of England and Ireland in the Diocese of Quebec, in Synod assembled, gladly avail ourselves of the arrival of Your Royal Highness on our shore to testify our deep and fervent loyalty towards that sceptre which in good time we trust you are destined to succeed, and also express our heartfelt gratification that the Heir Apparent to the British Monarchy has for the first time in its history visited that great and important Province in which our lot is cast. We believe that in this auspicious event is implied much more than the mere graceful recognition of the request made by our Canadian legislators for the presence and sanction of the greatest work of engineering skill the world has seen. We view it rather as an evidence of the more ultimate union which is growing between the mother country and the Canadian offshoot, and as a pledge that that union will be developed into an enduring and indissoluble unity. And moreover we prize the more highly the presence of Your Royal Highness amongst us, as we shall thereby be enabled to add the feeling of personal acquaintance and attachment to that abstract loyalty which we have always cherished in the cause of your progress. Your Royal Highness will be in a position to judge of the rapid advance in material prosperity which the country has made in the last few years. Amidst the busy scene, the Church of England may seem to have been remiss in her work, and to have done little to keep pace with the rapid motion of the world around. We have, it is true, comparatively few marks of outward prosperity. We have no state privileges, no great cathedral, no opulent endowments, and in this part of the Province we are scattered and few in number; yet we are endeavouring as best we may, and by God's blessing we trust with some measure of success, to reproduce in the new land all that is essentially important in the doctrine and discipline of that pure and refined branch of Christ's Holy Catholic Church, which in England entwines so closely with the very foundations of the Throne; and we pray you to remember, that the petitions for the welfare and prosperity of Your Royal Highness will continue to be offered, and with not less fervency from our humble friends as from those splendid fabrics which the wealth and piety of our ancestors have reared at home for the worship of the Almighty. That God may have you in His holy keeping; that He may conduct you on your way, and restore you to your native land in health and safety, is our sincere and earnest prayer. To His care we recommend you; may He ever bless, preserve, and keep you; may He fill you with the richest gifts of His Holy Spirit, and finally bring you to everlasting life, through Jesus Christ our Lord.

REPLY.

GENTLEMEN,—It is a source of no little pleasure to me to receive from you these words of welcome, and to hear from the lips of your Bishop the assurance that your prayers are offered, for my future usefulness and happiness, within the walls of your Cathedral. I have joined in the petitions offered for the Queen; and I am convinced that the ministers of the church from which this Address emanates, do not fail to inculcate these principles of loyalty which are so characteristic of this Province. I trust that it may be my lot, whatever be the future reserved for me, to realize the hopes which you have expressed, and to secure the beneficial results of this my first acquaintance with the Canadian people.

COUNTY OF QUEBEC.

To His Royal Highness Albert Edward, Prince of Wales, &c., &c.

MAY IT PLEASE YOUR ROYAL HIGHNESS,—

We, the Warden, Mayors, and Councillors of the Corporation of the County of Quebec, avail ourselves of the happy event of the arrival of Your Royal Highness in Canada, to approach Your Highness with the assurance of our most sincere and hearty welcome to this country, and with the expression of our most devoted attachment to the person of Your Royal Highness, and of our loyalty to our most Gracious Sovereign, Your Royal Highness's royal mother, through whose beneficent and constitutional sway, we enjoy prosperity and peace under the powerful protection of the British Nation. The County of Quebec which we represent, comprises a territory which has been the theatre of the most important event in the history of our country, the scene of its earliest settlement, and, though once the battle-ground of those two great nations from which we spring, now happily presents the spectacle of their fusion into one race, through the influences of peace and the ties of family.

Interesting from historical associations, our country is remarkable for its picturesque scenery, its lakes, rivers, and fruitful soil, the aspect of which cannot but favourably impress Your Royal Highness; the peculiar, but as yet unemployed, facilities which it possesses for the important purposes of manufacturing industry.

We fully appreciate the great honour conferred upon our country by the visit of Your Royal Highness, and its important social and political consequences to ourselves; and hope that it will prove a source of unalloyed pleasure with satisfaction to Your Royal Highness, certain, as we are, that it will leave a recollection never to be effaced from the hearts of the Canadian people. And we beg most respectfully to offer to Your Royal Highness, our sincere congratulations on your happy voyage, and our heartiest welcome on your auspicious advent to our shores.

And have the honour to be,
Your Royal Highness's
Most obedient, humble, and devoted servant,
JOHN ROSS,
Warden County of Quebec.
Quebec, 14th August, 1860.

REPLY.

Quebec, 21st August, 1860.

SIR,—I have the honour to acknowledge the Address presented to His Royal Highness the Prince of Wales by the Warden, Mayors, and Councillors of the Corporation of the County of Quebec, and to convey to you the thanks of His Royal Highness for the terms in which it is expressed.

I am, Sir,
Your obedient servant,
NEWCASTLE.
John Ross, Esquire, Warden.

THE MAGISTRATES' ADDRESS.

To His Royal Highness Albert Edward, Prince of Wales, &c. &c.

MAY IT PLEASE YOUR ROYAL HIGHNESS,—

We, the Magistrates of the City and District of Quebec, in special session assembled, beg leave humbly to approach Your Royal Highness, to congratulate you on your safe arrival in the ancient capital of Canada, —the keystone of Her Most Gracious Majesty's British North American possessions; and to bid you welcome to scenes that are mixed up with some of the most important events in the history of the glorious empire of which we are proud to form a portion; welcome to ground rendered classic by many past associations, among which the visit of Your Royal Maternal Grandsire is remembered with pride and pleasure.

We beg to assure Your Royal Highness that in no part of Her Majesty's dominions, has she a more zealous or loyal body than they who have the honour to bear commissions in Her Majesty's name, for the preservation of the peace, in this city and district; and we hail with peculiar satisfaction the circumstance of Your Royal Highness's visit to this part of the British Empire, as a proof of the affectionate interest taken by Her Majesty and Your Royal Highness in the welfare of Her dominions; and we trust that the recollection of it will be as agreeable and satisfactory to Your Royal Highness, as it will ever be proudly remembered by us, when it becomes an event of the past.

QUEBEC, 4th August, 1860.

REPLY.

GENTLEMEN,—I receive with sincere gratification the Address which you have presented to me.

You welcome me to a city of which you speak with just pride,—to a city once famous in war and now prosperous in peace,—to a city ennobled by heroic deeds and enriched by honorable industry, hallowed of old by the blood of Wolfe and Montcalm, shed in the struggle of nations, but now blessed by the hand of commerce, and knowing no rivalry but such as is carried on with the rest of the world, by the united energies of a happy people.

That such may long be the condition of this city and district, and that your labours as Magistrates may be lightened by the good order and contentment of those around you, is my earnest hope and expectation.

ADDRESS OF THE URSULINE NUNS, AS TRANSLATED.

MAY IT PLEASE YOUR ROYAL HIGHNESS,—

The Ursuline Nuns will always regard as a signal honour the visit of Your Royal Highness to their ancient Convent, and thus humbly ask that they may be allowed to lay at your feet, in a solemn manner, the homage of respect and devotion. Although they live in the cloisters, they are indifferent to nothing which is of interest to their country. They have always been among the most thankful and faithful of Her Majesty's subjects in British America ; how then should they not partake of the public joy on this occasion, the felicitous arrival of Your Royal Highness in this Province ? Twice already have princes of the glorious House of Brunswick visited this country ; and when this most ancient educational establishment in British America, and the annals of the Convent, mention these events with happiness as being of good omen, with what enthusiasm shall we then not add to these illustrious names that of Albert Edward, Prince of Wales. It would be useless to try to repeat now what rumor says of the goodness of Your Royal Highness, and of all the other qualities which will entitle you one day to sit upon one of the grandest thrones of the universe ; but the Ursuline Nuns will endeavour to preserve intact, and to transmit to their successors, the remembrance and the impressions of this gracious visit. May Heaven continue to shower favours on our august Sovereign, and may the ever-increasing prosperity of her reign be a happy presage of the glory which the future is preparing for the Heir Apparent to the brilliant Crown.

MONTREAL.

CHURCH OF ENGLAND SYNOD.

MAY IT PLEASE YOUR ROYAL HIGHNESS,—

We, the Bishop, Clergy, and Laity of the United Church of England and Ireland in the Diocese of Montreal, in Synod assembled, beg respectfully to assure Your Royal Highness of our sincere attachment to the person, respect for the character, and devotion to the Crown and authority of Your Royal Mother our beloved Sovereign. As Her Majesty's Representative and Heir Apparent to the Throne, we feel it a high privilege to welcome your arrival amongst us; but at the same time we wish to testify our respect for Your Royal Highness's own character and person, and to express our confidence that the anxious care of your royal parents in preparing you for that exalted station which you yourself hereafter, we trust at some very distant day, may expect to be called on to fill, has not been without the most satisfactory results, and in that course of preparation to have seen with your own eyes those magnificent transatlantic possessions of the Crown of England, and to have become personally acquainted in their own countries with many of their inhabitants, will have been no unimportant event. For ourselves, as a Church, we neither occupy the same position as our brethren at home, nor can we be named in comparison with them for our numbers or our wealth, but we still feel we are members of the same body. We teach the same truths, we offer up the same petitions on behalf of the Queen and all that are in authority under her, and ever pray for Your Royal Highness that Almighty God will be pleased to endue you with His Holy Spirit, enrich you with His Heavenly Grace, prosper you with all happiness, and bring you to His everlasting kingdom for Jesus Christ's sake.

REPLY.

GENTLEMEN,—I thank you from my heart for this Address, presented by your Bishop, on behalf of the Synod of the Diocese of Montreal, which has been so lately constituted the Metropolitan See of the Province of Canada. It is most agreeable to my feelings to receive such proofs of welcome to myself, and of loyalty to the Queen, from members of a Church to which it is my happiness to belong; but it would be most unjust if I were to forget, that, since my arrival in this country, the professors of every creed have given ample assurance that all join in one common sentiment of devotion to the Crown of England, and that all co-operate in the one great duty of enforcing obedience, not only to heavenly laws, but to those of earthly origin. I shall never cease to rejoice that I have been enabled to visit this distant portion of the Empire, and to become acquainted with a people of which I shall carry back with me most pleasing recollections. I trust that on your part the prayers of which you remind me will henceforth be offered up in the churches of the land with even an increased earnestness.

CROSSE CLUB.

To His Royal Highness Albert Edward, Prince of Wales, &c. &c.

MAY IT PLEASE YOUR ROYAL HIGHNESS,—

The Crosse Club of Montreal respectfully approach Your Royal Highness to express with sentiments of deep gratification a cordial welcome to this portion of Her Majesty's dominions.

The members of this Club are not insensible to the great encouragements which all manly sports and athletic games have received from the patronage and example of Your Royal Highness.

In our city it has also pleased Your Royal Highness to be present at our game of Crosse.

It is scarcely necessary to mention that this game is one peculiar to Canada; derived from the aboriginal Red Men of the forest, and pre-eminently adapted to test their swiftness of foot, quickness of ear and vision, and powers of endurance.

The Crosse Club of Montreal being sincerely desirous of promoting the interests of this game, and, feeling assured of the value of Your Royal Highness's appreciation of their efforts, request that Your Royal Highness will be graciously pleased to receive a *Crosse* offered for your acceptance by the Club with feelings of the warmest devotion, of the highest admiration, and the most ardent wishes for Your Royal Highness's continued happiness.

On behalf of the Crosse Club of Montreal,

G. H. KERNICK,
President.

REPLY.

BAY OF QUINTE, Sept. 5, 1860.

SIR,—I am directed to thank you and the members of the Crosse Club at Montreal for your Address; and for the intention you there express of presenting to the Prince of Wales a Crosse, of which His Royal Highness will accept with much pleasure as a memorial of the occasion of his witnessing that interesting game.

I have the honor to be, &c.,

R. BRUCE,
Major General

COLLEGE OF PHYSICIANS AND SURGEONS OF LOWER CANADA.

To His Royal Highness Albert Edward, Prince of Wales, &c., &c.

MAY IT PLEASE YOUR ROYAL HIGHNESS,—

We, the President, Vice-Presidents, and Governors representing the

College of Physicians and Surgeons of Lower Canada, possessing privileges and powers nearly similar to those of the Royal Colleges of Physicians and Surgeons of England, desire to take this opportunity of welcoming Your Royal Highness to Canada, as the Heir Apparent to the Throne of England, and the Representative of Her Most Gracious Majesty, with every assurance of our loyalty to the Queen, affection for Her family, and grateful appreciation of the blessings which we enjoy under Her wise and patriotic rule.

And we are the more pleased at being allowed the privilege of making this assurance to Your Royal Highness, because we feel confident that you will rightly estimate the character and importance of such a Corporation as that in whose name we now appear; that you will understand how wide is their sphere of action, how great their influence upon the community at large. And we trust it will always be our endeavour, as it is certainly our duty, so to labour in our vocation, that we may not only promote the physical improvement and bodily health of Her Majesty's subjects, but also contribute in every way to the welfare and greatness of Canada, that so Her Majesty may have increase of glory in the growth and prosperity of this bright jewel of Her Imperial Crown.

MASTERS AND WARDENS OF THE TRINITY HOUSE.

To His Royal Highness Albert Edward, Prince of Wales, &c., &c.

MAY IT PLEASE YOUR ROYAL HIGHNESS,—

We, Her Majesty's dutiful and loyal subjects, the Master, Deputy Master, and Wardens of the Trinity House of Montreal, approach Your Royal Highness with our respectful congratulations on your safe arrival at this flourishing portion of Her Majesty's dominions.

As one of the numerous colonial offshoots, performing, so far as to our position pertains, the duties of a Corporation, whose origin in Britain dates from antiquity anterior to public records, intituled "the Master, Wardens, and Assistants of the Guild, Fraternity, or Brotherhood of the most glorious and undivided Trinity, and of St. Clement in the parish of Deptford Stroud, in the county of Kent," a Corporation which has had the high honour of mentioning, among other illustrious personages, as its master, our late revered sovereign, William IV., and is now presided over by your illustrious father,—the presence of Your Royal Highness, the lineal heir to the throne of this mighty empire, is to us the source of especial gratification, in addition to that we entertain in common with all Her Majesty's subjects.

We fervently hope that Your Royal Highness's visit to Canada may be productive of as much satisfaction to youself as it is to the entire population of every class, creed, and origin.

ANDREW SHAW, *Master.*
W. BRISTOW, *Dy. Master.*
W. EDMONSTONE,
J. L. BEAUDRY,
H. STARNES,
V. HUDON,
T. MORLAND,
P. COTIE,
} *Wardens.*

E. D. DAVID, *Registrar.*

M'GILL COLLEGE.

To His Royal Highness Albert Edward, Prince of Wales, &c., &c.

MAY IT PLEASE YOUR ROYAL HIGHNESS,—

We, the Governors, Principal, and Fellows of the University of M'Gill College beg leave to congratulate Your Royal Highness on the safe arrival which Divine Providence has granted you in this distant part of the Empire, and to express our gratitude to Her Majesty the Queen and Your Royal Highness for the condescension and graciousness implied in this visit to her Majesty's subjects in Canada.

We call to remembrance, with great satisfaction on the present occasion, that we owe it to the Imperial Government, from the interest which it has taken in education in this part of the dominions of our Sovereign, that the University with which we are connected possesses the Royal Charter, which gives authority to its public acts for the advancement of sound learning and science. And, although this University, the oldest in Canada, may be said to be still in its infancy, and in this, as well as on account of the obstacles which in a new country impede its progress, does not bear comparison with the venerable institutions of like nature in the mother country, particularly with that of which Your Royal Highness is an Alumnus, we nevertheless beg to assure Your Royal Highness that it possesses in common with them the affection and sense of obligation that are due to our Sovereign Lady the Queen, and the happy part of the Empire over which she immediately reigns.

We pray that Your Royal Highness may find this present visit in every way agreeable, and fruitful of pleasing thoughts throughout many years to come.

SIGNED by the Hon. Charles Dewey Day, LL.D., President; the Hon. James Ferrier, M.L.C., Governor; the Hon. Peter M'Gill, M.L.C., do.; Thomas Brown Anderson, Esq., do.; David Davidson, Esq., do.; Benjamin Holmes, Esq., do.; Andrew Robertson, M.A., do.; Christopher

Dunkin, M.A., M.P.P., do.; William Molson, Esq., do.; Alexander Morris, M.A., do.; John William Dawson, LL.D., F.G.S., Principal; Rev. Canon Leach, LL.D., Vice-Principal, and Dean of the Faculty of Arts; Andrew F. Holmes, M.D., LL.D., Dean of the Faculty of Medicine; Henry Aspinwall Howe, M.A., Rector of the High School; J. J. C. Abbott, B.C.L., Dean of the Faculty of Law; Brown Chamberlin, M.A., B.C.L., Fellow; Walter Jones, M.D., do.; W. B. Lambe, B.C.L., do.; Sir William E. Logan, LL.D., F.R.S., F.G.S., do.

MONTREAL BOARD OF TRADE.

MAY IT PLEASE YOUR ROYAL HIGHNESS,—

We, the President and Council of the Montreal Board of Trade, a body corporate, respectfully approach Your Royal Highness to offer our sincere and dutiful welcome on your arrival in Montreal, and to assure you of our loyal attachment to the person and government of our gracious Queen, your royal mother.

As a Corporation more particularly concerned in the commercial interests of our city, which are intimately connected with those of the whole country, we feel assured Your Royal Highness will permit us to lay before you very briefly the nature of the geographical position we occupy, of the commercial intimacy maintained with neighbouring kindred States, as well as our own trade-relations with the Mother Country.

The recent abolition of all Imperial statutes protecting Colonial trade and navigation, and the inauguration of a system of freedom from former regulations and preferences, has necessarily introduced a new era for the Colonies as well as for the parent State. In a country situated as Canada, there devolved the necessity of turning to the utmost account whatever natural advantages it possessed, under the penalty of being wholly distanced in the race of American progress and prosperity. Under this conviction, an extensive canal and railway system has been constructed; the natural channel of our river between Quebec and Montreal has been excavated, so as to admit merchant ships of the heaviest burden; an Ocean Steamship Line has been generously subsidized by the Province; and other means taken to attract through the route of the St. Lawrence a share of the vast and ever-increasing exports and imports of Western Canada, and the Western United States. In the same spirit, the Treaty of Reciprocity with the United States was entered into; the general result of which has proved advantageous to both the parties to its negociations.

As part of the same general scheme, that magnificent structure has been thrown across the St. Lawrence, which Your Royal Highness has so graciously crossed the ocean formally to open. Even that great work and the others alluded to, may, however, be considered but as links in

P

the chain; for, although the efforts to attract a large share of the interior trade through the St. Lawrence has not yet been attained, we confidently hope that the same spirit of enterprise inherited from our ancestors, which has already accomplished so much, will not rest satisfied till it has demonstrated the inherent superiority of the St. Lawrence route over all others, as a means of intercourse between this continent and Europe.

Placed as Montreal is, at the head of ocean, and the foot of inland navigation, being at once three hundred miles nearer to England than New York, and nearer to the interior lakes than any United States Atlantic port, and with the vast water-power at our command for manufacturing purposes, we cannot doubt, that, with other necessary improvements effected, and its position properly understood, it must become in time one of the most important commercial cities in Her Majesty's dominions. Nor could we, consistently with our duty, representing, as we do, large interests, actual and prospective, refrain from submitting to one in Your Royal Highness's eminent position the importance to the Empire of the timely improvements of those geographical advantages to which we have just alluded.

We beg leave to be permitted to add, that every exploration has demonstrated the existence of the most direct and most practicable railway route to the Pacific from those Eastern Provinces of the Crown which Your Royal Highness has so recently visited, and consequently to the transit of that immense eastern commerce which now seeks for outlets by circuitous channels, or through foreign territory. The construction of such a continuous road through British American territory, from the Atlantic to the Pacific, tending, as we are convinced it must, to the increase of commerce, and the spread of civilization, is a subject which we humbly trust may not be found unworthy of Your Royal Highness's consideration.

We beg further to assure Your Royal Highness, that your auspicious visit will stand as a memorable event, and will be gratefully remembered as of the grace of our beloved Queen your royal mother. We believe it to be fraught with the most important results, and we rejoice in the assurance of the warm and heartfelt welcome which awaits Your Royal Highness throughout Canada.

JOHN YOUNG,
President.
JOHN G. DINNING.
Secretary.

Montreal, August, 1860.

REPLY.

MONTREAL, August 27, 1860.

SIR,—I have the honour to convey the thanks of His Royal Highness the Prince of Wales for the Address presented by the Board of Trade of Montreal.

I have the honour to be sir, your obedient servant,

NEWCASTLE.

The Hon. John Young.

NATURAL HISTORY SOCIETY.

To His Royal Highness Albert Edward, Prince of Wales, &c., &c.

MAY IT PLEASE YOUR ROYAL HIGHNESS,—

We, the President, Vice President, Council and other members of the Incorporated Natural History Society of Montreal, ask leave respectfully to address Your Royal Highness, with every assurance of our loyalty and affection, on this occasion of your visit to this city, as the representative of Her Majesty, and Heir Apparent to the Imperial Crown of England.

Having been a frequent attendant at the meetings of "The Royal Institution" in London, and at others of a kindred nature, Your Royal Highness will be able fully to appreciate the benefits to be derived from such societies; and especially in a new country, where the necessary business of active life is so pressing, and but few individuals are found who have the inclination or the time to devote themselves to what are looked upon as the unremunerative pursuits of literature and science.

We have been encouraged, during the past few years, by the increased success of our Society, and by the growing interest manifested in its operations. A large and commodious building has been recently erected by our Society, containing ample accommodation for our library and museum, to which some valuable additions have lately been made; and we also have a spacious lecture-room, for our annual course of lectures, which are fully attended. And, to exhibit to Your Royal Highness some proof of the talents and acquirements of our members, we beg to be allowed to present to you the four volumes of the *Canadian Naturalist*, a bi-monthly periodical, which has been in existence these last four years, edited by the Society, and which has been favourably received and noticed by scientific persons on this continent and in Europe. Almost all the articles, many of them upon important subjects connected with the Geological, Meteorological, and Natural History of British North America, have been contributed by members of the Society; and the plates are engraved in this city, where the work is printed.

At the same time, we desire to present to Your Royal Highness, on behalf of Dr. Smallwood, Professor of Meteorology in McGill College, and a member of our Society, a volume entitled "Contributions to Canadian Meteorology."

F. MONTREAL.

President.

Museum of the Natural History Society, Montreal, July 26th, 1860.

His Royal Highness expressed his thanks for the Address by a written communication through his Grace the Duke of Newcastle.

THE VETERANS OF 1812.

To His Royal Highness Albert Edward, Prince of Wales, &c., &c.

PRINCE,—

The Veterans of the Militia of Lower Canada crave permission to approach your person to tender to Your Royal Highness the homage of their respect and of their prayers.

The Battalions formed in our Counties, in our Villages and in our Towns, for the defence of our country, during the war of 1812, number now but few among their ranks.

Our companions have fallen, some on the field of battle, others under the scythe of time; for, Prince, years have rolled by since then. Then we served your ancestors.

We, their survivors,—soon no doubt in our turn to pass away like them,—cherishing religiously in our hearts the memory of that eventful period, seize with delight this auspicious occasion—the last we can hope to have—to present to Your Royal Highness, and in your person to your august mother, our beloved Queen, the assurance of our unaltered loyalty and devotion.

Prince, most of those who fought at Lacolle and Chateauguay are gone from among us, and the blood of their survivors courses in their veins more feebly than of yore; but we rejoice to say that the race of 1812 has its successors, and that the youth of Canada know the history of their sires, and, should occasion arise, will not belie it.

Montreal, 25th August, 1860.

(Here follow the signatures of a number of officers and men.)

REPLY.

NIAGARA FALLS, Sept. 18, 1860.

SIR,—I have the honour to communicate to you the thanks of His Royal Highness the Prince of Wales, for the loyal Address presented to him by the Veterans of the Militia of Lower Canada.

It is very gratifying to His Royal Highness to receive these expressions of devotion and attachment to the Queen from gallant men, who, in years gone by, have deserved so well of their country. He only regrets that so few now survive to testify to their ancient spirit.

His Royal Highness accepts this Address with the more pleasure, because happily we can now look upon the deeds of our brave countrymen without any other feelings than those of friendship and regard for the nation against whom they fought. Hostility to our neighbours is buried the plains where they struggled for victory, but the honour of each nation survives for ever.

I am, Sir,
Yours faithfully,
NEWCASTLE.

Colonel the Hon. Sir Etienne Taché, A. D. C.,
&c., &c., &c.

DICKINSON'S LANDING.

To His Royal Highness Albert Edward, Prince of Wales, &c., &c.

MAY IT PLEASE YOUR ROYAL HIGHNESS,—

We, the inhabitants of the Township of Osnabruck, County of Stormont, hail the opportunity now afforded us, to welcome to this rising Province of the British Empire, the son and representative of that good Queen, whom all love, and the Heir Apparent to that Crown on which Her Majesty sheds so much lustre.

Many of us are the descendants of that illustrious band of patriots,—the United Empire Loyalists,—who, rather than surrender their allegiance to Great Britain and her King, fled, with their families, from their homes and possessions, and took refuge in this land, then a wilderness. Our lot is cast in more pleasant and peaceful times than theirs, and, while enjoying the fruits of the privations which they underwent, as well as of their hard toils, we rejoice to be able to testify to your Royal Highness our loyalty and devotion to the British Crown.

We feel sure that Your Royal Highness will this day experience unwonted pleasure in descending the far-famed Rapids of that noble river on whose banks we dwell; and we trust that when, on your return home, Your Royal Highness tells Her Majesty, the Queen, of the magnitude, resources, and natural beauties of this Province, Your Royal Highness will also vouchsafe to assure Her Majesty of the entire devotion of our rural population to Her Majesty's person and crown.

SHERBROOKE.

UNIVERSITY OF BISHOP'S COLLEGE, LENNOXVILLE.

MAY IT PLEASE YOUR ROYAL HIGHNESS,—

We, the Vice Chancellor, Principal, Professors, and other members of the University of Bishop's College, Lennoxville, having received our charter privileges as a University by the gracious act of our beloved Queen, respectfully ask leave, on this occasion of Your Royal Highness's visit to Canada as representative of Her Majesty, and Heir Apparent to the throne, to express our gratitude for the same, and our veneration for the person, and loyalty to the Crown and authority of our Sovereign.

Having arrived here fresh from a course of study at the most ancient university in England, Your Royal Highness can well appreciate the advantages of such institutions, and the effects they are calculated to produce upon the character of the people.

As far as our limited means and opportunities will enable us, in these days of the infancy of our University, it will be our endeavour to promote sound learning and true religion amongst the inhabitants of this province, and to train up the rising generation in feelings of affection for the mother country and loyalty to their Sovereign; so that, whenever it shall please Almighty God that Your Royal Highness shall succeed to the responsibilities and greatness of the Imperial Throne of England, we may hope that you will find in these noble transatlantic possessions hearts as true and loyal to you as as they now are to your august mother, Her Most Gracious Majesty Queen Victoria, whom God preserve.

OTTAWA.

RAFTSMEN OF THE UPPER OTTAWA.

To His Royal Highness Albert Edward, Prince of Wales, &c., &c.

We, the Raftsmen of the Upper Ottawa, constitute a body of 13,000 men, the bone and sinew of Canada.

We take advantage of meeting Your Royal Highness upon a raft, respectfully to offer you our hearty welcome, and to express our loyalty, our devotion, and our affection for the Queen. God bless you.

May Your Royal Highness long remain the Prince of Wales.

COUNTY OF CARLETON.

To His Royal Highness Albert Edward, Prince of Wales, &c., &c.

MAY IT PLEASE YOUR ROYAL HIGHNESS,—

The Warden and Corporation of the County of Carleton beg leave most respectfully to tender to you, in the name of those whom they represent, a sincere and hearty welcome to this section of Canada, which has lately been so highly honored by our most gracious Sovereign as selecting the same as the metropolis thereof; and at the same time, to convey to Your Royal Highness, as the son of our august and beloved Queen, and Heir Apparent to the Throne, their unwavering attachment to British Institutions, and unshaken loyalty to the British Crown.

They trust that the visit of Your Royal Highness to this extensive dependency of the empire may be fraught with important and beneficial results to the country in general, and that your tour through Canada may be as gratifying to Your Royal Highness as your visit is to the inhabitants of this loyal country.

In conclusion, they desire to tender through Your Royal Highness, to our most beloved Sovereign, our loyal attachment to her person, and to express the hope that the richest blessings of Divine Providence may be vouchsafed to you during your sojourn on this continent, and return you in safety to the heart of that illustrious family of which your Royal Highness is so great an ornament.

JOSEPH HINTON,
Warden of the County of Carleton.

REPLY.

OTTAWA, Sept. 1st, 1860.

SIR,—I have the honour to convey the thanks of His Royal Highness the Prince of Wales for the Address presented to him by yourself and the Corporation of the County of Carleton.

I have the honour to be, Sir,
Your obedient servant,
NEWCASTLE.

Joseph Hinton, Esq.,
Warden County of Carleton.

GLENGARY.

MAY IT PLEASE YOUR ROYAL HIGHNESS,—

We, Her Majesty's dutiful and loyal subjects, duly deputed by the freeholders and other inhabitants of the County of Glengary, avail ourselves of the present joyful occasion of the visit of Your Royal Highness to this flourishing portion of Her Majesty's wide-spread dominions, to tender to Your Royal Highness our heartfelt congratulations on your safe arrival, and to renew the expression of our devoted attachment to the person and Government of your most august mother.

The county, whose homage we now humbly present, was settled in 1784 by a small number of individuals, mainly of Highland Scottish descent, who, faithful in their attachment to the throne and their national institutions, after the severance from the British Empire of a large number of her colonies on this continent, preferred to brave the rigours of a Canadian climate and the hardship of an uncleared wilderness, rather than swerve from their allegiance. These few pioneers of the forest, strengthened and increased by successive tides of immigration, have grown up into a rich and flourishing county, numbering at this time about twenty-five thousand inhabitants.

As in the infancy, so in the progress and manly growth of the settlement, the "Men of Glengary" have evinced, in the War of 1812 with the neighbouring nation, and on every other occasion where their services were required, their unwavering attachment to the institutions of their fatherland, and their reverence and love for their sovereign. With heartfelt gratitude do we now receive the high proof of Her Most Gracious Majesty's condescension and regard for her faithful subjects in this portion of the Empire, afforded in her acceptance of the invitation tendered by the Legislature of this Province, and more especially in deputing to represent Her Royal Person, Your Royal Highness, the lineal successor to the Throne.

We fervently trust that the hearty manifestations of loyalty with which Your Royal Highness will be greeted in every portion of this country that you may be pleased to honour with your presence, will render your stay as agreeable to yourself as it is gratifying to your people; that the information which personal observation will afford you of the capabilities of the country, as well as of the character of its inhabitants, will strengthen those favorable impressions of both you have been pleased to pronounce; and that the effect of your visit amongst us may be to cement more strongly the mutual ties of interest and affection that now happily unite these British Provinces with the Parent State.

Glengary, 13th August, 1860.

REPLY.

MONTREAL, Aug. 27, 1860.

SIR,—I am directed to express the thanks of His Royal Highness the Prince of Wales for the loyal Address presented by the inhabitants of the County of Glengary.

I have the honor, to be,
Sir,
Your obed't serv't,
NEWCASTLE.

D. A. Macdonald, Esq., M.P.P.

PRESCOTT AND RUSSELL.

To His Royal Highness Albert Edward, Prince of Wales, &c., &c.

MAY IT PLEASE YOUR ROYAL HIGHNESS,—

We, the Warden and Council of the United Counties of Prescott and Russell, have the honour to present to Your Royal Highness, our cordial welcome and congratulations on your safe arrival in the Canadian portion of the British territory. While we desire to assure Your Royal Highness of our continued and steadfast loyalty and attachment to the throne and government of your august and illustrious mother, our most beloved and gracious Queen, we would also most respectfully and dutifully, as Canadians, and particularly as inhabitants of the valley of that grand and romantic river on whose banks lies the site of the future capital of Canada, express to Your Royal Highness our feelings of deep satisfaction for the just selection made by the kindness and condescension of Her Most Gracious Majesty, of the city of Ottawa, as the seat of the Government of these United Provinces. The free laws under which we have the happiness to live, granted us by the most liberal and enlightened of all governments in the world, a noble instance of which is afforded us in our own municipal institutions, tend to strengthen and cement more strongly and closely, if possible, than ever, our respect, regard, and attachment for the British Crown and Constitution. We cannot conclude this humble and respectful Address to Your Royal Highness without uniting, in the fervent prayer of our fellow-subjects in Canada, that God may spare our most gracious Queen, long to reign over us; and, at the same time, assuring Your Royal Highness, that, should Providence so ordain it that you shall survive your royal mother, we shall only vie with each other in testifying our loyalty and allegiance to Your Royal Highness, as the rightful heir and sovereign of the British Empire.

Signed, on behalf of the Municipal Council of the United Counties of Prescott and Russell,

JOHN HAMILTON, *Warden.*

REPLY.

OTTAWA, Sept. 1st, 1860.

SIR,—I have the honour to thank you, by desire of His Royal Highness the Prince of Wales, for the Address presented to him by the Warden and Council of the United Counties of Russell and Prescott.

I am, Sir, your obed't serv't,

NEWCASTLE.

John Hamilton, Esq.

BROCKVILLE.

MAY IT PLEASE YOUR ROYAL HIGHNESS,—

We, the Mayor, Town Councillors, and Inhabitants of the Town of Brockville, respectfully approach Your Royal Highness to tender our grateful acknowledgment of the kindness and condescension which have induced you to accept the invitation of the Canadian people to visit this country, and thus witness the universal joy which the presence of the heir to the Crown was sure to evoke. As citizens of Brockville, a town which has shown its loyal attachment to the Crown by perpetuating the name of the gallant General who fell fighting to maintain the integrity of the Empire, we now beg to offer Your Royal Highness a heartfelt welcome to this portion of the wide-spread dominions of our Sovereign; and to assure you, that the same sentiments of attachment to British soil which prompted the first settlers in this place to seek here an asylum from a hostile country, at the sacrifice of all they possessed, still animates their descendants. We beg Your Royal Highness to believe that the enthusiasm which renders your tour through this Province one triumphant progress, does not wholly arise from laudable gratification that the vast resources of the most important colony of the Empire are seen by our future monarch, nor yet by temporary excitement caused by an unprecedented event; it is the expression of the deep-seated affection for the Crown and Constitution of the United Kingdom, which constrains us still to call the old country our home. It shall be our earnest prayer that Your Royal Highness may live long to adorn the lofty position which you so worthily fill, and that the colonists of the Empire may be enabled hereafter to feel towards their King the same emotions of loyalty and affection with which the virtues and wise government of your Royal Mother is spoken of throughout that Great Kingdom over which she providentially reigns.

WM. FITZSIMMONS,
Mayor.

REPLY.

GENTLEMEN,—I thank you sincerely for the Address which you have presented to me. In the Queen's name I acknowledge the expressions of your loyalty to Her Crown and person; and for myself I am grateful to you for this welcome to your neighbourhood.

KINGSTON.

PRESBYTERIAN CHURCH OF CANADA.

MAY IT PLEASE YOUR ROYAL HIGHNESS,—

The Synod of the Presbyterian Church of Canada in connection with the Church of Scotland, beg to approach Your Royal Highness with our respectful and cordial welcome on the occasion of your arrival in this part of the dominions of our beloved sovereign, the Queen. We hail with the most lively satisfaction the appearance amongst us of so important a member of the royal family as the Heir Apparent to the throne, regarding as we do the presence of so distinguished a visitor as adding another to those numerous links of sympathy and affection which already bind the North American Provinces so firmly to the British Crown. We are persuaded, that, in your tour through the Province, amid much that may manifest the infant state of the country, Your Royal Highness will observe with satisfaction the progress that has already been made in the development of its material resources and the numerous indications of a yet greater advancement. Feeling assured that without the influence of religion presiding over national advancement, true prosperity cannot be enjoyed by any people, it is our care, as a branch of the Church of Scotland from which so large a portion of the population have come to this new land, and it shall be our endeavor in the exercise of the duties of our sacred office, to keep the adherents of our church in the path of piety and virtue in which their fathers walked; and whilst thus, in our own sphere, doing our part to promote the spread of pure and undefiled religion, we are also persuaded that we thereby take the surest means of cherishing in their hearts sentiments of loyalty to the Sovereign and respect to her government That Almighty God may bless Your Royal Highness with length of days and all other temporal and spiritual blessings, and that He may finally call you to the inheritance of that crown of rejoicing which is laid up for those, whether of high or low degree, who shall serve the Lord, shall be our earnest prayer.

REPLY.

It is with much satisfaction that I receive the Address which you have presented to me on behalf of the Presbyterian Church in connection with the Church of Scotland. You are too well acquainted with the views and feelings of the Queen, not to be aware how anxious she is for everything that can promote the religion and morality of her people, and how earnestly she watches the results of the labors of those who devote themselves to teaching the word of God. She will therefore rejoice to learn from your own lips that the ministers of your persuasion are training their people in the paths of piety and virtue, and in habits of loyalty to the Sovereign and obedience to the laws. I trust that their efforts, in common with those of the other churches of this land, may long prosper, and that under their care a population may be reared fearing God and honoring the Queen. I beg you to accept my thanks for imploring the blessing of Heaven on my behalf.

ST. PATRICK'S SOCIETY, KINGSTON.

To His Royal Highness Albert Edward, Prince of Wales, &c., &c.

MAY IT PLEASE YOUR ROYAL HIGHNESS,—

We, the St. Patrick's Society of Kingston, do most cordially welcome Your Royal Highness to this Province.

We rejoice at the opportunity afforded us of expressing to Your Royal Highness our attachment and loyalty to the British Throne, and to unite with our fellow-colonists in the enthusiastic greetings that have accompanied Your Royal Highness in your progress through this Province.

With heartfelt pleasure we hail the arrival amongst us of the Son of Our Beloved and Most Gracious Sovereign, whose virtues have added lustre to the British Crown, and who lives in the hearts and affections of her people.

The prosperity of the people under the mild sway of Our Beloved Queen, in this distant portion of the Empire, is in a great measure attributed to the freedom they enjoy; and we are gratified to believe that the presence of Your Royal Highness will strengthen (if possible) the ties that so happily unite us to the mother country.

We earnestly hope that your visit may be attended with much pleasure; and that, upon your return home, you will be pleased to convey to Your Royal Mother renewed assurances of the loyalty and devotion of all classes of Her Majesty's Canadian subjects.

J. O'REILLY,
President St. Patrick's Society.

The Prince in reply said that he was well assured of the loyalty of the people of Kingston, and regretted that anything should have occurred to prevent his visit to it.

FRONTENAC, LENNOX, AND ADDINGTON.

To His Royal Highness Albert Edward, Prince of Wales, &c., &c.

MAY IT PLEASE YOUR ROYAL HIGHNESS,—

We, the Chairman of the Court of Quarter Sessions of the United Counties of Frontenac, Lennox, and Addington, and Her Majesty's Justices assigned to keep the peace therein, beg leave to approach Your Royal Highness for the purpose of expressing our respectful regard for Your Royal Person, and our feelings of loyal attachment to Her Majesty's person and government. We, in common with the rest of the inhabitants of North America, hail the arrival of Your Royal Highness among us as an event of great national interest,—an event which we feel assured will prove an additional guarantee that the union so happily subsisting between Her Majesty's North American dominions and the mother country, will be perpetual; that the intended presence of His Royal Highness the Prince of Wales as the representative of Our Most Gracious and Beloved Queen, at the opening of the Victoria Bridge, presents in a truly gratifying manner the interest which Her Majesty feels for the progress and material prosperity of this highly-favored Province of Her Empire. As we are severed from our Sovereign and the mother country by the broad Atlantic, we deem it a high privilege to be able to tell His Royal Highness the Prince of Wales, at this place, near our own homes, that we are, from feelings and conviction, proud of being the free subjects of the greatest and most enlightened empire in the world; and how highly we prize the right to participate in the rich inheritance of British freedom, British triumphs, and British civilization. We earnestly pray that the present royal visit to this country may prove, as we feel certain it will, an enduring advantage to the best interests of the nation, and a source of pleasure and gratification to Your Royal Highness personally.

REPLY.

GENTLEMEN,—I thank you sincerely for the Address you have presented to me. In the Queen's name I acknowledge the expressions of your loyalty to Her government and service; and for myself, I am grateful to you for the welcome to your neighborhood, although circumstances which I deeply deplore prevent my landing and visiting this city and the United Counties.

BELLEVILLE.

MAY IT PLEASE YOUR ROYAL HIGHNESS,—

We, the inhabitants of the town of Belleville, beg to express to Your Royal Highness our loyalty and devotion to the Throne of Great Britain, and our heartfelt regret, that, when Your Royal Highness condescended to visit us, untoward circumstances, deeply deplored, deprived us of the long and eagerly looked for opportunity of meeting Your Royal Highness with an expression of our devotion to our beloved Queen and the Royal Family.

From earliest infancy we have been taught to regard our title to the time-honored name of British subjects as a heritage dear to us as life. We feel deeply humiliated, and we pray that Your Royal Highness may, by forgetting the circumstances alluded to, enable us again to exult in the unfolding of that flag around which cluster the historic glories of ten centuries.

Do not leave Canada without testifying, in some way, the faith of Your Royal Highness in our devotion,—without bearing home to Your Royal Mother, our beloved Queen, the assurance, that, notwithstanding the unfortunate events of the 6th September, Her honor and Her interests, reverential love for Her person and Crown, pride in the power and glory of Britain, and an undying determination to preserve the integrity of the Empire, are most dear to us. We entreat Your Royal Highness, if possible, again to visit Her Majesty's loyal subjects in Belleville, and to relieve us from the unhappy position in which we are placed; thus restoring to us the right to feel that we are in the opinion of the world, but more especially in the sight of Your Royal Mother, and Your Royal Highness, lovers of peace and order, and loyal British subjects.

On behalf of the inhabitants of the town of Belleville,

W. HOPE, *Mayor*.

Belleville, 8th Sept., 1860.

REPLY.

GENTLEMEN,—It gives me the most sincere pleasure to receive this very numerous and influential deputation from Belleville, and to hear from your lips the assurances and explanation contained in your Address. All painful feelings occasioned by the proceedings in your town on a recent occasion, which I knew were heartily disapproved by the great majority of the inhabitants, are now entirely removed.

The only regret which I now experience is that I am unable to comply with the strongly-expressed wish of your citizens and those of Kingston, that I would go back and pay them that visit which was so unhappily prevented last week. My engagements to other places will not admit of such a change as a return so far eastward would necessarily entail, and I cannot break faith with those who have so kindly made preparations to receive me. It causes me real sorrow to leave Kingston and Belleville behind me unvisited; but I will not fail to inform the Queen of your protestations of loyalty and devotion, nor to add my own conviction of their entire sincerity.

COBOURG.

VICTORIA COLLEGE.

To His Royal Highness Albert Edward, Prince of Wales, &c., &c.

MAY IT PLEASE YOUR ROYAL HIGHNESS,—

We, the Senate, Alumni, and Students of the University of Victoria College, present to Your Royal Highness our loyal greetings and most cordial welcome.

The visit of Your Royal Highness to this humble seat of learning, will ever be remembered by us with gratitude and pride; and the annual recurrence of the day, celebrated with festivity and joy, will enable us to give renewed expression to those feelings of devoted attachment to the British Throne, which it is our duty and happiness to cherish.

Our infant University cannot boast of architectural grandeur, or of princely endowments; but we may refer with pleasure to the fact, that, although established and chiefly sustained by voluntary contributions, she was the first university in actual operation in this colony, while she is, we believe, second to none in the number and character of her graduates.

Founded as our institution is by royal charter, and honoured with the name of our illustrious and noble Queen, we desire that loyalty, patriotism, and religion may unitedly animate the education imparted within her walls; and that the study of the unrivalled literature of our fatherland, combined with the teachings of the great masters of Greece and

Rome, may render Canadian youth not unworthy of their Saxon origin and language.

We implore upon Your Royal Highness the Divine blessing. May you live to become the Sovereign of this great empire, and may your reign be as happy and benign as that of your august and revered mother.

REPLY.

GENTLEMEN,—Accept my thanks for an Address which, proceeding from the Senate and Students of a College which bears the name of the Queen my mother, and is devoted to the education of the youth of this Province, affords me peculiar pleasure.

I wish your University every success; and earnestly hope that in future years it may spread the blessings of a sound education to the rapidly-increasing population in the midst of which it is erected.

ST. ANDREW'S SOCIETY.

To His Royal Highness Albert Edward, Prince of Wales, &c. &c.

MAY IT PLEASE YOUR ROYAL HIGHNESS,—

We, Her Majesty's loyal subjects, the members of the Cobourg and County of Northumberland St. Andrew's Society, eagerly avail ourselves of this opportunity of giving vent to the expression of our feelings on this occasion of the visit of Your Royal Highness to the town of Cobourg.

As Scotchmen, born in Her Majesty's Kingdom of Scotland, or as the descendants of Scotchmen who have emigrated to this favoured portion of her dominions, we joyfully tender to Her Majesty, through Your Royal Highness, the assurance of our unalterable attachment to her crown and person.

It is our sacred duty, may it please Your Royal Highness, ever to bear in mind the heroic deeds of our ancestors in defence of the honour and independence of the ancient Crown of Scotland. With feelings of delight, therefore, which we find it impossible to express in words, we welcome amongst us the Heir Apparent of the British Crown, and the descendant of that long line of our Scottish Kings, by whose side our forefathers in the days of yore,

"Through hostile ranks and ruined gaps,
Old Scotia's bloody lion bore."

The memories of the Scottish past crowd thick upon us on an occasion so auspicious as the present; but we would assure Your Royal Highness that our Scottish right hands have not forgotten their ancient cunning, but that they will be found

"Ready, aye, ready,"

as they were of old, to defend the honour and dignity of the Crown of our beloved Sovereign.

Earnestly praying Almighty God to bless Your Royal Highness, and that He will long preserve you as the pride and hope of all ranks and conditions of the British people, we most dutifully subscribe ourselves Her Majesty's devoted subjects, the members of the St. Andrew's Society of the Town of Cobourg and County of Northumberland, Canada West.

Signed in the name and on behalf of the Society,

CHARLES HOPE MORGAN,
President.

REPLY.

TORONTO, September 8, 1860.

SIR,—I have the honour to convey to you the thanks of His Royal Highness the Prince of Wales for the Address presented to him by the members of the Cobourg and County of Northumberland St. Andrew's Society.

I am, Sir,
Your obedient servant,
NEWCASTLE.

Charles Hope Morgan, Esq.,
President.

PETERBORO.

To His Royal Highness Albert Edward, Prince of Wales, &c., &c.

MAY IT PLEASE YOUR ROYAL HIGHNESS,—

Second only to the presence amongst us of a Queen whom all nations honor for the integrity which has marked Her whole public and private career since Her advent to the throne of these realms, is the presence of Your Royal Highness, the Heir Apparent to the Crown of England, in our midst this day.

The inhabitants of Cavan bid Your Royal Highness welcome. They trust that here, as elsewhere in Canada, you will perceive that there is a sincere attachment to Great Britain prevalent among the people; that a near relationship between England and this part of Canada exists in feeling as in fact; and that the only wish of the latter is the continuance of a connection which is alike profitable and honorable to both.

The fostering care of England, under which the Colony has grown and flourishes, and the interest taken by our Queen in all that concerns the welfare of Canada, have received new proof in the kindness and condescension which have prompted the visit of Your Royal Highness.

The inhabitants of Cavan trust that a visit, as auspiciously commenced, and which has, during its progress, given as much pleasure to yourself, as to those whom you have so highly honored, will continue equally happy to its conclusion.

It is our fervent prayer that God Almighty may grant to our Queen your mother, a long, prosperous, and happy reign ; and that He may guide Your Royal Highness successfully through life.

In the name of the people of the Township of Cavan, in Canada West.

JOHN SWAIN, *Reeve.*

PORT HOPE.

To His Royal Highness Albert Edward, Prince of Wales, &c. &c.

MAY IT PLEASE YOUR ROYAL HIGHNESS,—

We, the inhabitants of the Municipality of the Town of Port Hope, in Upper Canada, beg leave to approach Your Royal Highness to offer the expression of our sincere congratulations upon your visit to this portion of the dominions of our Most Gracious Sovereign, and we heartily bid you welcome.

We tender you the assurance of our steadfast loyalty to the Person and Crown of your Royal Mother, the Queen of Great Britain and Ireland, and of our devoted attachment to the British Constitution.

We regret that the limited time at the disposal of Your Royal Highness may prevent your making a sufficient stay in this town and neighbourhood to be able personally to judge of its beauties and attractions ; amongst which we might direct your attention to the viaduct of the Grand Trunk Railway crossing this place, being second in extent and importance in the line only to " Victoria Bridge," and named after your Royal father, the " Albert Bridge."

We trust that your progress through the land may be one of unmingled gratification to Your Royal Highness, as it must be of pride and pleasure to its inhabitants, most of whom, from their great distance from their fatherland, now behold for the first time a member of the Royal Family of England.

We cannot take leave of Your Royal Highness without the expression of our thanks to Her Majesty, our Most Gracious Sovereign, for this testimony of her affection for her people in this distant part of her dominions, in permitting Your Royal Highness to visit us ; and we pray that Her Majesty may long live to govern her vast empire with that wisdom and justice for which her reign has been so preëminently distinguished.

Dated the first day of August, one thousand eight hundred and sixty.

Signed and sealed on behalf of the Municipality,

JAMES SCOTT,
Mayor.

REPLY.

GENTLEMEN,—I thank you sincerely for the Address which you have presented to me.

In the Queen's name, I acknowledge the expressions of your loyalty to her Crown and Person; and for myself I am grateful to you for this welcome to your neighbourhood.

TORONTO.
CANADIAN INSTITUTE.
To His Royal Highness Albert Edward, Prince of Wales, &c., &c.

MAY IT PLEASE YOUR ROYAL HIGHNESS,—

The President, Council, and Members of the Canadian Institute, incorporated by Royal Charter for the promotion of science and literature in this Province, humbly approach Your Royal Highness with loyal and affectionate greetings, and tender to you with unfeigned respect their welcome on this auspicious occasion.

While the energies of this Province are chiefly directed to the development of its vast agricultural capabilities, and to the fostering of trade and commerce, as the essential sources of its material prosperity, the Canadian Institute specially devotes itself to investigations and researches such as lead to the discovery of abstract truths in science, but which ultimately tend to the intellectual and social progress of man. While, therefore, uniting with their fellow-subjects in this Province of the Empire, in welcoming Your Royal Highness with grateful and hearty loyalty, as the Representative of their beloved Queen, and the Heir Apparent to the British Throne, they beg leave respectfully to tender their loyal congratulations unitedly as an Institute devoted to objects and pursuits specially fostered by Her Majesty's countenance, and to the furtherance of which the illustrious Prince Consort has extended his highest favor and influence.

Enjoying as they do all the priceless blessings derived from institutions by right of which Her Gracious Majesty rules over a free and united people, and sharing in the glories and sympathizing in all the interests of the empire, of which this Province forms no unimportant member, they hail with loyal satisfaction the presence of Your Royal Highness, on whom rests the future hopes of this great empire. Their earnest prayer is, that, endowed with all nobles graces and divine blessings, trained in sound learning, and gifted with a liberal love of science and arts, you may be eminently fitted for the high trust of which you are the heir. May He who is the King of Kings, long spare to you, as to them, her who, while, commanding honor from Your filial heart, lives not less fondly in the affections of a willing people. On her sceptre the virtues of their loved and gracious Queen have conferred a might more potent than ever ruler achieved by conquest. Under its genial sway science and letters have accomplished triumphs which will render the Victorian era illustrious in all future ages ; and while other nations are struggling to attain such privileges as her subjects freely enjoy, the British Empire —the sceptre of which they trust will hereafter be no less illustrious in your hands than in those of their beloved Queen—has girdled the world with a glorious confederacy of Provinces, alike united in freedom and intellectual progress, and in loyal devotion to their Sovereign Head.

In their united capacity, as an institution incorporated by Royal Charter, and specially recognized by the Provincial Parliament as representatives of the interests of science and letters, the President, Council, and Members of the Canadian Institute renew their assurance of devoted loyalty to Her Gracious Majesty, and of cordial welcome to Your Royal Highness.

DANIEL WILSON, LL.D.,
President.

CHURCH OF ENGLAND SYNOD.

MAY IT PLEASE YOUR ROYAL HIGHNESS,—

We, the Bishop, Clergy, and Laity of the Diocese of Toronto, in Synod assembled, beg permission to offer to Your Royal Highness a cordial welcome on your arrival amongst us.

The position in which the United Church of England and Ireland has lately been placed in this country, as being self-governed, and dependent for support on the dutiful liberality of her children, does but serve to enhance our appreciation of the inestimable benefits which we enjoy as subjects of the British Empire, and as an integral part of that Reformed Communion which, under the good providence of Almighty God, is becoming, in every portion of the globe, the instrument of invaluable blessings to mankind.

We strongly feel that since the ties which have connected us with the Civil Government of this Colony have been severed, and the Church thereby rendered independent of the State, this independence, in respect of material interests, must be compensated by a closer and more conscious sympathy with the land of our origin, and with the glory of that land, our Spiritual Mother.

Nor can we ever forget, that, as the Church of Christ, in all ages and in all climes, has taught her children not only to fear God but to honour the King, so has our Church been pre-eminently distinguished by Christian constancy, and by a high-souled loyalty which religion only can inspire.

It is our fervent prayer to Almighty God, that these virtues may ever live and flourish amongst us ; and that, as faithful servants of the King of Kings, we may ever seek the honour of our earthly rulers, and the welfare of the people at large, by presenting, in our several stations, an example of dutiful allegiance to our Sovereign, and a grateful recognition of the signal virtues by which our beloved Queen has purchased for herself, among all nations of the earth, an imperishable name.

JOHN TORONTO.

(Attested) STEPHEN LETT, LL.D., Trinity College, Dublin, *Clerical Secretary.*

JAMES BOVELL, M.D., Trinity College, Toronto, *Lay Secretary.*

REPLY.

GENTLEMEN,—I am grateful for the assurance of your loyalty to the Queen, and for the welcome to me conveyed in your Address.

I am a member of the Church of England, and as such I rejoice to meet in this distant land and in so important a diocese, the representatives of that body in whose creed I have been nurtured and trained.

I trust that Almighty God will aid in your efforts to maintain the efficiency of the Church, under the guidance of the benevolent prelate who has so long presided over your diocese.

COUNCIL OF PUBLIC INSTRUCTION.

MAY IT PLEASE YOUR ROYAL HIGHNESS,—

The Council of Public Instruction for Upper Canada beg to unite with the many thousands of our fellow-subjects in welcoming you to a country first selected as a home by United Empire Loyalists of America. To us, as a body, has been assigned the task of establishing Normal and Model Schools for the training of Teachers, of making the Regulations for the Government of Elementary and Grammar Schools throughout the country, and of selecting the text-books and libraries to be used in them; while on one of our number has been imposed the duty of preparing and administering the School Laws. It has been our aim to imbibe the spirit and imitate the example of our beloved Sovereign in the interest and zeal with which Her Majesty has encouraged the training of teachers and the establishment of schools for the education of the masses of Her people; and we have been nobly seconded in our efforts by our Canadian fellow-subjects at large. At the commencement of our labors in 1846, our meetings were held in a private house, the number of our schools was 2,500, and the number of the pupils in them was 100,000. At the present time we have the Educational Buildings now honored by the presence of Your Royal Highness, where teachers are trained, and Maps, Apparatus, and Libraries are provided for the schools; and those schools now number 4,000, attended by 300,000 pupils. In the song and text books of the schools, loyalty to the Queen and love to the Mother Country are blended with the spirit of Canadian patriotism, and Christian principles with sound knowledge are combined in the teaching and libraries of the schools.

With all our Canadian fellow-countrymen, our earnest prayer is "long live the Queen;" but whenever, in the order of Providence, it shall devolve on Your Royal Highness to ascend the Throne of your august ancestors, we trust the system of public instruction now inaugurated will have largely contributed to render the people of Upper Canada second to no other people in your vast dominions, in virtue, intelligence, enterprise, and Christian civilization.

REPLY.

GENTLEMEN,—The progress of Canada has excited my admiration; but there is no subject in which your efforts appear to have been more glorious than in the matter of public education. You have, I know, the assistance of an able administrator in the person of your Chief Superintendent; and I hope that the public education of Upper Canada will continue to emulate the principles of piety, obedience to law, and Christian charity among a thriving and industrious population. Accept, Gentlemen, my thanks, for the welcome now offered to me within the the walls of this great and important establishment.

HORTICULTURAL SOCIETY.

MAY IT PLEASE YOUR ROYAL HIGHNESS,—

We, the Directors of the Toronto Horticultural Society, desire, on behalf of the Association, to express our gratification of the high honor conferred upon the Society by the visit of Your Royal Highness to our gardens.

In prosecuting the work of laying out these grounds, now for the first time to be opened to the Public, the Society have been actuated by a desire to promote the interests of Horticulture, and, at the same time, to provide a new source of healthful recreation and rational enjoyment for their fellow-citizens.

The encouragement which has always been accorded to undertakings of a similar nature in our Fatherland, both by Her Most Gracious Majesty and the Prince Consort, have emboldened us to hope for the countenance and favor of Your Royal Highness upon the present occasion; and we now, on behalf of the Horticultural Society, most respectfully request that Your Royal Highness will be graciously pleased to inaugurate these gardens; and, at the same time, to leave a lasting memorial of your visit by planting in our gardens a Canadian maple, which may long continue a living monument, both to us and to our children, of the gratifying events of this day, as well as of the high honor conferred upon our country by the visit of the Heir Apparent to the British throne.

REPLY.

GENTLEMEN,—I shall have great pleasure in doing anything which will tend to encourage amongst you a taste for the cultivation of gardens, such as may increase the comfort and enjoyment of the citizens of Toronto.

I shall be content if the tree which I am about to plant, flourish as your youthful city has already done.

KNOX'S COLLEGE.

MAY IT PLEASE YOUR ROYAL HIGHNESS,—

We, the Principal, Professors, and other members of the Senate of Knox's (Theological) College, beg leave to offer our cordial congratulations on Your Royal Highness's visit to this part of Her Majesty's dominions.

We gladly embrace the opportunity which it affords of testifying our dutiful regards for our gracious Queen and the royal family, and our appreciation of the protection we enjoy under the shield of the British laws in the prosecution of our literary and religious labors. We assure Your Royal Highness of the one sentiment of loyalty to the British Crown, which animates alike teachers and pupils in the Institute we preside over. We trust we shall aim at making some fitting return for the invaluable civil privileges afforded to us, by Divine Providence, by training the youth committed to our charge, in such sound religious and moral principles as may qualify them to diffuse among others the knowledge of that righteousness which exalteth a nation.

Accept the expression of our fervent wishes for your Royal Highness's protection by sea and land; and of our earnest hopes that the visit you now make to these parts of the world may be no less gratifying to our royal visitor, than it is fitted, we are persuaded, to strengthen the ties that bind us all to the British throne, and to subserve your Royal Highness's preparation for the high ulterior position to which Divine providence may one day call you.

In name, and by appointment of Senate,

MICH. WILLIS,
Principal.

PRIMITIVE METHODIST CHURCH.

MAY IT PLEASE YOUR ROYAL HIGHNESS,—

We, the Ministers and Laymen of the Primitive Methodist Church, assembled in our annual Conference in this Province, unanimously agreed on your auspicious arrival in this country to present our most sincere congratulations.

The Primitive Methodist body in Britain and her Colonies have ever shown an unalterable attachment to the royal household and to the beloved Sovereign that rules her vast empire with such distinguished grace and wisdom.

As one of the Branches of the Protestant Church in Canada, devoted to the dissemination of religion in the community, we have evidence of the fact, that, whilst our teaching elevates in personal and social happiness, it secures all necessary obedience to the Throne and Constitution of our country.

We therefore trust that Your Royal Highness will be greatly interested in your visit to this colony, and in receiving expressions of loyalty from the people of all ranks and degrees; and we most earnestly pray the Giver of all good to continue you his gracious protection, and grant you all happiness in this life and that which is to come.

WM. ROWE, *President*.
JOHN DAVIDSON, *Secretary*.

ROYAL CANADIAN YACHT CLUB.

To His Royal Highness Albert Edward, Prince of Wales, &c. &c.

MAY IT PLEASE YOUR ROYAL HIGHNESS,—

We, the officers and members of the Royal Canadian Yacht Club, while joining with all our hearts in those manifestations of devotion to the Empire and attachment to the Crown which have everywhere greeted Your Royal Highness, feel that we have especial reason to be proud of this opportunity of extending to Your Royal Highness in person the loyal sentiments which animate us in common with all classes of your fellow-subjects.

We are grateful for the kindness which has enabled us thus to afford a hearty welcome to the son of that Gracious Sovereign to whose favour we are indebted for the honour of being entitled to the privileges of a Royal Club.

We are also happy in being able to greet in Your Royal Highness one who can fully sympathize with us in our desire to promote those noble pursuits which we believe to be among the most effectual means of perpetuating in these Provinces that manly spirit which has contributed in no small degree to the national supremacy in which it is the pride of every Canadian to participate.

Associated for the encouragement of the great national sport of the British Empire,—a sport so intimately connected with its naval pre-eminence,—we feel that the condescension of Your Royal Highness in receiving this expression of devotion to yourself and your august mother will constitute hereafter an epoch in the existence of the Club, to which we shall ever look with pride and gratification.

In conclusion, we beg Your Royal Highness to accept our earnest assurances of respect and devotion, and our heartfelt prayers for the happiness of our beloved Queen, and your own prosperity and success in the discharge of the exalted duties, to which, in God's providence, Your Royal Highness will hereafter be called.

REPLY.

GENTLEMEN,—I assure you that I take a lively interest in those manly sports which distinguish England and her Colonies, more especially when they are connected with that element on which has been seen so much of the glory of our common country. I thank you for the expression of your loyalty and devotion to the Queen my mother, and for your good wishes in my behalf.

ST. GEORGE'S SOCIETY.

MAY IT PLEASE YOUR ROYAL HIGHNESS,—

The St. George's Society of Toronto crave permission to approach Your Royal Highness on this auspicious occasion to express their devoted loyalty to their beloved Queen, and their homage to Your Royal Highness as the illustrious Heir to the Crown of that mighty Empire "on which the sun never sets."

In the progress of Your Royal Highness through this great dependency of the British Throne, Your Royal Highness has witnessed that unity among the subjects of Her Gracious Majesty who have made Canada their home, and has received that undivided outpouring of Canadian love and loyalty which may render it matter of surprise that societies, possessing features of individual nationality, exist among us. May then the St. George's Society of Toronto, an association composed as well of Englishmen as of the sons of that great principality from which your Royal Highness takes your august title of "Prince of Wales," be permitted to quote from their Charter of Incorporation the main object of their organization, namely:—"The affording relief to such natives of England and Wales in this country as from sickness or other causes have fallen into distress." Such an object we feel assured will excite the sympathy of Your Royal Highness as England's future Sovereign,—as the Welshman's noble Prince.

But while alluding to "benevolence" as the main object of their association, the St. George's Society of Toronto also seek, by periodical commemorations, to keep alive the remembrance of the achievements of their forefathers, under the banner of their Patron Saint; and on such occasions it is their especial pride to know (how closely!) the time-honored cry of "St. George for Merrie England!" The adopted motto of the Society is associated not only with their beloved father-land and its numberless public and charitable institutions, but still more with the ancient residence of its kings; the title of their beloved Queen, as

"Sovereign of the order of the Garter," reminding them that Windsor's proud Castle became, on its restoration by William of Wykeham, the cradle of England's most illustrious order of Knighthood, and that an enduring alliance was then inaugurated between the nobility of birth and the nobility of virtue in the Hall and Chapel of St. George.

That the same power that guided the spear of the valiant knight of Christendom may ever be the guardian and defender of Your Royal Highness, is the fervent prayer of the St. George's Society of Toronto.

SAMUEL B. HARMAN,
President.
JOHN P. FULLJAMES,
Secretary.

SYNOD OF THE PRESBYTERIAN CHURCH.

To His Royal Highness Albert Edward, Prince of Wales, &c.

MAY IT PLEASE YOUR ROYAL HIGHNESS,—

We, the Ministers and Elders of the Synod of the Presbyterian Church of Canada, in Synod assembled, beg leave most respectfully to offer to Your Royal Highness our cordial salutations, and those of the church which we represent; and to tender the assurance of our hearty attachment, in common with all loyal Britons, to the person and throne of our Sovereign. Occupied as we are in the wide field of this church's operations, both in Eastern and Western Canada, in the duties of the pastoral care, and meeting from time to time as church judicatories for the discussion of matters of importance affecting the order and government of the church, we recognize the duty of joining, with our other inculcations of Christian truth, the obligation on all to respect those who are in authority over us; and we appreciate gratefully the protection which, under the shield of the British Constitution, is secured to us in the exercise of our social rights, and liberty of Christian profession. This Synod hails Your Royal Highness in your visit to these parts of the American continent, recognizing in you the representative of a Sovereign, who, no less by her example of domestic virtue, than by her mild and prudent exercise of her queenly prerogative, has secured the hearty homage of her subjects, and the universal respect of the civilized world.

Permit us only to add our best wishes for the protection of Your Royal Highness in your journeying by sea and land; and to assure Your Royal Highness of our continued prayers, as a portion of the religious community, for a family and dynasty, associated in our minds with the preservation of whatever is dear to us as Britons and as Protestants.

REPLY.

GENTLEMEN,—Among the characteristics of our parent land, and of this important colony, is the perfect freedom of religious creeds. I recognize in your position the assertion of this right, associated with the doctrines of that church which has long guided the people of Scotland.

I thank you for your Address, and for your prayers offered in behalf of the Queen my mother, and myself.

TEMPERANCE ORGANIZATION.

To His Royal Highness Albert Edward, Prince of Wales.

MAY IT PLEASE YOUR ROYAL HIGHNESS,—

On behalf of the various Temperance organizations of Upper Canada, numbering some tens of thousands of loyal hearts, we desire to welcome Your Royal Highness with feelings of ardent attachment to our Sovereign the Queen, whose condescension in having permitted the Heir Apparent of the British Throne to visit this portion of her vast dominions, we gratefully acknowledge.

We rejoice that our allegiance is due to a Sovereign whose glorious reign has never been tarnished by the excesses of former Courts, but that the truly Christian example of your Royal Mother has called forth universal commendation.

Emulating the Christian graces of our Queen, many thousands of youth are banded together to check the current of intemperance ; and we look forward to a brilliant future for Canada, because in the youth of the present day the principles and practice of Total Abstinence are growing with their growth and strengthening with their strength.

We sincerely trust that the visit of Your Royal Highness may be in every respect agreeable ; and that when you are welcomed home, Your Royal Highness may be enabled to assure Her Majesty, that, amongst the glorious institutions of the Province enjoyed by a free and happy people, none seem to be more blessed of Heaven than those established to discourage intemperance.

As it has pleased the Almighty long to spare the Queen, to wear unspotted the brightest crown of modern nations, so may she hereafter wear an everlasting crown of life ; and when it shall please the King of Kings to call her hence, may it be the fondest desire of your heart to wear unsullied that crown which has so long adorned the brow of our beloved Queen, whose goodness and whose virtues will form the choicest page of England's history.

ROBERT SPENCE,
President Temperance Reformation Society, Toronto.
Toronto, Sept. 8, 1860.

REPLY.

TORONTO, 8th Sept., 1860.

SIR,—I have the honor to convey to you the thanks of His Royal Highness the Prince of Wales, for the Address presented to him by you on behalf of the various Temperance organizations of Upper Canada.

I am, Sir,
Your obedient servant,
NEWCASTLE.
To the Hon. Robert Spence.

TRINITY COLLEGE.

MAY IT PLEASE YOUR ROYAL HIGHNESS,—

We, the Chancellor, Masters, and Scholars of the University of Trinity College, Toronto, beg to express to Your Royal Highness our heartfelt congratulation on the occasion of your visit to this Province, and our grateful sense of the kindly interest which you have thus discovered in the welfare of the College.

While we gladly recognize the many obligations under which we lie, in common with all our fellow-subjects in this Province, to loyal attachment to the Throne of Great Britain, and to its present most gracious occupant, it is our especial duty to acknowledge the distinguished favor which Her Majesty the Queen has conferred upon us, by conveying to us, under the Royal Charter, the full privileges of a University.

Her Majesty, in that character, has been pleased to declare her willingness "to promote the more perfect establishment within the Diocese of Toronto of a College in connection with the United Church of England and Ireland, for the education of youth, in the doctrines and duties of the Christian Religion, as inculcated by that Church, and for the instruction in the various branches of science and literature which are taught in the Universities of this Kingdom."

It will ever be our pride, as it must ever be our duty, faithfully to execute the trust which has been thus graciously confided to us, both by the inculcation of sound religious principles, and by the communication of all useful secular learning. In attempting to discharge this duty, we are assured that we can propose to ourselves no better model than that of the ancient Universities of England, with the studies of one of which Your Royal Highness is already familiar, while we learn with satisfaction that it is your design to form a like intimate acquaintance with the other. It will be our aim, by the blessing of Almighty God, to perpetuate in this Colony that spirit of English faith and loyalty, by which the members of our communion have ever been distinguished at home, and by which we trust that they will still be recognized in every land in which our Church is planted under the protection of the British Crown.

REPLY.

GENTLEMEN,—I thank you sincerely for the expression of loyalty and attachment to the British Crown contained in your Address, and for the welcome which you have given me to this City.

The Institution from which the Address proceeds is one of the utmost importance to the Colony, inasmuch as it is destined to train those to whose care are committed the spiritual interests of the members of the Church of England.

I know the difficulties under which you have labored, and I sincerely hope that you may successfully surmount them.

UPPER CANADA BIBLE SOCIETY.

To His Royal Highness Albert Edward, Prince of Wales, &c., &c.

MAY IT PLEASE YOUR ROYAL HIGHNESS,—

We, the President and Directors of the Upper Canada Bible Society, in behalf of that Institution, desire to express our grateful sense of the distingnished honour which has been conferred upon this Province by the visit of Your Royal Highness, and rejoice to have the opportunity of testifying our devoted loyalty to the Queen, and our warm attachment to British connection.

The great and good work for which we are associated, has long excited the warmest interest amongst the inhabitants of the United Kingdom; and Her Majesty, ever ready to encourage undertakings calculated to promote the glory of God, or advance the welfare of man, has evinced her appreciation of the British and Foreign Bible Society by graciously accepting the patronage of one of its Branches. Animated by the success of the Institution in the Parent Country, and impressed with the conviction that the noblest characteristics of our glorious Fatherland is the prevalence of those principles which the Holy Scriptures inculcate, we have directed our humble efforts towards the dissemination throughout the Province of the same Blessed Volume, in the well-gronnded hope that through its instrumentality the same happy results may be manifested in the diffusion of that righteousness "which exalteth a nation" and "establisheth the throne."

Nor have the Society's operations been altogether confined within the limits of this Province; but we have endeavonred, from time to time, as God has put it into the hearts of our members, to aid by special contributions to the Parent Society, in spreading abroad the knowledge of the Blessed Gospel in distant lands.

Permit us, in conclnsion, to assure Your Royal Highness, that our earnest prayer to the Giver of all good is, that He may pour His choicest blessings npon our Qneen, the Prince Consort, and every member of the royal family, and especially that He will take under His protecting care and guiding influence the Heir of the British Crown, that so he may, when called upon to rule over the Empire, walk in the steps of our present honoured and beloved Sovereign.

GEO. WILLIAM ALLAN,
President.
JAMES S. HOWARD,
WM. REID, A.M., } *Secretaries.*
J. G. HODGINS, LL.B.,
Minute Secretary.

REPLY.

GENTLEMEN,—It is particularly pleasing for me to receive an Address from those whose efforts are directed to the spread of Divine knowledge and the circulation of the Holy Scriptures. I wish you every success in the mission you have undertaken, and I thank you very sincerely for the welcome which you have given me to this city.

UPPER CANADA COLLEGE.

MAY IT PLEASE YOUR ROYAL HIGHNESS,—

We, the Principal and Masters of Upper Canada College, beg to approach Your Royal Highness with sentiments of devoted loyalty to Her Most Gracious Majesty the Queen.

The Institution with which we are connected is amongst the earliest of the educational benefits conferred upon this Province by the enlightened liberality of your illustrious relative, His Majesty King George IV. Established in 1829 by Royal Charter, Upper Canada College has since continued to discharge a most important work in the education of many hundreds of Canadian youth, numbers of whom have been enabled, under the Divine blessing, to serve their country and the Empire with credit in various honorable positions.

The Danube, the Crimea, and the still more recent battle-fields of India, stained with their life-blood, have witnessed the daring and devotion of Upper Canada College boys ; and among the officers of that Regiment which boasts Your Royal Highness's name, are several whose career in Upper Canada College gives promise of good service to their country, should opportunity offer.

It is our grateful duty and our privilege, along with the sound and religious training which characterizes the time-honored Grammar Schools of England, to inculcate in our Canadian youth attachment to the land and Institutions of their forefathers, and so to educate both mind and body that they may be fitting and useful members of the great Empire to which it is our pride to belong.

In those of our youth who are now passing under our care, we cannot on this happy occasion forget that we see many who are destined to take prominent parts in the future of this young country, at a time, when, in the order of Providence, Your Highness shall hold the sceptre, which is now so benignly swayed by your august mother; and the recollection of this royal visit will, we fervently trust, stamp an indelible impress of reality on the abstract sentiment of loyalty, and knit the hearts of the rising generation inseparably to the youthful heir to the mightiest Empire in the world.

YORK AND PEEL.

MAY IT PLEASE YOUR ROYAL HIGHNESS,—

We, the Council of the United Counties of York and Peel, on behalf of the municipalities we represent, respectfully approach Your Royal Highness to offer the hearty welcome of Canadian Yeomanry to the son of our beloved Queen, and the Heir Apparent to the British throne.

Through your Royal Highness, we desire to express to our gracious Sovereign our feelings of attachment to the British Constitution, and loyalty to the British crown; and our hope that her reign, so happy and prosperous, may be long continued.

We trust that this visit may prove an agreeable one to Your Royal Highness; that the opportunity of personal observation on the part of yourself, and the distinguished noblemen who accompany you, may prove beneficial to this and the mother country; and that, in after years, amidst other scenes, Your Royal Highness may at times revert with satisfaction to your recollections of Canada and the Canadians.

D. REESOR,
Warden.

Council Chamber, 7th September, 1860.

COLLINGWOOD.

To His Royal Highness Albert Edward, Prince of Wales, &c., &c.

MAY IT PLEASE YOUR ROYAL HIGHNESS,—

We, the Mayor and Council of the Town of Collingwood, on behalf of ourselves and our loyal townsmen, beg respectfully to approach Your Royal Highness with assurances of esteem to yourself, and loyalty to our gracious and beloved Sovereign, your august mother.

In doing so, we avail ourselves of this your visit to the most northern town of British North America, to offer you a hearty and loyal welcome and to sincerely thank Your Royal Highness for the honour conferred upon us by this your visit to this our youthful Municipality.

We trust that the visit of Your Royal Highness to the shores of the majestic Huron, the great highroad to our Sovereign's extensive dominions in the North-west, stretching as they do to the mighty Pacific, will not be among the least pleasing reminiscences of the sojourn of Your Royal Highness with Her Majesty's loyal Canadian subjects.

We pray that Your Royal Highness will be pleased, on your return to the Mother Land, to convey to our gracious Queen the assurances of our continued attachment to Her throne and person, and our unwavering fidelity to the British Constitution.

JOHN McWATT,
Mayor.

BARRIE.

MAGISTRATES OF SIMCOE.

MAY IT PLEASE YOUR ROYAL HIGHNESS,—

We, the Magistrates of the County of Simcoe, in Session assembled, are grateful for the opportunity of approaching Your Royal Highness with our tribute of respect both to Her Majesty whom you represent, and also to yourself personally.

We would hope that your progress through the Province, as it has drawn closer the ties which unite us and the land of our fathers, by adding feelings of personal interest in yourself, may have also assured you that the Crown of England has, in Canada, as loving and faithful subjects as any in the British Isles. The blood which throbs in England's heart, circulates through every member of Her mighty empire.

As ministers of justice, we take pride in informing Your Royal Highness, that, whether congregated in towns or villages, or secluded in the depths of the forest, Her Majesty's Canadian subjects are a law-abiding people; that our laws, nearly identical with those of England, are, throughout our borders, valued and obeyed.

We see in Your Royal Highness's visit a graceful and welcome recognition of Canada as an integral and important portion of the empire; and trust that the recollections you may bear from our shores will be as suggestive to you of our country's devotion to the Crown and to your person, as the remembrances you leave behind you are assuring to us that the throne which your noble mother our good Queen has long set up in the hearts of her subjects, will rest on the same enduring foundation of respect and love when you become our King.

REPLY.

GENTLEMEN,—I thank you sincerely for the Address which you have presented to me.

In the Queen's name, I thank you for the expressions of your loyalty to her crown and person; and for myself, I am grateful to you for this welcome to your neighbourhood.

GUELPH.

To His Royal Highness Albert Edward, Prince of Wales, &c., &c.

MAY IT PLEASE YOUR ROYAL HIGHNESS,—

The Mayor and Council, on behalf of themselves and the inhabitants of Guelph, proudly welcome Your Royal Highness to this town, which bears the family name of the illustrious House of Brunswick,—a town which has risen in thirty years from an unbroken forest.

We thank Your Royal Highness for the honor of this visit, and the opportunity thus afforded of expressing our loyalty and devotion to the person of our Queen, and attachment and fealty to the free institutions of the great Empire of which we are proud to form an integral part.

We entertain a profound sense of Her Majesty's kind and gracious consideration for Her Canadian subjects, in delegating Your Royal Highness to visit Canada; and are deeply sensible of our obligations to Your Royal Highness in encountering the fatigues and perils of an Atlantic voyage to come amongst us.

Our warm affections will follow Your Royal Highness, and our earnest prayers to Almighty God for your safe return to that empire whose future hopes and expectations, in common with our own, are bound up in Your Royal Highness.

JOHN HARVEY,
Mayor.

REPLY.

GENTLEMEN,—I thank you sincerely for the Address which you have presented to me.

In the Queen's name, I thank you for the expressions of your loyalty to Her Crown and person; and for myself, I am grateful to you for this welcome to this the chief town of so fertile and beautiful a district, bearing, as it does, the name of my own family.

LONDON.

BOARD OF TRADE.

To His Royal Highness Albert Edward, Prince of Wales, &c., &c.

MAY IT PLEASE YOUR ROYAL HIGHNESS,—

We, as representing the gentlemen composing the Board of Trade in the city of London, C.W., most respectfully approach Your Royal Highness with a cordial welcome on this auspicious occasion; and we do so the more readily because you have high claims on our loyalty, not only as the Heir Apparent of the British Throne, but as descended from our illustrious sovereign, whom we, in common with all her subjects, revere and love. It is the aim of our Board to encourage every species of legitimate trading and manufacture, and thereby to co-operate with all other classes in the community in advancing the prosperity of our youthful city, and of the Province at large; therefore, it is with no ordinary pleasure that we address Your Royal Highness at a time when this portion of the colony, justly called "the garden of Canada," is steadily recovering from the late commercial crisis, and when a singularly abundant harvest has cheered the entire population, who had been much discouraged by the failure of the crops of past years, causing a general depression of business.

Although inhabiting a distant part of the British dominions, we continue to preserve the most devoted attachment to the crown and person of Her Most Gracious Majesty.

It is our sincere prayer, that, when the day arrives for Your Royal Highness to leave the American shores, you may be carried over the deep in safety, and that your life may be long, glorious, and happy.

With profound respect,

D. FARRAR,
President,

CHAS. HUNT,
Vice-President, of the Board of Trade,
London, C.W.

COUNTY COUNCIL.

To His Royal Highness Albert Edward, Prince of Wales, &c., &c.

MAY IT PLEASE YOUR ROYAL HIGHNESS,—

We, the Warden and Municipal Council of the County of Middlesex, heartily welcome Your Royal Highness on your arrival within this county. Forty years ago, Middlesex was a dense forest, within which scarcely a civilized being could be found; but, through the energy industry, and untiring perseverance of the pioneers of the wilderness, that forest has receded, and has been mainly converted into cultivated lands, the comfortable homes of a loyal, free, and independent people.

We gladly avail ourselves of this opportunity to beg Your Royal Highness to convey to Her Gracious Majesty the assurance of our admiration of the high qualities which so conspicuously adorn her character, and the devoted loyalty of the people of the County of Middlesex to the Crown and Constitution. We trust that your visit to Canada and sister Provinces may prove agreeable to Your Highness; and that, on your return to the parent land, you may be pleased to represent to Her Majesty that her transatlantic subjects have already made considerable progress in material comfort, and in the arts of civilization; and that a further advancement will doubtless continue to be made, under the wise and liberal policy pursued by the parent State, in the benefits of which this important dependency of the British Empire has largely participated.

REPLY.

GENTLEMEN,—I thank you sincerely for the Address which you have presented to me.

In the Queen's name, I acknowledge the expressions of your loyalty to her crown and person; and for myself, I am grateful to you for this welcome to your neighbourhood.

ST. ANDREW'S SOCIETY.

To His Royal Highness Albert Edward, Prince of Wales, &c., &c.

MAY IT PLEASE YOUR ROYAL HIGHNESS,—

We, the office-bearers and members of the St. Andrews' Society in the city of London, Canada West, most respectfully present to Your Royal Highness our cordial welcome to this city, with the expression of our deep affection for you as the Heir Apparent of that vast empire under the dominion of our Beloved Queen.

To relieve the wants of our indigent countrymen who have emigrated to this soil, is the first aim of our Society; and as Scotsmen, and the descendants of Scotsmen, in this portion of Canada West, we cherish towards the illustrious family of which you are the hope, an attachment loyal and devoted as that which animates the hearts of Caledonians at home.

We continue to regard with undiminished satisfaction those domestic virtues which adorn the character of Her Most Gracious Majesty; and we respectfully request that Your Royal Highness will convey to the Queen the unalloyed pleasure we feel in uniting with our fellow-subjects throughout the empire in maintaining the stability of her throne.

May the Almighty bestow on you length of days and happiness, and, by making your life a blessing to the whole British territories, make you a blessing to the world at large.

REPLY.

LONDON, C. W., 14th Sept., 1860.

SIR,—I have the honor to convey to you the thanks of His Royal Highness the Prince of Wales for the Address presented to him by the members of the St. Andrew's Society.

I am, sir, your obedient servant,

NEWCASTLE.

J. Wilson, Esq.,
President St. Andrew's Society.

SYNOD CHURCH OF ENGLAND.

To His Royal Highness Albert Edward, Prince of Wales, &c., &c.

MAY IT PLEASE YOUR ROYAL HIGHNESS,—

We, the Bishop, Clergy, and Laity of the Diocese of Huron, in Synod assembled, approach Your Royal Highness to offer to you the homage of our unfeigned respect, and to evince our devoted loyalty to the crown and sceptre of Great Britain.

Attached by principle and by strong affection to the British Throne, we rejoice to welcome amongst us the son and representative of our beloved Queen, whose many virtues have shed a lustre upon the high position which, in the providence of God, she has been called to fill.

Though separated from Great Britain by thousands of miles, we rejoice to feel that we are under the British crown, and an integral part of the United Church of England and Ireland. We earnestly desire that the supremacy of the Sovereign of Great Britain over us, as a portion of the Church of England and Ireland, may be ever maintained, and that we and our posterity, to the latest generations, may enjoy the high privilege of being united to that pure and reformed church, which, under God, has conferred the highest blessings upon our fatherland.

We are thankful that God, in his providence, has watched over Your Royal Highness, and protected you in your travels by land and by water; and we earnestly pray that the same protecting power may be extended over you throughout your gracious visit to this remote portion of the British Empire.

We shall ever continue earnestly to entreat our Heavenly Father, the King of Kings and Lord of Lords, the only ruler of Princes, to endow you with His Holy Spirit, to enrich you with His heavenly grace, to prosper you with all happiness, and to bring you to His everlasting kingdom, through Jesus Christ our Lord.

REPLY.

GENTLEMEN,—The formation of this new Diocese of the Province of Canada, appears to show the vitality of the Church of our Fathers in this distant land.

It is clear that the ministry of her clergy, and the paternal care of her bishop, are sought for, and appreciated.

I thank you very sincerely for the warm expression of your loyalty and affection for the Queen my mother; and I feel the value of those prayers which you will continue to offer on her behalf, and on my own

It is true that I shall not have heard, within the walls of your cathedral, the preaching of the word of God; but I shall bear away with me from this city a lively recollection of the welcome which has been given me by the clergy, and the members of that church to which I belong.

THE MAGISTRATES.

To His Royal Highness Albert Edward, Prince of Wales, &c., &c.

MAY IT PLEASE YOUR ROYAL HIGHNESS,—

We, Her Majesty's loyal and dutiful subjects, the magistrates of the county of Middlesex, in Upper Canada, in general Quarter Sessions assembled, beg leave to approach Your Royal Highness with an assurance of our devoted attachment to the person and government of our most gracious sovereign, and to congratulate Your Royal Highness upon your safe arrival amongst us, and to assure you of the grateful sense we entertain of the condescension of Your Royal Highness in submitting to the many inconveniences necessarily attendant upon visiting this portion of Her Majesty's dominions.

We sincerely hope that Your Royal Highness,—the descendant of a long line of illustrious ancestors, whose memory will be ever dear to Her Majesty's Canadian subjects,—after having viewed as much of this great continent as your time and convenience will admit, may be blessed by the Almighty with a safe return to your native land ; and that, when, under the dispensations of an All-wise Providence, you shall be called, in the course of time, to reign over us, you may remember (as we ever shall, with feelings of pleasure) Your Royal Highness's visit to this favored and flourishing portion of the British empire.

THE MILITIA.

To His Royal Highness Albert Edward, Prince of Wales, &c., &c.

MAY IT PLEASE YOUR ROYAL HIGHNESS,—

We, the loyal Militia of the 8th Military District of Canada West, comprising the counties of Middlesex, Elgin, Norfolk, Brant, and Oxford, and numbering upwards of thirty thousand of all ranks, are most happy in the opportunity given to us by your august mother and beloved Queen of assuring Your Royal Highness in person of our firm and devoted attachment to her person and crown ; and offering to Your Royal Highness, as the son of so admirable a mother, and as the Heir Apparent to that crown, a warm welcome to our home in the forest.

We are indeed rejoiced to see amongst us, in these remote backwoods, the first (with the exception of your illustrious grandfather, the Duke of Kent) of the Princes of the House of Brunswick ; and next to the gratification which Her Most Gracious Majesty in person would have given to us, in common with our fellow-subjects in British North America, we esteem the advent of Your Royal Highness.

It has been the good fortune of Canadians, from the time since Canada became an appendage of the British Crown, to have served in the armies of Britain, both in the ranks and by commissions from the sovereign ; and it is a proud reflection for us that Canadians have ever, in such positions, no less truly than their fellow-subjects, fought the battles of their parent land ; and from the militia of Canada (partly of this district) there was recently added to the British army, as your Royal Highness is aware, the regiment which has your title as its own distinctive name. We can, therefore, confidently assure Your Royal Highness that if, in the course of events, our beloved mother country, and that throne to which, in loyalty and devotion, we will give place to none, should need to call to her aid the sons of her colonies, many such bands as that gallant regiment will be found, who, leaving for the time their axes, their ploughs, and their peaceful occupations in the forests, and slinging their rifle,—the weapon of the Canadian militia-men,—will gladly, side by side with the loyal volunteers of England, strike a blow for the honor and glory of that empire with which it is our pride to be identified.

Again we ask Your Royal Highness to accept a hearty welcome, and our best wishes for your future welfare, your health and happiness, and for a safe return to the shores of Old England.

THE WELSHMEN.

To His Royal Highness Albert Edward, Prince of Wales, &c., &c.

MAY IT PLEASE YOUR ROYAL HIGHNESS,—

The natives of the ancient principality of Wales, and their descendants, settled in this vicinity, proud of the traditions of their country, have appointed us a deputation on this auspicious occasion to receive and welcome their royal Prince to this young and rising inland city.

We therefore, in their name and in our own, beg leave to express the hearty and unfeigned joy we all feel at the consummation of an event now so long and ardently looked forward to. From the hour in which Your Royal Highness first arrived in these Provinces, we have marked with great pleasure the enthusiastic loyalty and devotion with which all classes of our fellow-subjects have testified their attachment to your royal person, as the representative of our beloved sovereign and her august family. And we beg leave to assure Your Royal Highness, that our hearts respond in unison with the many warm tributes of admiration so justly earned and so universally accorded to those Christian and domestic virtues that have so eminently adorned the life and reign of our good Queen, and increased, if possible, the attachment of her subjects to the British Throne and to British institutions.

We are happy also in the opportunity thus afforded us of conveying to Your Royal Highness our sense of the admirable prudence, judgment, and wisdom displayed on all occasions by your royal father during his long and happy connection with the British Empire.

We earnestly hope that Your Royal Mother has yet many years to reign over us; and that from the satisfaction which Your Royal Highness has been graciously pleased to express at all you have seen during your progress through this Province, as well as from the ease and rapidity with which the distance separating us from Great Britain can now be traversed, we may be permitted to indulge a hope that this short visit is but the first of a series, increasing both in frequency and duration, which Your Royal Highness may be induced to undertake before reaching that high destiny to which God has appointed you, that you may with your own eyes mark from time to time that rapid progress which is so peculiar a feature of this part of Her Majesty's dominions.

May God in his infinite mercy guide and watch over you.

REPLY.

LONDON, C. W., Sept. 14, 1860.

SIR,—I have the honor to convey to you the thanks of His Royal Highness the Prince of Wales, for the Address presented to him by the natives of the principality of Wales, settled in the vicinity of London.

I am, Sir,

Your obedient servant,

NEWCASTLE.

To Benjamin Nash, Esq.

SARNIA.

To His Royal Highness Albert Edward, Prince of Wales, &c., &c.

MAY IT PLEASE YOUR ROYAL HIGHNESS,—

We, the Mayor and people of Sarnia, most respectfully approach Your Royal Highness to bid your welcome to our young town, and offer our congratulations on your having now reached, in health and safety, the western boundary of Her Majesty's Canadian dominions.

We are glad of the opportunity thus afforded us of giving expression to the sentiment of loyalty to the British Crown and Sceptre, which, although "Borderers" geographically, we strongly hold, and have uniformly evinced in past years; and which we also enjoin our children to maintain, in time to come, esteeming their union and identity with the mighty British nation as their chief boast and greatest glory.

As the substitute and representative of our gracious and beloved Queen, sent to visit Her transatlantic subjects in response to their invitation, we pray you to accept our warm thanks for this special mark of her royal consideration, and convey to her the heartfelt tribute of our admiration of the many excellencies that adorn her private character, and of the wisdom and beneficence that characterize her widely-extended government.

As the Heir Apparent of the British Throne, we trust that you will be preserved and guarded by a watchful Providence, to become a future blessing to the multitudes, in many lands, who shall yet own allegiance to your inherited authority, and promote, in their day and generation, the strength and splendor of the kingdom.

As a traveller for recreation and instruction, we trust that you will see much to please, and more to profit by, in the course of your journeyings through the Queen's American possessions, and subsequently through those of our republican neighbors; and that you will carry with you and preserve, after returning to your native land, many agreeable recollections of your visit to this Western Hemisphere.

We have not very much to show Your Royal Highness in Sarnia, as evidencing the prowess of the people in the subjugation of the rude native elements to the uses of civilization; but when we say that there are standing here to-day many of the pioneers who first, in this locality, cleared homes for themselves in the unbroken forest, destitute then of any roads, and railroads all unhoped for,—even steamboats uncommon on that beautiful river in front,—it may be acknowledged, after all, that we still inherit a portion of the energy and perseverance which make the Anglo-Saxon a conquering race on every soil upon which they undertake to live and labor.

In name and on behalf of the inhabitants of Sarnia,

THOMAS W. JOHNSTON,
Mayor.

HAMILTON.

HIGHLAND SOCIETY.

To His Royal Highness Albert Edward, Prince of Wales, &c., &c.

MAY IT PLEASE YOUR ROYAL HIGHNESS,—

We, the President, Directors, and Members of the Highland Society of Hamilton and Canada West, desire most respectfully to approach Your Royal Highness for the purpose of assuring Your Highness of our devoted attachment to the person and throne of our beloved Queen, of expressing our affectionate regard for your Royal Person, and of tendering to you a Highland welcome to our Canadian homes.

As sons of the garb, associated together for the purpose of perpetuating in the land of our adoption, the language, music, and martial spirit of our forefathers, it is not possible for us to witness the presence in our midst of the descendant of "Caledonia's Royal Race," without giving utterance in a few inadequate words to the feelings of intense delight and satisfaction with which we have viewed the cordial and enthusiastic manner in which he has been received by all classes of Her Majesty's subjects since his arrival on our Western shores; and especially to the feelings of delighted pride with which we, in common with all the sons of the "land of the mountain and the flood," hail his arrival in this distant portion of Britain's glorious Empire.

We feel as if we had a territorial interest in Your Royal Highness, distinct from political considerations, distinct from constitutional theories, or even from regard to those personal qualities which we are proud to know you possess, and which, of themselves, would command the homage of our esteem.—We recognize in Your Royal Highness the unquestioned heir of Scotland's ancient Kings; we *render* to you the homage due to him through whose veins runs the blood of the heroic Bruce, the defender of Scotland's liberties; we *hail* you as one whose Royal brow, we humbly trust, shall at some distant day be adorned by Scotland's Virgin Crown, that old diadem which, through ages of darkness and danger, has ever been the holy rallying-light to bravery, to patriotism, and honour; and we welcome you amongst us as the son of a monarch endeared to Scotsmen all over the world, above all other monarchs that ever sat upon Britain's throne, for the loving interest she has ever manifested in the land they love so well.

We cannot sufficiently give utterance to our feelings of gratitude for the consideration and kindness which prompted our August Sovereign to depute Your Royal Highness as her representative to visit Her North American dominions; and the importance of the visit cannot, we think, be over-estimated.—We know and believe that her object has been to show her colonial subjects that she loves us, and to gratify our loyal love to her and to her race. We fondly hope that both objects have been happily accomplished. Our people are not of those who hurry from their homes, their farms, and their workshops to gaze upon a senseless pageant: they hurry to do homage to the son of their Queen; they wish him to see how happy they are in having him amongst them; to see for himself the placid aspect of a people grateful to God for the position they hold among the Nations,—who know their own worth, and, knowing it, feel that they have a Sovereign of whom Canada may well be proud, and to support whose Throne thousands of them are prepared to bring hands steeled by the labours of a life of hardihood and freedom, and hearts fearless of man in the fear of God.

By giving expression to our earnest prayer that to Your Royal Highness a long and happy life may be vouchsafed, that an all-wise Providence may ever have you in its gracious keeping, and that you may prove a blessing to the people over whom you are destined to rule, we conclude. With these hopes, in the language of our fathers, we tender you " *Cead mille failte.*"

Signed in the name, and by authority, of the Highland Society of Hamilton and Canada West.

Hector Munro, *President.*

Hamilton, Canada West, 19th Sept., 1860.

MAGISTRATES AND YEOMANRY.

May it please Your Royal Highness,—

We, the Magistracy and Yeomanry of the County of Wentworth, desire to approach Your Royal Highness with the expression of our heartfelt attachment to Her Majesty the Queen, and to the Royal Family.

We deeply value the high honor which has been conferred upon this Province in the presence of Your Royal Highness among us as Her Majesty's representative; assuring ourselves that Your Royal Highness's visit will excite in the people of this Province, if possible, a yet higher regard for British institutions, and an increased attachment to British connexion. The Exhibition of the Provincial Agricultural Association will have developed in some degree the resources and capabilities of this Province in agricultural products, and, we trust, has proved, that it is not without the promise of much success in manufactures, or wholly wanting in the cultivation of the fine arts ; and we venture to express the hope, that the opportunity which has been afforded to Your Royal Highness of visiting this section of the Province, has impressed Your Royal Highness with the assurance, that, although occasionally oppressed by the failure of its harvest, Wentworth and its adjoining counties possess the elements of future prosperity as the reward of steady industry.

We heartily bid Your Royal Highness welcome ; and when the period of Your Royal Highness's return to the " Old Country " shall have arrived, we venture to hope that Your Royal Highness will convey to our Queen the assurance of our loyalty, and that Your Royal Highness will ever retain a pleasing remembrance of the visit with which we have been favoured.

By desire of the County and on its behalf,

E. CARTWRIGHT THOMAS,
Sheriff.

15th Sept., 1860.

MILITIA.

To His Royal Highness Albert Edward, Prince of Wales, &c., &c.

May it please Your Royal Highness,—

We, the officers and men of the 7th Military District of Upper Canada, beg leave to offer to Your Royal Highness, our congratulations upon the safe arrival of Your Royal Highness in this portion of Her Majesty's dominions, where loyalty and attachment to the Throne, and veneration for the country whence our forefathers came, are the predominant sentiment of its inhabitants. These have ever been the marked characteristics of the people, whether engaged in their various occupations, contributing to the material advancement of the Province, or assembled together in arms to repel the attacks of a numerous and gallant foe.

As loyal subjects of Her Majesty, and in our capacity of Militiamen, we hope we may be pardoned by Your Royal Highness, if, upon this auspicious occasion, we refer to the deeds of our forefathers, who were ever ready to rally round the throne at the first sign of danger.

During the war of 1812 the enrolled militia of Upper Canada, with the aid of a few troops of the line, repeatedly defeated a well-appointed and much more numerous body of the enemy's regular troops; and not only succeeded in repelling invasion, but carried the war into the enemy's country, and thus contributed to preserve this noble Province to the British Crown.

Many hard-fought battles, including the crowning victory of the storming of Fort Niagara, and the capture of the whole of the Niagara frontier, exhibited instances of the courage, endurance, devotion, and ability of the Militia of Upper Canada; and we, as their representatives, beg leave to assure Your Royal Highness, that that loyalty and devotion to their Sovereign and their country which so distinguished the militia of those days have been inherited by their descendants, and that we shall ever be ready to devote our fortunes and our lives to the same cause, wherever occasion may arise.

We trust that the tour of Your Royal Highness through these noble dominions of Her Majesty, and through the States of the adjoining Republic, may have a pleasant and happy termination; that the result of Your Royal Highness's visit may tend to unite more closely the British American Provinces to the great Empire of which they form a part; and that the friendly alliance with the United States of America may be strengthened, and made lasting and permanent.

We pray, that it may please an All-wise Providence to conduct Your Royal Highness in safety to the shore of Great Britain; and that Your Royal Highness will be pleased to assure our beloved Sovereign the Queen, of the heartfelt devotion of Her Militia of Upper Canada.

Signed at Hamilton, on behalf of the officers and men of the 7th Military District of Upper Canada, this 4th day of September 1860.

TRUSTEES OF THE HAMILTON CITY SCHOOLS.

MAY IT PLEASE YOUR ROYAL HIGHNESS,—

We, the Chairman and members of the Board of School Trustees for the city of Hamilton, beg to approach Your Royal Highness with all loyal and dutiful respect, and, in our own name, as also in the name of all the Teachers and pupils in the several schools under our care,— the highest of which you have deigned to honor with your presence,—

we most heartily and loyally greet you on your auspicious arrival in our city, and gratefully bid you a joyous welcome.

Amid the great manifold blessings we enjoy under the benign sway of our most Gracious Sovereign, your august and honored mother, we specially prize the system of general education established in the province, which, if matured and maintained, will soon render a good common education,—the young Canadian's birthright,—altogether irrespective of his class, color, or condition, and free access to the schoolhouse, the privilege of all. In all our schools, and in their appropriate lessons, the great principles of religion and patriotism, loyalty and charity, are kindly but faithfully inculcated. And we feel assured that the condescension of Your Royal Highness in visiting this and other schools of learning in the Province, will not only greatly encourage the work of education, but will also foster and perpetuate in the hearts of the young, that profound sentiment of devoted loyalty which endears the tie that unites us, as a people, to the British Crown, and which will hereafter strengthen the pillars of that illustrious throne, which, in the providence of God, you may be called to occupy.

We gladly avail ourselves of the occasion to renew our assurances of loyalty to the Queen, and our personal regard for Your Royal Highness.

May the recollections of your present extended tour, be to you a future satisfaction; may your further journeyings be prosperous, and your return home safe and happy.

W. L. BILLINGS, M.D.,
Chairman of Board of Trustees.

WATER COMMISSIONERS.

MAY IT PLEASE YOUR ROYAL HIGHNESS,—

The Water Commissioners of the City of Hamilton beg leave to express their feelings of love and loyalty to the person and throne of your august mother, and their devoted attachment to yourself.

They would not have ventured to request that Your Royal Highness would inaugurate these works at this point, had they not been aware of the distance travelled by Her Majesty the Queen to perform a similar ceremony at Loch Kathrine.

They also know the interest which Your Royal Highness, as well as your illustrious father, manifests in the industry and social well-being of the people; and they are happy to have this opportunity of exhibiting a system of Water Works which they believe to be as complete as any on this continent.

These works have been planned and executed under the direction of Thomas C. Keefer, an engineer born and educated in this province; and the engines to which the attention of Your Royal Highness is directed, are specimens of Canadian workmanship, the most powerful and highly-finished of their kind in the province.

The fact that a city of twenty-five thousand inhabitants has carried to completion an undertaking of such magnitude, shows that protection of life and property from fire, sanitary considerations, and social comfort, are as well understood and as highly appreciated here as in larger and older communities.

The inauguration of these works by Your Royal Highness is a most gratifying event to the Commissioners and the people whom they represent. They hope that the present will not be the last visit of Your Royal Highness to this country; but if it should be, rest assured that the interest manifested by Your Royal Highness in their enterprize will ever be gratefully remembered by the citizens of Hamilton.

ADAM BROWN,
Chairman.

WELLINGTON.

To His Royal Highness Albert Edward Prince, of Wales, &c., &c.

MAY IT PLEASE YOUR ROYAL HIGHNESS,—

We, the Municipal Representatives of the County of Wellington, in County Council assembled, gladly avail ourselves of the opportunity presented by this visit of Your Royal Highness to our County Town, to testify in word, as we are ever ready to do in our daily lives, our devotion to the Crown and person of our illustrious and beloved Sovereign; while with others we cannot avoid the expression of our regret that the duties appertaining to the high position held by Her Gracious Majesty, have prevented her acceptance of the invitation proferred by our Legislature, and from becoming personally acquainted with the fervent feeling of loyalty pervading this portion of her dominions. We gratefully acknowledge the readiness with which she has met the prayer of her Canadian subjects, by deputing as her representative, one who, at some distant day, will wield the sceptre now held by her. In doing this, we beg to congratulate Your Royal Highness upon the enthusiastic and hearty reception which has greeted you during your tour through the Province; and can assure you, that, in the backwoods of this peninsula, thousands of miles from the parent state, where the hardy pioneer is busily engaged in battling with the difficulties of a fresh settlement in a forest land, there burns as strong a feeling of attachment to the Throne, as in those " happy homes of England " in the midst of which you dwell.

And our pleasure in welcoming you to this section of Canada, is only marred by the reflection that the limited time at your disposal does not permit you to travel through the interior of the noble country spreading from this town northward to the shores of Lake Huron; and to witness how the labors of less than a score of years have converted the wilderness into a land teeming with plenty, and filled with a prosperous and contented people.

In conclusion, we pray Your Royal Highness to convey to our beloved Sovereign this expression of the feelings of devotion and esteem which animate the people of this country; and an assurance, that, should occasion ever call for more active proofs of loyalty, the men of Wellington will be found worthy of the illustrious name which they proudly bear.

WILLIAM WHITELAW, *Warden.*

UNITED STATES.

DEPUTATION FROM NEW YORK.

To His Royal Highness Albert Edward, Prince of Wales, &c., &c.

MAY IT PLEASE YOUR ROYAL HIGHNESS,—

On behalf of the citizens of New York, we have the honor to request your acceptance of a ball upon the occasion of your visit to our city, at such time as may suit your convenience.

We hope that in view of the deep and universal admiration felt throughout our land for the public and private virtues of your royal mother, and for the high respect entertained for yourself, as the heir to the throne of a great country, united to our own by so many ties of history, language, consanguinity, and common interests and principles, you will accept the invitation which we now tender you.

JOHN A. KING, *Chairman.*
HAMILTON FISH.
JOHN JACOB ASTOR, Jr.
ROBERT B. MINTURN.
WILSON G. HUNT.
ROBERT L. KENNEDY.
M. B. FIELD, *Secretary.*

REPLY.

GENTLEMEN,—I thank you very much for your invitation to the ball, and accept it with great pleasure. For any details I must refer you to Lord Lyons and the Duke of Newcastle, who will be most happy to confer with you.

BUFFALO.

BUFFALO, Wednesday, Sep. 5, 1860.

To the Prince of Wales,—

The citizens of Buffalo, understanding that Your Royal Highness contemplates visiting some portions of the United States, have appointed a committee to invite you, if convenient, to take Buffalo in your route.

That committee, in obedience to the desire of our citizens, is happy to extend to Your Royal Highness a most cordial invitation to visit our city at such time as may suit your convenience.

While our people, as an independent nation, cannot be supposed to feel that loyalty which has been enthusiastically and justly expressed in Canada, yet there is a bond of sympathy between the United States and Great Britain arising from their common origin, consanguinity, language, and literature, and the great similarity of their religion, laws, and government, differing more in form than substance, and more especially from the proximity of our city to Her Majesty's colonial possessions, and the friendly and social intercourse existing among the people, which will, we are confident, insure Your Highness a most cordial welcome by our citizens; and the committee, without any burdensome ceremonial or ostentatious display, will be most happy to show to Your Royal Highness whatever may interest a stranger in our young but growing city.

Should this invitation be accepted, the committee would esteem it a favor to be informed at as early a day as possible of the time fixed by Your Royal Highness for the visit.

With assurance of the high regard and consideration of the committee, I have the honor to be Your Highness's most obedient servant,

MILLARD FILLMORE, *Chairman.*

REPLY.

GOVERNMENT HOUSE, TORONTO, Sept. 11, 1860.

SIR,—I have received your letter of the 5th of September, and have laid it before the Prince of Wales. His Royal Highness regrets exceedingly that the arrangements already made, and the shortness of the time at his disposal, will prevent him from accepting your invitation, for which His Royal Highness feels much obliged.

The reason for his not doing so have been more fully explained to the gentlemen composing the deputation.

The Prince of Wales is greatly gratified by a letter from so eminent a person as yourself, as he is pleased to have received the invitation of the citizens of Buffalo.

I am, Sir, your very obedient servant,

To Hon. Millard Fillmore. NEWCASTLE.

PITTSBURG.

To His Grace the Duke of Newcastle,—

Learning through the ordinary channels of public intelligence that the contemplated tour of Lord Renfrew over a portion of the United

States will be extended to the Ohio River and adjacent country, it would certainly prove a singular gratification to the citizens of Pittsburg to seize the opportunity of manifesting in the person of Her son their profound respect and admiration for the virtuous and exalted Sovereign of that great nation from whom, as a people, we are mainly descended.

At the instance, therefore, of very many of our most worthy citizens, and in accordance and in behalf of their and my own earnest wishes as their chief magistrate, I have the honor to present through your Grace a cordial invitation and most hearty welcome to Lord Renfrew and suite, on a visit to this city.

Nor would such a detour on the part of his Lordship be devoid of some historical interest, in view of the present visit to the Canadas of the heir to the Crown of England, when it will be remembered that it was the seizure by France, in 1754, of this position, commanding the navigation of the Ohio in the then Province of Pennsylvania; the establishment thereon of Fort Du Quesne; its subsequent recapture by the arms of Great Britain, and final discomfiture of the hostile and ambitious combination of France and their Indian allies, for the possession of the Ohio and the West; the construction of Fort Pitt on the ruins of the French fortress of Du Quesne, forming, with their aggression, the primary cause and commencement of that long and eventful war terminated by the treaty of Paris in May, 1763, by which the conquest of all the Canadas, achieved by British valor, was secured in perpetuity to the Crown of England.

Trusting the facilities of intercourse with this city in journeying to, or returning from points further West, will in no wise interfere with the convenience of his Lordship, while it will afford to us a grateful occasion to render his presence in Pittsburg agreeable to himself, it will at the same time supply for record in the future annals of our city (bearing the name and on its official seal the arms of one of England's most renowned and liberal statesmen), one more to the manifold incidents of interest arising out of the visit of his Lordship to this continent, which has so strikingly moved the hearts and awakened the kindred reminiscences and sensibilities of so large a portion of this nation.

With profound respect and consideration,
GEORGE WILSON,
Mayor.

[We exceedingly regret that we have been unable to obtain the whole of the Addresses presented.]

www.ingramcontent.com/pod-product-compliance
Lightning Source LLC
Chambersburg PA
CBHW031947230426
43672CB00010B/2078